Collection Management Handbook

Collection Management Handbook

The Art of Getting Paid

THIRD EDITION

A. MICHAEL COLEMAN

WILEY

John Wiley & Sons, Inc.

Library of Congress Cataloging-in-Publication Data:

Coleman, A. Michael.
   Collection management handbook : the art of getting paid / A. Michael Coleman.—3rd ed.
     p. cm
   Includes index.
   ISBN 0-471-45604-7 (cloth)
    1. Collecting of accounts.   I. Title.

  HG3752.5.C65 2004
  658.8'8–dc22

                                                                                        2004057667
Printed in the United States of America

10 9 8 7 6 5

Dedication

This volume is dedicated to the thousands of professionals charged with the formidable task of converting credit sales into bank deposits. Whether they are titled as bookkeepers, customer service reps, salespeople, entrepreneurs, credit managers, collection agencies, attorneys, or bill collectors—they all play a pivotal and important role in our economy. Without the combined, dedicated efforts of the people assigned to this function, charge-offs would metastasize to catastrophic dimensions, sufficient to drive our economic infrastructure to certain calamity. Fortunately, however, in our untiring quest to fulfill the credit sale—getting paid—equilibrium is maintained, enabling stimulated circulation of currency, while in turn invigorating our economy.

This volume is dedicated to these indefatigable souls, who for whatever hats they may wear ensure that customers dutifully honor credit terms, and in so doing, contribute to our economic well-being.

About the Author

Reducing the complex to the simple is one of the most difficult aspects of writing biographies of people who are at or near the pinnacle of their chosen field. When the subject is Michael Coleman, the challenge is even greater. A grade-school dropout (his last year in the classroom was the seventh grade), Mr. Coleman traded a basic education for "riding the rails" in the pre-Amtrak era armed with an illegitimate pass. He accumulated thousands of rail miles as a teenager, and by age 21, he acquired seven vintage rail cars—all on credit. A tumultuous sales career during his twenties resulted in him settling for a menial job in a tomato packing plant.

Along the way, Mr. Coleman built the foundation for his incredible rise to success, attaining paralegal status representing himself in hundreds of consumer lawsuits, achieving an enviable record of accomplishments—all without an attorney. These lawsuits ranged from minor fender bender mishaps to complicated jury trials. Mr. Coleman consistently secures monies in difficult cases on which attorneys have given up, including the recovery of voluminous judgments.

By age 35, he became an accomplished bill collector authoring a best-selling book, *The Art of Getting Paid*, published by Prentice Hall and later updated and published by John Wiley. He took to the lecture circuit, delivering more than 200 free talks before being paid a $500 fee. Five years later, Mr. Coleman earned accolades as a professional speaker. Simultaneously, he parlayed a $35,000 investment (mostly borrowed money) into a multimillion-dollar real estate portfolio. Today Mr. Coleman has delivered hundreds of speeches for America's most respected corporations and has authored countless articles and three books: *A Passion for Trains, Consumer's Day of Retribution,* and *The Art of Getting Paid.*

He is a collector of antique automobiles and a die-hard ferro-equinologist ("ferro" = iron, "equin" = horse, "ologist" = study)—the study of iron horses—a railroad buff. Mr. Coleman is also an avid international train traveler and serves as general partner to numerous real estate trusts.

Contents

Preface

Credit sales are interwoven in the fabric of corporate culture—a necessary evil that, if combined with an aggressive recovery effort, yields maximum dollars. If we are to achieve optimum conversion of receivables into cash, debt collection skills must be honed.

Proportionate to risk taking, corporations hope to realize profits sufficient to offset bad debt write-offs. To the degree that they extend credit, simultaneous with the customer's having the wherewithal to pay, other factors also determine success. The process can either produce a dollar bonanza or end in a bottom line written in red ink. Management of receivables is related to selling but differs in that debt recovery is making a sale after the sale (i.e., getting paid).

Companies place great emphasis on marketing but practice only a haphazard effort in converting credit sales into bank deposits. In most cases, accounts receivable represents a company's most important asset, yet its management is often a neglected function. Why? The business landscape reverberates with sales and marketing know-how, but conversely, money procurement is shunned. Stated another way, debt recovery is closing up-front, a reverse selling process that gives would-be collectors the heebie-jeebies. Unfortunately for most creditors, conventional collection procedures do not yield results proportionate to those geared toward generating new customers.

The information age also has its drawbacks. Too many creditors focus on the information explosion, becoming fascinated by the parade of new gizmos, which offers more intrigue than the humdrum of calling recalcitrant debtors. Add to this the stomach-wrenching task of engaging in verbal warfare and it's obvious why debt collection takes a backseat to the positive aspects of selling. Like it or not, gladiatorial combat is a game with which creditors must reckon. It takes iron nerve and bulldog determination to extract money from nonpaying customers, a posture for which a collector must maintain momentum and self-motivation. It is not enough to educate collectors in customer service techniques because success depends on maneuvering many personality types into negotiable climates. Various laws, debtor attitudes, the cost of money, liberal credit policies, and increased competition have fostered a dog-eat-dog mentality.

Today's debtor attitudes do not respond to yesterday's dunning. Similarly, bombarding debtors with letters and phone calls, although sometimes effective, will not in itself yield substantial results. Nonpaying customers must be maneuvered into a negotiating mentality by zeroing in on their hot buttons. Yet despite their lack of bottom-line impact, most credit executives continue practicing the virtues of good customer service, applying them universally within their portfolios, falsely believing that a smile and goodwill can save the day. It will not! True, conciliatory appeals are preferred, but they don't work with nefarious types. There has been virtually no redefinition of collection methodology—until now.

This expanded edition elevates debt recovery to its highest level, incorporating many avenues of strategic creditor recourse. For the first time, accounts receivable practitioners have at their fingertips a treasure trove of awesome firepower. Among the new weaponry are easy-to-implement techniques to utilize small claims courts nationwide, expanded investigatory resources, recovery of money judgments, and potent legal remedies—including how to initiate an impleader action, a clever device that turns the classic debtor's excuse "I can't pay you because I haven't been paid" (by legally extracting the money due from your customer's customer) into a creditor checkmate. Imagine the euphoria of legally ambushing your nonpaying customers (who make their financial problems yours) and euphorically proclaiming: "Make my day!" This revised edition also includes the ultimate creditor proficiency gauge: an accounts receivable exam/solutions that equips the reader with the legal knowledge and strategic ammunition to subdue—and collect from—even the most formidable scoundrels.

In the credit granting arena, this valuable resource includes several easy-to-implement techniques to *prevent* a bad debt, including venue, jurisdiction, exercising Long Arm Statutes, impleader, ACH electronic debit, and other devices that, if implemented, will veil creditors in an umbrella of protection. If an account does default, the safeguards illustrated within will maneuver a company's receivables into a secured position.

The art of receivables management is much more than applied psychology. The science goes beyond an ability to communicate. Successful debt recovery requires a mastery of numerous persuasion skills, including, but not limited to, negotiation, application of legal principles, customer service appeals, persuasion, street methodology, jailhouse lawyering, intimidation, guerrilla warfare, storytelling, barter, and even humor.

The collection agency industry is the ideal forum to gauge receivables management success because third-party agents' livelihood depends on converting credit sales into bank deposits. Professional collectors in the employ of agencies do not get paid unless they recover delinquent receivables. As a result, the collection agency industry has mastered the art par excellence. It is a marvelous learning forum. What better source to employ as mentors? Collection agencies typically operate on a "no collection, no fee" basis. Because they are paid only for what they produce, their income is proportionate to results; however, just because collection agencies are in the business of recovering bad debts, does not mean they are all experts. Of our nation's estimated 8,000 collection agencies, less than 5% practice the techniques in this extraordinary volume. Why? Just as in every profession, there are always the majority of mediocre types. The experts almost always excel. The techniques contained herein are practiced by the minority of supercollectors—individuals whose commission income is comparable to top Fortune 500 executives. Who would you rather learn from: the amateur collector who takes potshots at balloons (limiting debtor pursuit to letters and phone calls) or the strategist who skillfully maneuvers the intentional debtor into a vexing and embarrassing predicament by performing "mission impossible" accomplishments, without a traumatizing lawsuit?

This book is the result of exhaustive research, complemented with thousands of actual real-life cases. It is a treasury of vast experiences extracted from superachievers who have reached the highest levels of receivables management success. The principles in this book were extracted from the collection agency industry's most prolific talent—virtuosos whose modi operandi are in touch with today's debtor mentalities. Professional bill collectors have one objective: getting paid via the shortest, most direct route. This book reveals the path of least resistance relevant to virtually every conceivable problem. I absolutely guarantee that you will not find a more comprehensive how-to inventory of proven strategies than within these covers.

In the following pages, you will encounter an enormous inventory of cash-producing formulas derived from industry leaders who are at the head of their class in the complex world of debt recovery. These techniques will do much more than help you collect accounts; they will also multiply your bad debt recoveries and act as a springboard to new levels of achievement. Although the knowledge presented here is easy to digest, you will have to go through the process of not only learning new skills but also committing them to rote memorization. Only when these strategies become ingrained in your thinking, subject to instinctive recall, and eventually become habit will you, too, advance to the head of your class.

Put on your thinking cap and fasten your seat belt, for you are about to enter the fast track to accounts receivable success. Armed with a knowledge of what follows combined with practice and determination, your accounts receivable will transition from complacent to gold medal status—a quantum leap that guarantees maximum receivable penetration while yielding superior recovery. I challenge you to never again accept victimhood and write-offs as you squeeze every last dollar from your hard-earned credit sales.

A. MICHAEL COLEMAN

Harrisburg, PA

Acknowledgments

The author expresses sincere appreciation and gratitude to the following individuals who have been instrumental in the production of this book. Without their contribution, this learning experience would not have been possible.

Russell Case, Esq., former editor of the *Credit and Collection Management Bulletin,* Bureau of Business Practice

It was Russell Case, the BBP's prolific editor, who first recognized a need to introduce a success course on receivables management. Russ correctly surmised that too many books heretofore published on collection management were credit oriented and/or focused on conventional receivable procedures. Russ desired to reveal the recovery techniques of accomplished collection professionals via a comprehensive how-to manual. His insight produced the first edition in 1988, which is now recognized as the Bible in the debt collection industry.

The New York State Bar Association, Albany, New York

As a self-taught, pro se litigant, I relentlessly studied the techniques of virtuoso lawyers, particularly their verbal confrontation/persuasion skills, which I modified for debt collection purposes. These scorch-'em-speechless practitioners propound their spellbinding oratories on adversaries, which often yielded blockbusting acquittals/verdicts. If picturesque words shrewdly presented in opening statements and/or summations could win verdicts in the courtroom for accused felons, then why couldn't silver-tongued collectors motivate contumacious debtor types into satisfying their debts? The practical application of this technique is more than an oratorical dissertation—it's the powerful command of phraseology—picturesque words, metaphors, and quotes, which are at the cornerstone of persuasive debtor communications.

J. Douglas Edwards

Few professionals have influenced the art of making sales as has the great sales trainer, J. Douglas Edwards. As a salesman turned collector, I was inspired by Mr. Edwards' commonsense approach for maneuvering suspects into prospects and then into commissionable sales. J. Douglas Edwards taught salespeople how to increase their incomes via mastery of the assumptive tie down, shut up, closing question, alternate of choice, lost sale, storytelling, and phraseology techniques. Although the author takes no credit for introducing Mr. Edwards' world-renowned techniques, I was, however, one of the first bill collectors to recognize them—and apply them to receivables management. Virtually every book, seminar, and training manual on the subject of debt collection has failed to penetrate receivable recovery as a post-sale, closing process. In fact, the recovery of credit sales is a sale after the fact. The only difference between a professional salesperson and a collector is that the collector closes up front.

Corporate America

For more than 25 years, the corporate landscape has entrusted the author with an infusion of receivables that covered the gamut. Thousands of debtor types were relentlessly pursued, from condescending pathological liars (who tell creditors what they want to hear) to mastermind white-collar credit criminals who bilked millions of dollars via felonious manipulation. This author has successfully locked horns with them all. Many of these recoveries were "mission impossible" in demeanor. Whether the receivable was just a slow pay, conducive to customer service appeals, or ruthless, predatory credit criminals, thousands of receivables, representing millions of dollars in recoveries, has taught the author that the science of getting paid involves much more than the conventional approach of letter writing, phone calls, and legal intervention. The truly successful collector must be much more than an everyday fixture, dialing numbers and dunning deadbeats. A professional must be proficient in several callings: customer service, problem solver, troubleshooter, strategist, negotiator, communicator, investigator, asset locator, jailhouse lawyer, and even humorist. These are just a handful of the prerequisites necessary to achieve the accolades of the profession. From corporate America to a Main Street, Small Town, America, I am grateful to the armies of creditors who entrusted their no-pays to this streetwise collector. The sheer volume of receivables has, over the years, enabled the author to hone and perfect the art. The techniques in this volume are not based on theories or conjecture, but rather a three-decade-plus exposure to a landscape saturated with the most challenging and perplexing receivable problems.

To Sheck Cho and Stacey Rympa, of John Wiley & Sons, who had the foresight to publish this updated edition, a special vote of thanks. Sheck and Stacey recognized a need to provide creditors with a blueprint sufficient to convert no-pay receivables into bank deposit realities. They also converted stacks of documents and the original manuscript into the finished product. Many cash-starved creditors will profit handsomely owing to John Wiley & Sons' investment in publishing this manual.

A heartfelt thank-you is also due to Tom Williams of Investigations Unlimited. Tom's knowledge of information retrieval, particularly skip tracing, asset locating, and debtor profiles, has not only produced valuable information, which resulted in recoveries, but he also shared his knowledge with readers sufficient to impact their bottom line.

And last, but not least, to Lucy E. Trembone—the woman behind the author who painstakingly compiled mountains of gibberish into drafts and drafts into recognizable submissions. Lucy worked laboriously to write and rewrite the semifinal drafts. Without her commitment and support, I could never have fulfilled this arduous task, let alone meet intermittent deadlines.

CHAPTER 1

A New Collection Science Is Born

The title *collector* conjures up a very negative image. It connotes a cold, ruthless, insensitive individual whose only purpose is to extract monies from other human beings without emotion or feeling. A collector might be a credit manager, adjuster, accounts receivable clerk, bookkeeper—anyone who has been assigned the task of collecting delinquent accounts. Collectors are a valuable asset to any business, but, unfortunately, they are often viewed as a necessary evil.

Most collectors receive their training on the job—the prevailing theory being that experience is the best teacher. This cliché has some validity, but when collectors boast that they have 10, 15, or 25 years' experience, you can take that to mean their experience was accumulated in the first one or two years. After the break-in period, people tend to develop certain habits, which turn into prejudices. Experience is the best teacher, as long as you maintain an open mind and continue to grow. Develop a thirst for knowledge and continue to learn, always striving to reach ever-higher pinnacles of success.

We accept knowledge as an additive process. We believe that by acquiring new knowledge we increase our possibilities for success. What we fail to realize is that training for success is also a *subtractive* process. It may be necessary to eradicate poor habits that are barriers to higher levels of achievement.

If you want to grow a beautiful rose garden, you first plant the roses. Then you nourish and fertilize the plants. But this is not enough to produce beautiful roses. You also have to eliminate weeds and insect pests. So it is with the human mind. Our minds are cluttered, and that hinders our success mechanism. Let us approach the vital subject of collection management the same way we approach the rose garden—by tearing down old myths and shattering conventional theories that cripple our progress. The best way to point up the value of this philosophy is to prove to you that conventional collection techniques produce minimal results. (See Exhibit 1.1.)

If a new collector were to read every book, listen to every CD, network with other credit professionals, research every known source of information on collection management, and then work long hours applying conventional theories, a modicum of success would inevitably be realized. The collector might even attain expert status and recognition from peers. But this student of accounts receivable management still could not attain the

EXHIBIT 1.1   DAYS SALES OUTSTANDING (DSO):
A GRAPHIC SURVEY

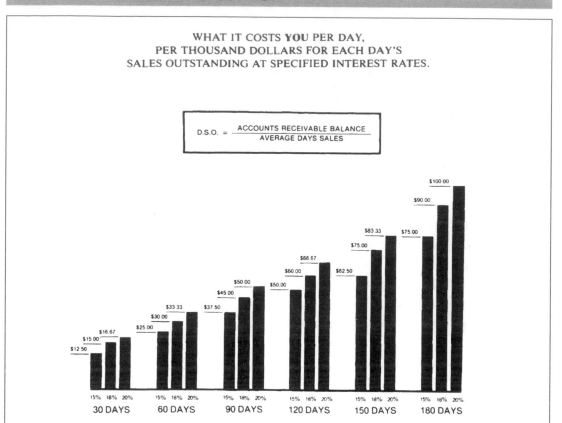

WHAT IT COSTS **YOU** PER DAY,
PER THOUSAND DOLLARS FOR EACH DAY'S
SALES OUTSTANDING AT SPECIFIED INTEREST RATES.

$$D.S.O. = \frac{ACCOUNTS\ RECEIVABLE\ BALANCE}{AVERAGE\ DAYS\ SALES}$$

As every financial executive knows, reducing the DSO is one of the most important functions of receivable management. The longer a company holds onto an uncollectable receivable, the greater its costs and thus the higher its DSO. However, this does not necessarily mean that a company should place its receivables early in the cycle, for the risk via conventional methods may cause customer alienation. This chart illustrates just how much money it costs for each $1,000 at varying interest rates, in 30-day intervals to 180 days.

high level of collection success that is possible using the techniques in this book. Why? Because my approach is unconventional and creative.

Many of the techniques and the knowledge presented in this book are new to the business of converting past-due receivables into cash. For example, assume that a customer owes $X and isn't paying because his customer isn't paying him—in effect making his problem yours. The conventional approach would be to wait and see. Even if you placed the receivable for collection, the same problem would ensue. The solution may be the extraordinary remedy of impleader—a potent legal maneuver that bypasses a nonpaying customer and establishes legal criteria to sue the customer's customer. This remedy, however, must be transaction related (i.e., the nonpaying customer's customer must be a beneficiary of your products or services), and there must be provable damages of your not getting paid if your customer eventually collects from his customer and then threatens not to pay you. Although not applicable in every situation, impleader is nevertheless a powerful solution.

Many frustrated collectors and credit managers have read books, attended seminars, and subscribed to the theories promulgated by their peers. But when they apply this knowledge to the real world, they find that the concepts they have learned do not work. Examine any book or seminar on collection technique, and you will find that they all offer the same information rearranged in slightly different forms. There is almost nothing new on this important subject.

PREVENTIVE REMEDIES FOR CREDIT GRANTORS

"An ounce of prevention is the best cure." Good advice, but tragically, most credit grantors fail in structuring their sales, leaving gaping holes for nonpaying customers to exploit them. Most companies emphasize marketing, competing vigorously while relying on flimsy credit applications and guarantees to support the sale. Once in default, the quality of sale origination documents will greatly impact recovery. How can a company ensure being paid *after* initiation of the credit sale? Take the time to perform a reference check augmented with executing documents to protect your interests.

For the credit grantor, structuring an airtight credit application and guarantees is the best preventive medicine. Numerous variations are possible, including ACH electronic debit authorization, creditor venue provision, impleader, interest and collection expense, recovery of chattel, and other variations. There are numerous safeguards, each intended to cure a specific contingency.

Remedies to consider incorporating into a credit application and/or sale origination document(s) include the following:

- *Creditor venue provision.* Provides legal wherewithal for creditors to sue from their locale, specific customer consent to venue, and "minimum contracts" requirement. Permits creditor to sue in their state.

- *Corporate debtor extension of liability to officers and/or third parties, assignment, or arbitrary sale of business.* Use where debtor sells business with intent to defraud creditors.

- *ACH electronic debit provision.* Never again be a victim of "the check is in the mail" syndrome. Preauthorization guarantee permits creditors to electronically debit primary or alternate accounts. Includes Social Security numbers and/or EIN. In the alternative, a search firm can develop this information in the event debtors changes the checking accounts.

Originating the Credit Sale and Payment Guarantee

Fortunately, most customers practice integrity. Nonpaying customers, however, represent a challenge—recovering monies *after* the gratification of merchandise and/or services have been tendered. Converting nonperforming receivables into cash depends on the credit application/guarantee; the security instruments that customers executed are instrumental. Tragically, for most creditors, their sale origination paperwork is as worthless as the paper it's printed on.

It's estimated that about 8 out of 10 credit applications/guarantees contain defects— inherent flaws—that seriously prejudice recovery. Why? Credit departments often rely on legalese written by corporate attorneys or copy language used by competitors. Credit applications and guarantees are often either out of date or inferior. The result is an origination document that *does not* protect the creditor. When an account proceeds into default, the real acid test of the guarantee is the leverage it maintains over nonpaying customers, particularly its enforcement. The object is not only to secure a creditor's position, but also to do so at minimum expense.

Another fallacy is fear, a stigmatized belief that the stronger the guarantee and its ramifications, the less likely it is that a prospective customer will sign it. Fear of the sale going to the competition paralyzes many creditors from protecting their interests.

Solution: The time to structure a creditor's position is simultaneous to the origination of the sale, or the "honeymoon" stage. Contrary to common belief, getting customers to agree to provisional remedies is *not* detrimental, provided they are presented properly. In situations where a customer refuses to cooperate, it may be better to deny credit (a reactionary customer is a sign of noncollectability). Transitioning a problematic account to a competitor may be better than gambling on uncertainty.

Neither does the customer have to execute a confusing clutter of paperwork to ensure safety. Depending on the complexity of the sale, dollar amount, and risk factors, documentation should average one and a half to three pages. The solution is to combine definitive legal provisions with psychology. Better to invest a few minutes with a new customer negotiating credit terms than to extend credit by the seat of the pants.

It is not the volume of paperwork, nor the legal mumbo jumbo, but rather a concise and definitive blueprint—an ironclad document—that will save the day. One sentence or paragraph can make the difference between recovery and write-off. Take the time to review these provisional remedies. By simply incorporating the correct legal language into a credit application, risk will be dramatically reduced.

Menu of Credit Sale Provisions

Consider the following clauses that can be incorporated into a credit application/guarantee:

- *Creditor venue clause.* Many creditors mistakenly rely on this typical language: "In the event of default, customer agrees to submit to the venue of *creditor's jurisdiction.*" Wording documents with this or similar language is fatal. Your customer can still move to dismiss your complaint.

Solution: A credit application must include a "minimum contracts" and "continuity and regularity" clause, making it impossible for a defaulting customer to circumnavigate jurisdiction. Establishing the right to sue within your locale is critical because it forces a non-paying customer to hire an attorney in your area. Statistically, 50% of nonpaying customers pay *without* expensive collection procedures when confronted with the reality of defending an out-of-state lawsuit. (Another advantage of this approach for creditors is that they can centralize legal intervention.)

- *Personal guarantee clause with privacy notice.* Recent changes in privacy laws have rendered language contained in conventional personal guarantees obsolete. Credit grantors are advised to restructure this critical document. Most personal guarantees are open ended, and while establishing personal liability, creditors fail to include a Social Security number and electronic search provision. New privacy laws make it illegal to access confidential information, thereby frustrating personal guarantee enforcement. You should close the gap by bridging the personal liability guarantee with a clause that permits accessibility to attachable assets, including waiver of privacy laws. What good is a personal guarantee if your customer transfers assets and/or conceals same? Worse, violate your customers' right to privacy, and you could be sued.

- *ACH electronic debit with site draft.* This remedy eliminates "the check is in the mail" syndrome and prioritizes remittances. Electronic transmittal of funds is the wave of the future This provisional remedy provides several options, including grace periods, discount incentives, and default remedies. One of the outstanding features of ACH debit and/or site draft is that if your customer goes bankrupt, a shrewd creditor can tap a bank account that was maintained for payroll and/or tax liabilities. A creditor armed with this provision only needs to perform an electronic search (i.e., Social Security number or EIN) on a bank account to debit funds. Because the ACH debit provision permits transfer of funds, it cannot be challenged by a nonpaying customer. If the creditor is armed with a personal guarantee, the wherewithal to electronically debit funds from *personal*—even joint or retirement accounts—is available. This provision is especially valuable if your customer goes out of business or transfers assets. Joint accounts can often be debited, much to the dismay of a nonpaying customer.

  As an added creditor recourse, you could add a site draft provision and/or credit card debit authorization. This provides a backup to the electronic debit feature. Site drafts are especially useful if a customer has a borrowing relationship with its bank. Typically, customers do not divulge nonreportable debts to their bank, thus jeopardizing revolving lines of credit.

  Modern creditors and landlords who convert to ACH swear by it; its usage has often yielded recovery where otherwise the account would have been written off, placed for collection, and/or litigated. See Exhibit 1.2 for a sample ACH authorization electronic debt form.

EXHIBIT I.2   CREDITOR AUTHORIZATION TO DEBIT BANK
               ACCOUNT: SAMPLE

PRE-AUTHORIZED CHECKING (PAC) AGREEMENT

INSTRUCTIONS
1. Sign the authorization using the signature(s) on file at your financial institution.
2. Attach a voided sample check.

As a convenience I hereby request and authorize the referenced financial institution to pay and charge my account for checks/electronic debits drawn on my account by _____ to its own order. This authorization will remain in effect until revoked by me in writing via certified mail, return receipt.

I agree that your treatment of each check/electronic debit, and your rights in respect to it, shall be the same as if it were signed by me personally. I further agree that if any such check/electronic debit be dishonored constitutes a breach of agreement.

DEPOSITOR(S)

Name of Depositor(s) listed on the account (Please Print)	Name of Bank
	Address of Bank
Signature of Depositor	City State Zip
Signature of Joint Depositor (if applicable)	Bank Phone
	Checking Account Number you wish to debit
	Bank Routing Number

- Attach a voided sample check -

TO: THE BANK NAMED ABOVE
So that you may comply with your depositor's request, this Company agrees:

1. To indemnify you and hold you harmless from any loss you may suffer as a consequence of your actions resulting from or in connection with the execution and issuance of any check/electronic debit, whether or not genuine, purporting to be executed and received by you in the regular course of business for the purpose of payment, including any costs or expenses reasonably incurred in connection therewith.
2. In the event that any such check/electronic debit shall be dishonored whether with or without cause, and whether intentionally or inadvertently, to indemnify you for any loss whatsoever.
3. To defend at our own cost and expense any action which might be brought by any depositors or any other persons because of your actions taken pursuant to the foregoing debits, or in any manner arising by reason of this authorization.

Creditor: _____   **Date:** _____

Address: _____

Phone: _____

UCC-1 Chattel Liens

Another misconception is UCC-1 chattel liens. Creditors properly execute and file them, but they fail to bridge these important documents with the credit application and/or guarantee. The effect is that if a customer arbitrarily sells your secured merchandise, you still have to sue. Contrary to common belief, the mere filing of a UCC *is not* a cure-all that protects your merchandise from conveyance. Unless the transferee undertakes a UCC search, a nonpaying customer will get away with illegally disposing of your merchandise! Although a UCC-1 is better than no chattel lien, creditors should provision their liens to extend voluntary surrender to transferees/purchasers, including ancillary liability.

Solution: Restructure your UCC-1s and credit application to include extended liability protection. Thus, if a customer illegally transitions your liened merchandise, you will gain substantial leverage over the purchaser/transferee. One carefully worded short paragraph will make the difference between write-off and recovery the next time a customer transitions your merchandise to third parties.

Impleader and Unjust Enrichment Provisions

"I can't pay, because my customer hasn't paid me." Sound familiar? For creditors, this is one of the most frustrating excuses to hear. Most creditors foolhardily keep calling their delinquent customers inquiring whether they have the resources to pay the debt. Even if your customer eventually gets paid from its customers, what guarantee do you have that it will pay you? Relying on your customer's customers' remittance is a dangerous game of Russian roulette.

Solution: Contrary to common belief, creditors can sometimes circumnavigate the nonpaying customer and derive payment *directly* from their customer. Because there is no "privity of contract" between you and your customers, customer liability is diluted; however, under certain conditions, two potent remedies are available, albeit only with specific legal criteria. Impleader recourse is one of the most misunderstood, yet effective, remedies. Tragically, naive creditors write off monies that could have been recovered. The following is an example of how an impleader action will short-circuit your nonpaying customer:

The Players

You are creditor "A." "B" is your nonpaying customer. "C" is your customer's customer who is beneficiary to your merchandise and/or services.

The Remedy

B goes out of business and defaults to A. C is indebted to B for merchandise or services that originated with A. Although A has no direct contract with C, the latter is nevertheless obligated to remit to B. Why? B, now defunct, still has a valid receivable relevant to C. However, once C pays B, your customer would likely pocket the money. A's conventional remedy is to sue B, but if B is a defunct corporation, A will likely secure an uncollectible judgment. A, however, would be wise to short-circuit C's remittance to B via an impleader action.

A's solution is to sue C for "unjust enrichment"—a legally prosecutable tort. Assume arguendo, that C pays B and B does not pay A. If A sues C for "unjust enrichment," C could still be held liable to A, maintaining a double liability having to pay A, although C paid B.

For C to legally extricate itself from multiple liability (i.e., to A and B), C, on the initiative of A's impleader complaint, simply deposits the monies that C owes B with the court; C is then legally discharged from its debt to B. The monies are then held by the court as escrow agent. B is then compelled to "implead" its claim against A, which would fail, because A has a superior contractual right to the proceeds as originating creditor. The effect of this power play is that B never gets his hands on the money C owes him. A gets paid, while C has eliminated multiple liability.

In its simplest terms, impleader is a legal strategy that, under certain conditions, may be exercised to circumnavigate your customer and proceed legally against their customer. Many of our clients are capitalizing on recoveries that would otherwise be written off.

Impleader solution: Although in some cases it's not legally necessary to compel a client to execute an impleader provision, its incorporation into a credit application/guarantee is important. Why? Assume that your customer goes out of business and you exercise this drastic remedy; your customer can *still* sue you per the Doctrine of Tortuous Interference of Contract (i.e., interfering with a contract in force with his client). The solution is to incorporate language that authorizes an impleader remedy, waiving tortuous interference of contract repercussions. By simply adding this language to an impleader guarantee, creditors gain a third-party resource (i.e., their customers' customers becomes an extension of the original creditor's liability).

Additional Safeguards

Another device is a blanket credit card debit. This remedy permits credit card debits for up to the full amount of the debt. Interestingly, a creditor does not necessarily have to obtain a copy of the customer's credit cards—or even their numbers and expiration dates—*only* a blanket authorization (although obtaining this information at the time of sale origination would expedite recovery). Then, if default occurs, the shrewd creditor need only employ a search firm to find the issuing bank and card number. For only a few hundred dollars, a creditor can access *all* of the nonpaying customer's credit cards and legally debit one or more until the debt is satisfied. *Warning:* The Truth in Lending Law provides for severe criminal and civil penalties for unauthorized credit card debits. Your waiver should include airtight language, together with a Section 212e dispute waiver.

Accessing Interest on Principal

One of the most common misconceptions is the wherewithal for creditors to charge interest on principal. Typically, creditors rely on printed invoices—usually 1.5% per month on the unpaid balance. In fact, a customer can legally refuse to pay interest even though it is emblazoned on the creditor's invoices. Why? Because the most fundamental aspect of contract law is violated: "a meeting of the minds." Unless your customer signs a statement agreeing to payment of interest, the creditor cannot legally collect it. The only exception is court-impounded interest, which is usually less than 11% and applicable only on obtainment of judgment. To legally compel your customer to pay interest on overdue invoices, it is recommended that an interest provision be incorporated *separately* in the credit application or guarantee and signed by your customer.

Reimbursement of Collection and/or Attorney's Fees

How many times have you prevailed at recovering collection and/or attorney's fees? According to statistics, more than 85% of creditors who attempt enforcement of this provision fail. Three reasons for this failure are as follows:

1. Litigation encourages settlement, usually for less than contract liability.
2. Collection agencies and attorneys are not motivated to recover their fees, preferring to deduct commissions off the top.
3. Creditors' guarantees usually contain unenforceable or defective language.

For example, suppose your guarantee is worded with a 33.33% attorney's fee reimbursement provision, but jurisdiction limits third-party fees to 20%. In this instance, it doesn't matter what your customer agreed to—you'd only recover 20%. Another fallacy is enforcement. If you or your collection agency ever tried to recover third-party recovery expenses, your customer will almost always refuse to pay it, although it was agreed to in writing.

Solution: Unfortunately, the solution is not as simple as preparing a universal document. The variables of state laws relevant to the recovery of collection expenses are diversified. The trick is to connect reimbursement provisions with venue. Generally, reimbursement provisions should not contain percentages (i.e., 25% or 33.33%) but rather language that is broad enough to satisfy most state laws, while specific enough to legally hold your customer liable for reimbursement.

HOW TO INCORPORATE PROTECTIVE LEGALESE INTO YOUR SALE ORIGINATION DOCUMENTATION

This section is intended to provide creditors with an arsenal of accounts receivable recovery strategies; it is a valuable resource for converting no-pays into bank deposits; it is *not* intended to be a course in credit granting. Nevertheless, prevention is always better than treatment. While the other side of the spectrum from recovering bad debts is prudent credit management, it is important to maintain a balance between safeguarding the credit sale and not resorting to overkill. Compelling your customer to execute a battery of legal

documents saturated with Latin terms will discourage even the most open-minded customer. Each potential sale must be weighed in relation to risk factors, potential loss, and
tolerance. As a crash course in preventive remedies, these provisions are included as a means
of introducing creditors to a menu of strategies, which if implemented will greatly reduce
risk. Space limitations do not permit a dissertation on this important subject, nor do the
following examples constitute a complete education.

The practitioner is referred to the National Association of Credit Management
(NACM). NACM-National and its network of affiliated associations are the leading
resource for credit and financial management, providing information, products, and services for effective business credit and accounts receivable information. (NACM, 8840
Columbia 100 Parkway, Columbia, MD 21045, phone: 410.740.5560, fax: 410.740.5574,
www.nacm.org)

LAW OF THE JUNGLE

The student of accounts receivable management is lured to the various techniques and
strategies by flowery claims and grandiose promises, most of which never pan out. You've
heard all the hype before, you have put the techniques into practice, and you have attained
some degree of success. At the risk of being considered an iconoclast, I suggest that the
game of receivables management is an intense game of strategy, a contest of egos, a struggle to survive. The game is played in a vicious jungle, where predators are constantly out
to get you. You cannot become complacent, not even for a minute. Survival depends on
your ability to structure a recovery remedy that pushes your nonpaying customer's hot button sufficient to prioritize remittance. Only the fittest endure. No doubt you have already
discovered that the theories you learned do not always work. The credit and collections
cycle is a constantly moving target. It is hard enough just to maintain the status quo, let
alone make progress.

Like many "experts," I fell into the trap of believing that my great reward would ultimately come if I continued to work hard and learn. Progress was made—until a complacent level was attained. Then, the rate of improvement leveled off and the sea of
complacency flooded in. Like everyone else, I analyzed my frustrations and harsh experiences. I finally concluded that many of the myths I blindly accepted could achieve only
minimal results. Experience was not necessarily the best teacher. What really surprised me
was how so many credit professionals could get hooked on so many illusory techniques that
in reality produce minimal results, if any (see Exhibit 1.3).

Conventional knowledge did not seem to provide any significant formulas for accounts
receivable success. Most collectors, even the so-called experts, seem to reach a plateau of
success, level off, and spend the rest of their lives on a merry-go-round—never really getting ahead. Could it be that these noted "experts" were too close to the trees to see the
forest?

But if we cannot rely on the traditional advice of experts, whom can we rely on? After
many years of trial and error, I became convinced that the only real solution was to develop

my own philosophy based on the realities of the jungle. I made it my business to study the principles of success used by the highest-paid professional collectors. I found that only 5% of top professionals in the collection agency industry earn a six-figure annual income. My battle plan was to study these top earners and find out what they were doing that the experts were not. What I learned was that virtually none of their techniques ever appeared in a seminar or a NACM publication. After all, if the so-called experts really understood the science of collecting bad debts, they would be earning CEO incomes. The experts are not earning anywhere near that kind of money, yet they are very willing to reveal their techniques to others. The best collectors are successful because they *apply uncommon solutions to common receivables problems*—solutions that are, in fact, practiced by only a minority of superachievers.

Why are these superstar collectors so successful when most of them ignore the rules promulgated by most experts? The conclusions are as follows:

EXHIBIT 1.3   COLLECTOR SELF-ANALYSIS TEST

Albert Einstein said, "Creativity and imagination rule the world." It has been said that there are three forms of creativity:

1. Rearranging what already exists—limited creativity.
2. Adding something to make an improvement.
3. Out of nothing something is created—the ultimate form of creativity.

Remember, *uncommon* collectors are implementing *uncommon* solutions to *common* problems. The following will test your creativity.

OBJECTIVE

Draw a straight line through all nine dots using only four straight connecting lines without removing your pen from the page. You may cross over lines, but you may not trace back over them.

STOP

If you have succeeded or if you have taken this test before and you know the answer—now try the same test using only three lines.

EXHIBIT 1.3   COLLECTOR SELF-ANALYSIS TEST (CONT'D.)

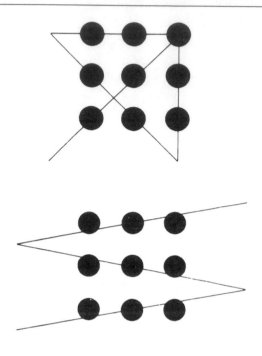

Now using smaller dots but with the same arrangement, place a piece of paper in a cylinder form and run a single line through all the dots.

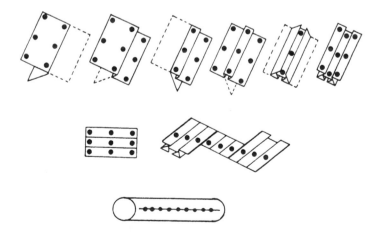

BE CREATIVE!

- Establishment experts continue to brainwash us with information based on success myths that have been handed down since the first credit transaction took place.

- We are still learning today by the outdated rules of yesterday. No one has even considered the effects of information in relation to strategy.

- The recognized experts and the myriad how-to books are not holding anything back. They simply do not know there are better ways to collect accounts receivable.

- The more information you secure on your nonpaying customer, the greater your chances of success.

Mozart Principle

Mozart was a genius. His ability to compose music has never been surpassed. What does this have to do with bad debts? Think about it. Here was one man who could achieve musical heights inaccessible to anyone else. By the same token, a small cadre of collectors effortlessly get results that apparently cannot be duplicated by their colleagues. The most successful collectors have a lot in common with Mozart—in short, an ability to get unparalleled results. Mozart was a gifted musician, but you do not have to be gifted to be a great collector. All you need is a desire to learn from the best. *To make a difference, you have to be different.*

Watermelon and the Transistor

Many years ago, the Japanese department of agriculture sent a team of experts to the United States to learn firsthand how we grow vegetables and fruit. The Japanese have always loved American watermelons, and they figured that this taste sensation would be a viable commodity in Japan, but there were several problems. Watermelons are clumsy in shape and difficult to store. They take up a lot of space and are expensive to ship.

The Japanese confronted the problem by designing a new process whereby watermelons grow to be square in shape. The results were marvelous. The Japanese calculated that if watermelons were easier to store, sales would increase—and they were right. Sales doubled. Because the square shape increased shipping capacity, the Japanese could ship 30% more watermelons for the same price.

Consider another example of Japanese ingenuity. In the 1950s, a group of Japanese businessmen negotiated a deal to purchase international patent rights to a transistor invented by Western Electric. The Japanese did not set out to create new technology. Their strategy was to improve existing technology and build quality products at a lower price. They made several modifications and improvements to the Western Electric transistor. Ultimately that $25,000 investment led to the great Japanese electronics boom. The rest is history. Apparently, it took a foreign nation with ingenuity and foresight to recognize what we had in our own backyard.

The same logic applies to individuals. One person earns $200,000 a year, working 6 hours a day. Another person earns $40,000 a year, working 10 hours a day. Is the first person smarter than the second? Not necessarily.

Consider this: Suppose we have arranged for a private race on the Indianapolis 500 track between you and a world champion race car driver. We place you in the driver's seat of a supercharged, high-performance Ferrari, with a top speed of 240 miles per hour. The professional driver goes behind the wheel of a Volkswagen Beetle—top speed: 85 miles per hour. The flag goes down, and you do eight laps. Who wins the race? You do! Why? Because your vehicle is faster. That is exactly my point. Ever since the first credit transaction took place, little has changed in the art of collecting, but the antiquated tactics of yesterday simply will not work in today's environment. It's not enough to call debtors or send letters.

What you have to do is find the vehicle that will carry you toward your accounts receivable objectives at the greatest possible speed and at the lowest cost. Why linger on the accounts receivable merry-go-round, struggling to keep pace? All you have to do is learn the advanced collection formulas that represent the best means to successfully manage your receivables.

As you study these advanced formulas, remember: You must not only learn them, but you must also practice them until they form themselves into new habits. Good habits can be acquired only via repetition.

BUILDING BLOCKS FOR COLLECTION SUCCESS

The average collector knows perhaps a dozen collection techniques. The professional collector, however, has mastered many high-powered collection techniques and uses them all. Knowledge is not enough in itself. You have to harness and direct that knowledge. It must be backed by a plan and affirmative action to achieve a specific purpose. The progressive structure of accounts receivable management can be likened to building blocks. Let us examine collection strategy as a step-by-step process and analyze appropriate techniques for each step.

1. *Establish communication and develop interest.* You must understand that your collection call, like any other call, is an interruption to the debtor, whose attention is elsewhere. When a debtor picks up the telephone, that person is not interested in you or your company. The debtor is certainly not interested in discussing the indebtedness. Therefore, you must set the stage for effective communication by making a *sale before the sale.* The mind is like a parachute—it works only when it is open. You must earn the right to make your presentation by neutralizing debtors' preoccupation with other matters and capturing their interest. You can succeed only if you have their undivided attention.

2. *Listen empathetically.* There is a big difference between sympathy and empathy. A sympathetic listener feels sorry for the other person. Listening with empathy, however, means you relate to the other person, understanding how that person feels in the circumstances under discussion. An empathetic person can develop relationships

with debtors under trying circumstances—a necessary skill in collections. Collectors must learn to listen and let debtors express opinions, remembering all the while that debtors can quickly direct conversations off the track. Level and tone of voice are very important. Your voice should be somewhat subdued and not unduly aggressive. It is okay to show a certain self-confidence, but do not have any preconceived notions about the debtor's sense of honesty or get so involved in conversations that you take what debtors say personally.

This book includes many empathy-building statements that acknowledge the debtor's point of view and provide a framework for better communication. Many collectors attend seminars, read books, and use other training forums to further their knowledge, but few have ever sought training to improve their *listening* skills. Yet listening is just as important to the collection process as selling. The ability to listen and decipher a debtor's excuses and frame a response is an absolute prerequisite to superachievement in collections.

3. *Use sales strategies.* Unfortunately, most collectors lack sales skills, relying instead on conventional collection protocol. But debtor mentality has undergone a tidal wave of change. Today's sophisticated debtor will not respond to antiquated terminology. The days when hard-line tactics were effective are today interwoven into a mixture of creative persuasion techniques. You need new collection strategies based on principles of effective sales. The secret is to be creative in terms of what you can do to persuade debtors to satisfy their obligations. To convince clients to pay, you must present your service or product in a manner that will result in monetary fulfillment of the obligation. If you can present your charges in light of the importance of your service or product to their business or personal happiness, you can persuade them to pay your bills before the others.

4. *Negotiate objections.* Few in the collection profession realize that their job description revolves around negotiation. Collection involves listening, problem solving, and persuasion—all components of effective negotiation. An unwillingness or inability on the part of collectors to negotiate is the reason a lot of money goes uncollected. Similarly, few collectors have the ability to distinguish between a "condition" (e.g., bankruptcy, loss of job, or other economic factors that make it impossible for the debtor to come to terms with the obligation) and an "objection" (an invalid or insufficient reason for nonpayment). Yet a collector who recognizes a debtor objection for what it is can overcome that objection and negotiate a settlement. A mastery of negotiation skills and an ability to distinguish between conditions and objections are essential.

5. *Follow up.* Follow-up is one of the most important, yet most neglected, phases in the collection cycle. A debtor's word that he or she will pay is not enough (especially after all of your customers defaulted on their original obligation). The collector must make sure the debtor follows through on that commitment. By doing so, the collector is making a sale after the sale. Too many collectors believe statements made

by debtors with the sole purpose of rushing the collectors off the telephone. A debtor's statement that he or she is going to mail a check or adhere to other agreements does not necessarily translate into funds on deposit in your account. It is critical to confirm the debtor's commitment and follow up the collection call if you are to keep broken promises to a minimum.

As the collector maneuvers the debtor, each preceding step must be completed and confirmed. Do not copy someone else's style. You are unique. Identify your own style. Develop your own message. You have a song to sing. You are on stage. You are an actor who directs, writes, and produces your own performance. Remember that every collection call is a performance, so give it your Academy Award best.

DEBTOR PROFILES

An understanding of typical debtor profiles will help a collector categorize a delinquent account, weigh collection potential, and map a collection strategy. The most common types of debtor include the following:

- *Prompt payer.* This debtor pays bills on time, is a good risk, and represents the majority of credit account holders.

- *Slow payer.* This debtor resorts to stalls, broken promises, and tends to procrastinate. There are two subcategories:
  1. The *unintentional* slow payer falls behind in meeting obligations because of circumstances, but ultimately does come to terms with creditors. The unintentional slow payer is the easiest of all collections to effect.
  2. The *intentional* slow payer initiates ploys to evade payment, has the earmarks of a potential skip, may be contemplating bankruptcy, or has taken steps to make himself judgment-proof.

- *Careless debtor.* This debtor is not concerned with details, is often negligent, and usually disregards payment notices.

- *Recalcitrant debtor.* This debtor takes the position that the debtor is in control. This debtor will pay debts at his convenience, on his own terms. This kind of person will challenge the creditor on every front, but ultimately will meet the obligation.

- *Impenetrable judgment-proof debtor.* This debtor is a virtuoso at the art of concealing assets, does not respond to pressure, makes a mockery of the legal system, and thrives on controversy.

- *Deadbeat.* This debtor never intended to satisfy the obligation. The debt was incurred with intent to defraud. This debtor is an out-and-out credit criminal.

- *Liar.* This debtor, a habitual or pathological liar, propounds reassurances. This person usually pays at the eleventh hour, when litigation ensues or when he fears other consequences in greater proportion to the amount of the debt.

- *Discretionary corporate debtor.* Maintains an exemplary payment history with select creditors (owing to maintenance of a relationship), but defaults on obligations where this mentality customer has no further use for creditors. Most common in corporate environment (i.e., officer pays his consumer debts but defaults on corporate obligations).

- *Skip.* Skips come in two categories:
  1. The *unintentional* skip moves out of town without paying, but leaves a forwarding address and is easy to locate. Usually, this debtor is easily motivated to satisfy the obligation.
  2. The *intentional* skip does not leave a forwarding address and covers his tracks. In this respect, the intentional skip, depending on the person's degree of expertise, can range anywhere from mild (i.e., minimal effort to locate) all the way to the "professional" skip, who initiates extraordinary maneuvers to evade creditors. Nonetheless, even the professional skip does leave a paper trail that a proficient skip tracer can follow.

- *Discretionary consumer debtor.* This debtor tends to pay primary bills (i.e., telephone company, utilities, prestigious credit cards) but ignores such other bills as department store invoices, minor charges, mail-order transactions, and so forth. This debtor is a "schizophrenic" personality, usually has a good credit rating, and knows which credit transactions are reported. An unsuspecting credit grantor might be misled as a result of this debtor's favorable credit profile. (See Chapter 8 for more on credit profiles.)

- *Intermediate credit criminal.* This debtor deliberately, and with actual malice, makes a livelihood by ripping off creditors.

- *Professional commercial "credit criminal."* This is the truly criminally minded debtor. Such a person resorts to elaborate, sophisticated schemes to procure hundreds of thousands of dollars' worth of credit. Usually this criminal establishes a shell corporation as a front, incorporating a name similar to that of another, legitimate business. The credit criminal, gifted with a "silver tongue," capitalizes on the legitimate business's good credit standing to lull creditors' suspicions and order hundreds of thousands of dollars in merchandise. The debtor will then liquidate merchandise quickly, usually below cost, on a grand scale, and walk away with megabucks, all the while shielded by a corporate umbrella. This professional credit criminal is definitely the most dangerous. Interestingly, this debtor pays most small, common obligations and usually has an impeccable credit history at the consumer level. This debtor may even be a well-respected citizen within a community. This scam is also known as a "bustout" scheme.

- *Transient debtor.* This debtor is a perpetual skip, moving frequently with the intent to evade creditors. This debtor moves out on a Friday night, leaving no forwarding address.

- *Threat-of-harassment debtor.* This debtor threatens creditors with a harassment suit, creates frivolous excuses, makes up disputes, and thrives on beating the system. An expert at fabricating stories as a smoke screen, this debtor is "always right." Another version of this mentality debtor will threaten a harassment suit by way of an attorney.

DELAY TACTICS

Aaron Burr said, "Never do today what you can put off till tomorrow. Delay may give clearer light as to what is best to be done." It would be impossible to review every one of the innumerable delay tactics used by debtors, but some of the most common are the following:

- *Defective merchandise.* The debtor claims merchandise is broken, inoperable, or unsatisfactory and uses the complaint as leverage to either evade payment or reduce the indebtedness.

- *Check is in the mail.* Creditors often nibble at this sour fruit. These "famous last words" take the wind out of the sails of the collector and effectively sidetrack creditors.

- *Broken promises.* A debtor may use a series of empty promises to string the creditor along. This just gives the creditor a false sense of security as the debtor leads the creditor down a garden path.

- *Honest debtor.* This debtor actually confronts the creditor, without being solicited. The debtor is trying to sidetrack the creditor with frivolous, ridiculous, untrue excuses, which may include ill health, problems at work, or other economic difficulties. This debtor attempts to secure the creditor's sympathy by offering assurances that the debt will be paid when the difficulty is resolved.

- *Letter-writing debtor.* This debtor has mastered the art of writing letters with excuses and promises to pay, but never follows through with paying the debt. Another version of this mentality is the debtor who provides creditors with grandiose marketing plans, projections, and so on.

A professional debtor will resort to numerous tricks either to buy time or to circumvent his obligation entirely. Every collector should be aware of the more familiar tricks debtors employ. Most of these evasion tactics involve the following:

- Distorting computer cards
- Writing back to the creditor and requesting an explanation of the debt
- Failing to sign a check
- Postdating a check
- Sending the check to the address of a subsidiary
- Sending a partial payment with an explanation or complaint
- Mounting frivolous excuses
- Placing a restriction on the debtor's check

A debtor might even have a relative or other accomplice send a partial payment along with a letter explaining some dire emergency. A collector should take the following steps:

- *Scrutinize checks.* A debtor will sometimes write a check in pencil, knowing that it will not be accepted, send the wrong check to a creditor "by mistake," stop payment, or write erroneous information on the check. Some debtors even use ink eradicator to erase one digit in the check's account number or otherwise scramble a check's account number to frustrate the bank's computer when the check is processed.

- *Be aware of the foreign country dodge.* Some debtors will provide the post office with a forwarding address in another country so that the creditor's letter, being forwarded, will end up in a distant country. If the creditor marks the envelope "Forwarding address correction requested," the post office is obligated not only to forward the mail, but also to send a card back to the sender (creditor) showing the forwarding address. The post office charges a fee for this service. Usually, the foreign country ploy is successful because most creditors that receive an address in another country will terminate pursuit.

INTEGRATED COLLECTIONS

The integrated accounts receivable recovery schematic in Exhibit 1.4 illustrates how to approach various collection problems and offers appropriate remedies. Note that most collection problems fall into three main categories:

1. Bad checks
2. Large balances
3. Small balances

This schematic together with the various footnotes will give you a broad perspective of various remedies and their application to collect accounts receivable.

PROBLEM-SOLVING TECHNIQUES

The Roman statesman Cicero said, "A problem well stated is half solved." If your debtor has a legitimate problem, you owe it to the person to listen. Display an attitude of interest. Convey your genuine concern and emphasize by saying that you are there to resolve a problem, not create new ones.

Problems you encounter can be real. But more often than not, they do not exist except in the debtor's mind. Debtors tend to blow things out of proportion. It is your job to distinguish between problems that are illusory and those that are real.

If a debtor's problem is valid, you should resolve it in an amicable fashion. If the debtor's problem is not valid, or if it is being used as a stall tactic, you can still deal with it effectively and maintain your company's integrity.

Debtors are human. They are subject to the same problems as the rest of us. They will react just like you or I. An astute collector recognizes this human tendency and will learn how to deal with it effectively.

EXHIBIT 1.4   INTEGRATED ACCOUNTS RECEIVABLE RECOVERY SYSTEMS

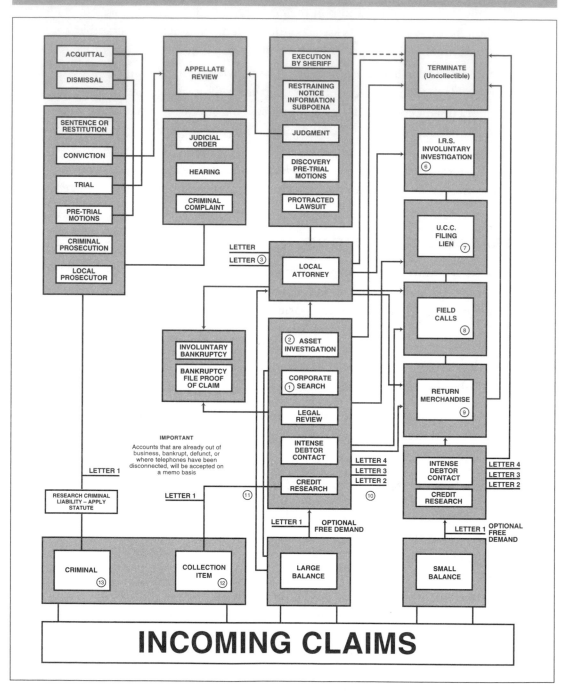

EXHIBIT 1.4   INTEGRATED ACCOUNTS RECEIVABLE RECOVERY SYSTEMS (CONT'D.)

Note 1: A corporate search is performed to verify the legal business entity of the debtor (i.e., corporation [no individual liability], partnership, and sole proprietor [limited and individual liability]).

Note 2: When legal action is necessary, first verify the legal business entity of the debtor. Then undertake a thorough and comprehensive investigation of the debtor's assets to uncover pending lawsuits, judgments, tax liens, foreclosures, bankruptcy proceedings, executions, assignments, priority creditors' liens, or other legal consequences that might render judgment uncollectible. All of this critical information should be investigated and verified before commencement of a protracted lawsuit. When a lawsuit is authorized, provide your attorney with a full investigative report containing in-depth and critical information on the legal status of your debtor. Armed with this knowledge, counsel can properly expedite and judiciously represent your best interests. Litigation is not recommended unless you can recover your monies after securing judgment. Do not throw good money after bad.

Note 3: In some situations, phone calls, letters, and personal contacts by a local attorney may be more productive and better serve the creditor's interests than immediate commencement of a lawsuit. Often, such localized contacts by an attorney will lead the debtor to settle the debt without recourse to costly litigation.

Note 4: Litigation can assume many forms, including attachment, summary judgment (accelerated judgment), injunction, or involuntary bankruptcy proceedings. Work closely with your attorney to intelligently explore all possible avenues in the litigation cluster that will yield maximum recovery.

Note 5: In certain jurisdictions, after judgment, an information subpoena and restraining notice can be served on the defendant (debtor). The subpoena can order the defendant to reveal pertinent information concerning the location of bank accounts, inventory, and other attachable assets. A restraining notice is a court order directing the debtor not to dispose of any assets pending execution by the sheriff.

Note 6: In extraordinary situations, it is possible to determine whether the debtor is engaged in financial transactions used to evade possible taxes. An involuntary audit can be commenced when appropriate, and a reward will be paid by the IRS for original information (Section 7623, Internal Revenue Code). But before you become too enthusiastic, you should know that you must submit a prima facie case to the IRS, and the IRS is legally bound not to reveal information on the taxpayer. You should contact the IRS for information on turning in tax cheats.

Note 7: Make sure to file a UCC-1 financing statement or a UCC-3 continuation statement as a protective measure.

Note 8: Person-to-person contact may be utilized when appropriate for greater debtor impact.

Note 9: Where merchandise is resalable or when monies cannot be recovered, merchandise may be returned, subject to the creditor's approval. An action in replevin can also be commenced to recover chattels in lieu of a money judgment, in appropriate situations.

Note 10: While letters do not generally make collections, they are an intrinsic element of the overall collection process when effectively combined with manual efforts. Do not use form letters on larger balances (as is the practice of most agencies). The correspondence factor is critical to achieve the best possible results and should be pursued with the utmost professionalism—with an emphasis on individuality. Use a collection agency that will uphold your good image.

Note 11: There may be instances when it is appropriate to direct your account to a local attorney for immediate attention. (See Chapter 9.) Your collection agency or your attorney will initiate a corporate search and asset investigation to assist the prosecution.

Note 12: Contrary to public opinion, passing bad checks does not necessarily constitute criminal culpability. In situations where bad checks have no criminal liability, they should be pursued as collection items.

Note 13: When a bad check is in violation of a criminal statute, initial correspondence should incorporate the appropriate criminal statute. If necessary, file a complaint with the local prosecutor's office. The decision whether to commence criminal prosecution will depend on many factors, including amount, how the check was returned, state, venue, and evidence rules. Keep in mind, however, that passers of bad checks are rarely prosecuted. Most often, the criminal justice system provides for punishment, not recovery. Another downfall is that many states render one form of punishment vis à vis criminal/civil forfeiture for the other.

Note 14: Where claims are placed for collection and the debtor ultimately files for protection under bankruptcy laws, the creditor must prepare and file a proof of claim. Consider filing an involuntary bankruptcy petition in cases where assets are being fraudulently conveyed or where creditors are given preferential treatment. A thorough credit investigation can determine legal remedies.

Your calls to a debtor are interruptions. The debtor might well be involved in other matters that are more important to him. A debtor encountered in the midst of another problem will not be in the friendliest of moods. Try this formula to deal with the problem:

- Show the debtor you are interested and listen attentively.

- If a problem is unrelated to the balance owed to you, empathize with the debtor's situation, but do not offer any advice. Acknowledge that you understand the problem, then get the debtor back to the business at hand. If you offer advice, you might trigger a lengthy conversation. Be courteous, be empathetic, but collect the debt.

- If the debtor voices a problem that does concern the debt, do not interrupt, but pay close attention. After the debtor has explained the situation in detail, tell the debtor that you are very much interested in the problem. In fact, say you are so concerned about what this person has to say that you would like to retrieve your notebook and take copious notes, so you can bring the grievance to the attention of management. This implies genuine concern.

- Then tell the debtor that you have a pad of paper. Ask the person to repeat *everything*—because the problem is important to you. There is good reason to use this formula. Normally, we speak at 125 to 150 words per minute. But in moments of emotional outburst, we speak much more rapidly. When asked to repeat something, the chances are the person will calm down and speak more slowly. Then you can reason with the debtor.

- If the debtor does not change his or her viewpoint, do not make any offers to resolve the problem. Instead, ask what the debtor expects you to do. If the proposed solution is reasonable, then you can treat the situation as a customer service matter. If the problem cannot be readily resolved, or if the debtor demands too much, you have at least put the debtor in a more agreeable frame of mind.

The key is to empathize with your debtor. Show a keen interest in the debtor's situation and encourage him to talk. The more a debtor talks, the better! In most cases, complaints can be resolved amicably.

Remember, you want to get paid. But sometimes debtors have legitimate complaints, and you have a responsibility to deal with complaints in a professional manner. The preceding formula will enable you to separate disputes that exist only in the mind of the debtor from disputes that are real. A collector must be a proficient problem solver.

OPENING STATEMENTS

No one has ever figured out how to get a second chance to make a first impression. Bear this truism in mind when you make collection calls. In many instances, collections are made or lost within the first 30 seconds. The most successful attorneys recognize the psychological impact of the initial impression. The outcome of a trial is often determined during the opening statement. Similarly, a receivable recovery is achieved during the initial conversation. In the following examples, consider how attorneys handle opening statements in their summations to the jury:

Example A: Typical Summation   "Ladies and gentlemen of the jury, we have now reached the conclusion of this trial. The case will now be turned over to you for deliberation. Judge Righteous will instruct you regarding applicable law . . ."

Analysis: The jury's attention has not been captured. The opening statement by the attorney is not compelling and fails to spark the jury's interest. Remember: People are interested in themselves, and juries are no exception. The members of the jury want to get on with their own lives. They are anxious to conclude this trial and go home. This opening statement is not wrong, but it can be improved.

Example B: Powerful Summation   "Ladies and gentlemen of the jury, you will make few decisions in your lives as important as the one that is about to be entrusted to you. Whether or not Frank Smith is convicted on the tenuous, flimsy, unsupported conjecture that has been brain-fed to you by the prosecutor, is in your hands. Whether Frank Smith is allowed to return to his loved ones—his wife and his family—or sentenced to the horrors of an unjust prison term, is in your hands! The decision as to whether Frank's family will be deprived of his love, affection, and support is one you will have to live with for the rest of your life."

Analysis: Notice the attention-grabbing "picture" words used to capture the jury's attention and humanize their role in the trial. The attorney emphasizes the great importance of the jury's decision. The defense counsel "humanized" his client by referring to him by name, but the district attorney was referred to as "the prosecutor." The defense counsel also suggested that the district attorney had "brain-fed" unsupported conjecture, implying that the members of the jury had been manipulated. The word "conjecture" was used instead of "evidence," since "evidence" implies guilt. Is there any doubt that the latter approach will persuade the jury?

The same psychology should be applied in communicating with debtors. Remember: The first words uttered to the debtor contact (the debtor, debtor's attorney, or assistant, or spouse) are the most crucial.

INITIATING A COLLECTION CALL

The following discussion provides various methods of initiating a phone call as well as an analysis of each method.

The conventional approach: "Mr. Pastdue, this is Mr. Rogers from XYZ Company. I am calling in reference to a debt incurred by you—a debt that remains unpaid. Your account is now 150 days past due, and I would like to discuss this with you . . ."

Analysis: Most collectors use this bland approach. The approach is not wrong, but it lacks ingenuity. It fails to arouse interest. Remember, debtors are human. They are caught up in their own concerns. You should say something that will capture a debtor's interest immediately.

A more powerful and compelling opening statement: "Mr. Pastdue? Mr. William Pastdue? Mr. Pastdue, this is Bill Rogers, and I am calling for a very important reason. Mr. Pastdue, I know your reputation in the community and that you value your creditworthiness. I would like to resolve a problem, for I know you have every intention of satisfying your long-outstanding unpaid balance with XYZ Company. Mr. Pastdue, I recognize that there may be reasons why this debt has not been satisfied, and I am calling to resolve this problem in good faith. Would you be good enough to process a check so that we can credit your account?"

Analysis: Notice the opening statement. Mr. Pastdue is referred to twice. Ask the first question ("Mr. Pastdue?") and pause for an answer. Then confirm with, "Mr. *William* Pastdue?" This sequence qualifies that you are talking to the right person. In the first question we ask the last name. In the second question we qualify, and identify Mr. William Pastdue. All this is done before we even identify ourselves. Debtors will often conceal their identities, and the two-name approach helps to qualify a responsible principal.

We repeat the name, Mr. Pastdue, for a third time after we confirm that we are talking to the right person. A person's name is very important. People like to hear their names. Note that Mr. Pastdue's name is intentionally repeated several times throughout the collection interview.

"I am calling for a very important reason." We know that the debtor is preoccupied when we call. The term "very important" suggests that the debtor should pay close attention to what we have to say. Our minds are like parachutes—they work only when they are open.

Our reference to "reputation" implies we know something about the debtor. People are interested in how other people feel about them. We have aroused the debtor's curiosity. Now the debtor wants to talk to us.

By expressing our interest in "resolving a problem" and in "creditworthiness," we imply that we are reasonable and concerned. Also note the assumptive statement, "I know you have every intention of satisfying this debt." This implies that the debtor will pay. Remember, it does not matter whether the debtor is a crook. We want to get paid. If that means appealing to the debtor's vanity, then let's do it. Remember, always make the sale before the sale.

WORDS AND PHRASES THAT SHOULD BE REMOVED

The following are examples of words and phrases that should be removed from collection language.

Be aware of nasty words: Whether you realize it or not, many of the words you use actually build resistance, create obstacles, and hinder your effectiveness. When you map out a collection strategy, you must be aware of the negative impact of "nasty words."

Assume that you have negotiated with the debtor to sign a *Confession of Judgment* or a note or other legal instrument. It will be difficult just to get a debtor to read such a document. It will be even harder to prompt the debtor to sign it.

What have you been told all your life about signing something? "Watch it," "beware," "don't sign anything," "read every word," "consult with an attorney." We have been conditioned not to sign any document. Yet there are collectors who constantly pressure debtors to sign legal papers. How can you use substitute words that will not create negative images?

Once an agreement is reached, you should encourage your debtor to "okay" or "initial" the "agreement" or "understanding." Debtors do not mind "okaying an agreement," but they are reluctant to "sign a contract."

The words "deal" and "proposition" are also nasty words that you should remove from your vocabulary. What do you mean when you use the word "deal" or "proposition"? These words have very bad connotations. They conjure up an image of a huckster making pitches on a street corner. What you really should say is "opportunity." We like to do business when there is an "opportunity." But we have been conditioned to beware of "propositions" or "deals."

Here is the correct way: "Mr. Debtor, I'm glad you recognize the opportunity to resolve this matter amicably."

Other nasty words: What about the words "pay," "payment," and "cost"? These words imply that the debtor is going to have to lay out money. No one likes to "pay"—no one wants to make "payments." To the debtor's mind, he or she is probably already "paying" too much. There is nothing that evokes a more negative reaction from a debtor than the word "pay." Professional salespeople have long recognized this principle, and have substituted a word such as "investment" for "pay," "payments," and "cost." Obviously, you cannot tell a debtor to make an "investment" by satisfying an obligation to your company. But you can use the word "investment" when referring to the merchandise or services your company provided where the customer profited. Here's how:

"Mr. Debtor, at the time you made the investment in our _____ it was important for you to have the benefits our products (or service) provided." This approach confirms the transaction as an investment and changes the debtor's base of thinking—bringing the person back to the state of mind that existed when the order was placed. There is no pride in being a "payer." But there is pride in being an "investor." Substitute the words "invest" or "investment" for words such as "pay," "payment," or "cost."

Condition debtors by asking for "remittance" or "the check" instead of "payment." Debtors do not like to "pay." They are more inclined to "make a remittance" for something in which they "invested."

Key phrases: Phrases are also very important. Have you ever heard a collector say "when you pay," or "after you've paid"? Never use this terminology. Instead say:

- After this matter is resolved . . .
- When you have cleared your account . . .

- When your account is brought current . . .
- When we have received your check . . .

These phrases give you a two-tiered psychological advantage. First, they imply that the debtor has already made payment (even though he has not). Second, they do not create a negative impression in the debtor's mind. Always use words and phrases that build your collection story. Paint pictures in the mind of the debtor.

Exhibit 1.5 shows both negative and positive climates created by collection management strategies.

EXHIBIT I.5   CLIMATES CREATED BY COLLECTION MANAGEMENT STRATEGIES

Strategies That Create Negative Climates:	Strategies That Create Positive Climates:
Subscribing to traditional collection management	Enhancing collection management by negotiation/innovation/creativity
Considering collectors as subordinates to be dictated to as a means to an end	Creating an atmosphere where collectors are participants working together in harmony toward promulgating the goals of the organization
Implementing rigid dictatorial policies that hinder productivity	Understanding human need, recognizing that building people, who in turn build the organization, is of paramount importance
Deeming the collection department as a "necessary evil"	Viewing the collection effort as the "sale after the sale" and positioning the collection department as a true profit center
Making little or no attempt to communicate or solicit input	Encouraging feedback, soliciting input, and rewarding employees for successful ideas
Not rewarding or encouraging creativity	Encouraging creativity and maximizing human potential
Governing with harsh discipline and rigid rules	Maintaining rules, but also incorporating flexibility and a belief in fairness
Governing only from above	Making each person feel like part of a team and recognizing that the collection department is an important part of the organization
Failure to provide incentives or rewards for quality work	Stimulating participation and rewarding for results

CHAPTER 2

Oratory and Advanced Communication Skills

Recovery of a delinquent account is an exercise in applied psychology. Influencing debtors—that is what it is all about. Bringing accounts current is a difficult and frustrating task. You must get debtors personally involved. You must stimulate and motivate nonpaying customers to accept your way of thinking.

There are many psychological techniques available to move a debtor into a productive frame of mind, but the bottom line is that you need to get the debtor's attention and inscribe a lasting impression. To accomplish getting paid, you must be skilled in the art of communication and persuasion.

Even with a structured approach, it can be difficult to get debtors to listen attentively. Remember, your calls are interruptions. You must capture their attention. In most cases, the debtor is aware of his indebtedness but has chosen to ignore the obligation. Regardless of the validity of the debt, you must use your imagination to elicit the debtor's interest. You must make a sale before the sale.

Words are easily misunderstood, or even ignored, and must be chosen carefully. It is imperative that you appeal to the common denominator that will prompt positive action—that is, payment of the debt. Sometimes silence can be far more effective than rambling on in a desultory fashion.

GRAB THE DEBTOR'S ATTENTION

When you get a debtor on the phone, you can safely assume that this person's thoughts are elsewhere. The debtor may not be consciously and attentively listening to you. It requires concentration to tune in to your message. Even if a debtor seems to be listening, it is likely that he is not. You are the last person the debtor wants to talk to. It is important to understand this, because it means that you have to develop attention-getters and use them skillfully, which requires using the following:

- A choice of compelling words
- Proper timing
- Powerful and persuasive communication techniques

The debts you are trying to collect may be valid and irrefutable in fact, but your ability to communicate effectively determines success.

Words and their psychological impact are important weapons in a collector's arsenal. That does not mean a torrent of verbosity will carry the day. Actually, quite the opposite approach is usually more effective. Picture words have impact. They will help communicate and persuade, when they are judiciously selected, applied in the right order, and coupled with effective listening to detect hidden meanings in conversations.

The art of communication depends on other people's perception of your words and their emotional impact. Words alone are not the rapiers of a collector's communication skills. They must be honed into persuasive motivaters by the deliberate use of tone and volume. Sometimes, humor is added to the ingredients.

You, the collector, are your employer's most important representative. The impression you make on debtors is going to have impact—one way or another. Your performance will either establish credibility or it will not. Credibility is created when debtors perceive that you are *confident*. Collectors who exude confidence, who impress debtors with this quality early in the collection cycle, have taken a giant step toward winning debtors over to their way of thinking. Confidence is the bullfighter who goes into the ring with mustard on his sword.

Match the Debtor's Background

Language is important. This does not mean that a master communicator always uses a lot of polysyllabic words or talks like a Harvard professor. A dignified member of the business establishment might be impressed with two-dollar words, but if you are talking to a hardcore debtor, streetwise language will carry a lot more weight. The point is, you must adjust your vocabulary and language to that of your listener. A rough-talking debtor with a scatological attitude will not take offense at streetwise terms—in fact, such a debtor will be more likely to be motivated by your message. If you give the impression that you come from a similar background, the debtor is more likely to identify with you and respond positively. A sophisticated debtor, on the other hand, would be alienated, if not offended, by such language. If you persisted in using streetwise terms, you would only widen the gap between you and the debtor. The point is, exercise language that zeros in on your debtor's hot button.

If you project an image that is inconsistent with the debtor's own background, you deemphasize the debtor's economic and social standing. That would be a cardinal mistake. You want to empathize with your debtor. Not all debtors are genteel citizens. There is some hostility inherent in relationships between collectors and debtors, but people of similar social status share at least some common ground.

BODY LANGUAGE CARRIES

Julius Fast, the noted authority on body language and one of the most successful attorneys in the collections area, states that most communication is nonverbal, perhaps as much as 60%. What's more, he reveals that body language can be transmitted over the telephone. Our gestures and expressions can be subconsciously conveyed through the voice. For example, if you were to communicate on the telephone while waving your arms and gesticulating, that physical exertion would affect your voice, tone, and control—and the transmission relayed over the telephone to your listener. Body language can be transmitted over the telephone. Always be conscious of this fact.

People communicate better when they are standing than when they are sitting. Many expert collectors have long extension cords on their phones. They freely walk the circumference of their desks while talking. So get up and stretch your legs when you are on the phone. This will help bring emotion to your conversations, and the added intensity will be perceived by your listeners.

VALUE OF COMMUNICATION SKILLS

Some people are paid small fortunes solely for their ability to communicate. Barbara Walters, Dan Rather, and Peter Jennings earn a million dollars a year because their ability to communicate effectively establishes their credibility as television journalists.

A collector's primary function is persuasion—the careful grouping and utilization of words and actions to achieve the desired result. Collectors who want to be as persuasive as possible use more than their mouths. They use their whole bodies. The way you dress, the way you articulate, your manners, even your hand gestures will be communicated and perceived by your listeners.

If you want to make a motion with your hand, or even with your body, to emphasize a point, then make it, but do not make gestures that have no purpose. Learning to use these nonverbal skills is an ongoing process. They take many years to develop.

It is very important to use the language of persuasion—language that will have the greatest impact. Words and gestures create pictures in the minds of listeners. Structure words and phrases to paint the picture you want to present. Debtors will respond more favorably to the following:

- Action verbs
- Color words
- Words and phrases that convey a sense of taste, touch, sound, or feeling

Your job is to persuade. Words that contain "picture meanings" will go a lot further toward persuading debtors than a plethora of meaningless jargon. Use words that have texture and substance. Choice of words is a significant factor in the art of communication and persuasion. The small minority of superstar collectors have mastered and effectively utilize this principle.

Start and Conclude on a High Note

Set the tone for your collection call by starting off with a key phrase that delivers a strong punch. People tend to remember the first and the last parts of a communication. The middle tends to get buried and is likely to be forgotten. Therefore, always start on the strongest point. Convey that point with feeling and emotion to captivate the interest of your debtor. By the same token, end on a high note.

A person's attention span dips as sentences become longer. The words in the middle tend to get cluttered. Some collectors like to build the collection strategy to a climax. Others like to start with a significant punch *and* end on a high note. There are no set rules. It all depends on what works best for you; however, if you remember to start and end with strong points, you will make deeper impressions, paint more pictures, and increase your chances for success.

How to Shape Questions

The way you shape your questions is of the utmost importance. By asking questions, you are developing information. As you learn to recognize the shape of your questions, you will develop new skills. These new skills will lead to more information, which will enable you to collect a significantly higher ratio of delinquent accounts.

Changing even one word in a single question can alter the response. Consider a court case in which it was important to determine whether a witness saw a particular vehicle. The attorney could phrase the question in one of two ways: "Did you see the car with *the* broken headlight?" or "Did you see the car with *a* broken headlight?" The choice of words in this case is extremely important. Most people will say they did see the car if "the" (the definite article) is used rather than "a" (the indefinite article). Using the indefinite article would pose a general question, to which the witness would be more likely to respond in the negative. A skillful attorney will recognize these tendencies and phrase questions with an assumptive attitude, taking it for granted that the witness will take the cue and respond in the manner that is most favorable to the attorney's client.

The same psychology should be applied in collection calls. Phrase your questions to encourage the response you want. Instead of asking debtors how much they can "afford to pay," for example, why not ask them how much they "are short"? This is a much more revealing question.

Nasty Words in Collection Calls

As you have seen, your choice of words is critical and can convey negative or positive images. An attorney would be wise not to use the word "accident" when representing a client in a personal-injury case. The word "accident" conjures up images of mistake, error, and being at fault. Repeated use of the word "accident" during the trial could paint a subconscious impression in the minds of the jurors that the victim was at fault. Better words, from the injured party's point of view, would be "occurrence," "incident," or even "smashup."

You can see how important it is to choose the right words. In collections, choice of words can spell the difference between success and failure. Such phrases as "We will turn your account over to a collection agency," "We intend to file suit," or "Please make payments" can actually diminish collection potential. Identify and eradicate nasty words from your speech.

Negative Words and Phrases

The following is a partial list of negative words and phrases that should be eliminated from your vocabulary.

Negative Words and Phrases	Comments/Substitute Words or Phrases
I, me, my, etc.	Debtors do not care about you or your problems.
I will turn you over to our collection agency.	"Your failure to satisfy your just and due obligation leaves us no alternative but to retain and implement third-party intervention."
	The phrase "third-party intervention" has greater impact than the phrase "collection agency" because it leaves debtors uncertain about whether you are referring to a collection agency or a law firm.
We will file suit.	The word "suit" has marginal impact. We live in a litigation-oriented society, and the threat of "suit" has been overworked. A better phrase would be:
	"Your failure to satisfy your just and due obligation has forced us to conduct an in-depth investigation into your business. It is our intention to commence and prosecute a protracted lawsuit in the courts seeking compensatory and punitive damages awardable by statute."

Words and Phrases Should Have Substance

Choose words and practice your speaking techniques to give your delivery substance and style. As you speak, vary your speed and intensity. Also, listen to your debtor, because as the debtor speaks, not only do you gain important information, but you can also structure an effective response. You must use your vocabulary in the context of the debtor's statements. Words in a vacuum have little meaning.

Paint a Picture

Communication is much more than a linear progression of words and phrases strung together to form sentences and paragraphs. Communication is the art of persuasion. The old Chinese proverb "One picture is worth more than a thousand words" is true. The converse may be equally true—one word is worth a thousand pictures. For example, the word "circus" would likely conjure a mental image of the big top, clowns, cotton candy, acrobats, three rings, and so on. Similarly, the word "baseball" might trigger memories of the crack of the bat, the green grass of the field, the excitement of the stadium at game time, or your favorite team—perhaps the New York Yankees or the Los Angeles Dodgers. The human mind thinks in terms of pictures, not words. This being true, why not use picture words that will reach out, touch, and motivate your debtor to do what you want? Avoid boring, stereotypical, unenticing words and phrases. Instead use graphic picture words with *content.*

Build a Collection of Impact Words and Phrases

The great sales trainer Elmer Wheeler once said, "Sell the sizzle—not the steak!" Radio, TV, newspapers, conversations with other people—these are excellent sources of impact phrases. Remember Senator Jackson's response to former President Ford's economic plan: "It's like moving chairs around the Titanic."

The media are full of such impact phrases—phrases that can be adapted to many collection situations. Keep a notebook in your car or beside you when you watch TV or listen to the radio. Listen for impact phrases and write them down. Later, transfer these phrases to a loose-leaf book and use them to build your collection vocabulary. Refer to this book often and practice your impact words and phrases in collection calls.

You will be surprised how quickly and effectively your ratio of collections improves. Largely through the use of impact words and phrases to motivate debtors. As a result of using picture words, I have recovered hundreds of thousands of dollars in debts that would otherwise have proceeded to litigation or remained uncollected.

Intimidation with Words

One case in my collection files clearly demonstrates the power of carefully chosen words and phrases. The debtor was an intentional and deliberate deadbeat who seemed to thrive on a life of writing bad checks and beating creditors. This hard-core deadbeat had retained counsel. In my initial contact, the attorney stated that his client "was an honest, ethical businessperson with an established reputation in the community." My prior investigation of the debtor had proved this was not the case, so when the attorney made this ridiculous, totally inaccurate statement, I responded:

"Counselor, the debt that your client has incurred is spotted with the leprosy of crime. Your client's word is a profanity. His statements are infected with lies, polluted with perjury, and contaminated with inconsistency. The truth of the matter, Counselor, is that your client went into this business with the echo of prison bars rattling in his ears."

Interestingly, the attorney was amused by my statement and even chuckled. He responded:

"Well, Mr. Coleman, I can see that you've done your homework, and you have a way with words."

I had caught the attorney in a false statement. But although I knew his portrayal of his client was a blatant lie and a gross misrepresentation, I realized that the attorney had an ethical and legal obligation to represent his client to the best of his ability, even if the debtor was a notorious criminal. The attorney knew I spoke the truth, and he was impressed, not only by my oratorical description of his client, but also by my knowledge. This productive conversation successfully maneuvered the debtor's attorney to act as my salesperson, for in the ensuing conversation we negotiated a very equitable payment plan that was backed by a confession of judgment (permitting judgment to be entered against him by the creditor) and a personal guarantee. It took six months to liquidate the obligation, but it was paid as a result of thorough investigation and powerful communication techniques.

How to Use Picture Words

Develop a treasury of impact words and phrases, and practice those picture words until you can retrieve them for instant use. Do not try to use all of them at one time. Rather, isolate one or two phrases and incorporate them into your conversations with debtors. You will have to make a conscious effort in the beginning. It takes the average person 7 to 21 repetitions to burn a word or a phrase into memory so that it becomes a natural part of his repertoire. Continue to collect your words and phrases on an ongoing basis to build your vocabulary. You will always come across new words and phrases you can use. This is a never-ending process. Do not make the mistake of thinking that just a few words are all you need. The more tools you have in your arsenal, the greater your chance of success.

Most collectors have never had exposure to these techniques, and they have no idea how to choose picture words or how to use them effectively, which explains why many collectors never escape the grasp of mediocrity. There are many powerful techniques in this book, but the selection and use of impact words and phrases is one of the most significant and one of the easiest to learn.

Become a virtuoso "word merchant," and your ratio of recovery will increase significantly.

It is not necessarily what you know that is important, but *how you use* what you know. Contrary to common belief, knowledge is *not* power. Knowledge is only potential power. It must be properly harnessed, backed up by an intense desire to succeed, and directed toward a specific goal.

There is no way of knowing in advance how particular words or images will be received. But the middle part of your communication with a debtor is not as important as the *beginning* and the *end*. The reason that the middle is not as important has to do with our attention span. You can string impact phrases together. Remember the famous statement made by President John F. Kennedy on January 20, 1961: "Ask not what your country can do for you; ask what you can do for your country." The great master of communication Winston Churchill used such phrases as "We shall not fail or falter." He was a man of "light and learning." "Let us do the task, to the battle, to the toil." This is persuasion!

Clichés Can Be Persuasive

Someone once asked Sir Isaac Newton, "Dr. Newton, how is it that you see things so clearly?" He responded, "I stand on the shoulders of men like Galileo." We all learn from one another, and we can learn about the art of persuasion from both the classics and modern oratory. Even clichés can be persuasive.

Avoid Overkill

It is important not to "overkill." Leave something to the imagination. It is not always necessary to paint a finished picture, presenting all the steps toward the conclusion you have reached. A good technique is to bring the debtor most of the way to your conclusion through the careful application of picture words. Then let the debtor's imagination take it from there. Debtors will be more convinced if they arrive at the conclusion themselves. Lead your debtors skillfully and persuasively to conclude that they should pay their debts, and they will pay. Remember KISS—Keep It Simple, Salesperson. A collector is a salesperson.

Strike the Jugular

Build to a climax. Use every available tool to persuade the debtor. Appeal to all the senses. Take the time to recognize key phrases as you hear them daily. Write them down, commit them to memory, compile notes, and retain them for future use.

COLLECTOR'S VOCABULARY

The following is a list of words and phrases that are commonly used in collections:

Abuse	An increasing segment of our practice involves . . .
Allegiance	
Allegiance factor	An investigation reveals . . .
Ammunition	Arson
A new broom always sweeps clean.	Battlefield

Beat them to death

Beat them until we draw blood

Bounty hunter

Breathes flames

Bulldog determination

Call a spade a spade

Can of worms

Can you afford to . . .

Cardinal mistake

Cast in concrete

Catch-22

Climactic moment

Colt .45

Come in from left field

Come up to bat

Complexities

Conviction

Convoluted

Corruption

Creative intellect

Crime

Crutch

Dead and buried

Declaration of war

Definitive

Demolition team

Destroyed

Dialogue

Direct hit

Dirty Harry

Disgusted

Dissolved by proclamation

Diversity

Dominant

Don't get stuck out in the rain.

Don't tell me what you can do—
show me!

Dynamite

Enforce

Explosion

Fat cat

Find a needle in a haystack

Fire our torpedoes

Foolproof

Forecasting

Forefront

For every day you allow this to remain
unpaid, you are . . .

From the grave

Fuse

Gladiatorial combat

Guerrilla warfare

Half-truth

Hall of fame

Hammer

Hard-line

Heavy hitter

How can we come to grips with this
problem?

I am interested in your success!

I am sure you recognize the inherent
changes in . . .

I appreciate your talking to me.

Idle threat

Immune

Indictment

Indoctrinated

Ingenious

Intermediate buffer

Intervene

Investigation

In your own best interests . . .

Ironclad

Irreversible

Isolate

Keep a lot of tools in the toolbox

Lends credibility

Lethal weapon

Leverage

Liability

Loaded gun

Lurking in my mind

Machinery in motion

Maneuver

Margin

Methodology

Misassumptions of underlying fact-corrections, erroneous explanations, inconsistent positions, blatant flaws of recollection

Mission impossible

More deadly than . . .

Muscle

99 times out of 100

Nitroglycerin

Nobody makes perfect copies.

Notorious

Nucleus

Off-the-wall statement

Once the personalities begin to blend, we can resolve the problem.

One-to-one

On target

Our research, investigation, and analysis of your business indicates that . . .

Our sincere desire is to resolve a problem, not create one.

Out of nowhere

Penetrate to the core

Perils

Perpetual

Perpetuate

Poison

Policing

Potent

Prisoner of credit

Progression cycle

Prosecution

Radical surgery

Red tape

Relish

Replete with error

Responsible to collect the money as quickly as possible

Restricted environment

Results

Safeguard your position

Shortchanged

Skeleton in the closet

Spill the beans

Spit in the ocean

Strike a nerve

Stuck out in the rain

Substance

Swat team

Tear gas

The instrument of a . . .

The instrument of a judgment is . . .

The intensity

The situation is uncompromising because . . .

The wheel that squeaks the loudest gets the most oil.

Time bomb

To accurately define . . .

Tortuous toxic tongue

To safeguard your interests by liquidating this debt, you can . . .

Turn the screws

Umbrella

Unfortunately, you have created a situation that will have long-term detrimental effects.

Value

Verbalization

Warlike

We are committed to resolving . . .

Wedge

When a torpedo hits you broadside, the water comes rushing in.

Would you prefer _____ or _____?

You cannot fight with one hand tied behind your back.

You can play an indispensable role in combatting . . .

You will feel better once you . . .

You won't fall prey
You (your client) incurred this debt spotted
   with the leprosy of crime. Your word is
   a profanity, your statements are infected
with lies, polluted with perjury, and
contaminated with inconsistency.
Your position is assured when
you . . .

I should point out that certain words have an extremely high picture content (e.g., "Dirty Harry," "Colt .45," "loaded gun") and should not be used incorrectly. For example, the term "loaded gun" does not mean that you should threaten to blow the debtor's brains out. You have to use such terms in their proper context. For example:

"Mr. Debtor, obviously, this is not going to be resolved without resort to litigation. Now, it is not our intention to commence a nonproductive lawsuit that would only result in an uncollectible judgment. Mr. Debtor, I have already communicated with several of your other creditors, and we discussed the possibility of forcing you into involuntary bankruptcy. Naturally, you are aware that an involuntary bankruptcy petition is a loaded gun, with immediate and long-term ramifications."

Analysis: The language was relatively strong, but I did not talk about filing a lawsuit. I used the implied threat of involuntary bankruptcy. The term "loaded gun" in the preceding illustration was not intended to be taken literally, but rather was a graphic illustration of a potential threat to the corporation (i.e., involuntary bankruptcy). The unpleasant connotations of the term could not help but make the debtor more uncomfortable with the situation. Carefully chosen, graphic words with intense picture meanings can help you manipulate your debtor into a frame of mind more amenable to the idea of resolving his indebtedness. They should not be used to threaten the debtor with violence. Use graphic words in a positive way.

Here's another example:

"Mr. Pastdue, obviously we are not engaged in 'warfare,' nor do I intend to create a 'battlefield environment.' We just want to resolve this matter to everybody's benefit . . ."

> *In my library are about a thousand volumes of biography—a rough calculation indicates that more of these deal with men who have talked themselves upward than with all the scientists, writers, saints and doers combined. Talkers have always ruled. They will continue to rule. The smart thing is to join them.*
> —Bruce Barton, 1886–1967, scholar, author, congressman, and founder of the ad agency Batten, Barton, Durstine and Osborn

VALUE OF HUMOR

Humor can be a potent tool in a collector's arsenal. Many collectors achieve noted success through the creative use of humor. If you can use an element of humor in your daily communications, you will not only make the debtors feel better, but you will also gain their confidence and enhance your credibility. When you build a debtor's confidence, you build your own success possibilities. Some collectors will dismiss this technique, labeling collections as serious business. That is true, and you should not take on the role of a comedian or humorist. Entertaining and telling jokes to debtors is not necessary, but try to be aware of potentially humorous situations, and use them to your advantage.

Everyone likes to laugh and to feel good. What better medicine is there than laughter? Norman Cousins, former adjunct professor at the University of California School of Medicine, was diagnosed to be in the final stages of a terminal disease and was given only a few months to live. Defying doctors' orders, Cousins checked out of the hospital and into a hotel. There he set up a projector and viewed every comic movie he could find. Over and over again he watched and laughed at the Three Stooges, Laurel and Hardy, W. C. Fields, Abbott and Costello, *The Honeymooners*, and many more. Behind those hotel doors, he watched and he laughed. He laughed so much that he literally laughed himself back to health! Think of it: The healing power of humor defied medical science and saved his life.

You might recall what former President Reagan said to reporters when he was shot by John Hinckley: "I forgot to duck!" Even as the president of the United States was being wheeled into the operating room, he jokingly said to doctors, "I hope you are all Republicans!"

Personally, I can recall many instances where a little humor established a rapport between me and the debtors, or even their attorneys, that enabled me to successfully recover what otherwise would have been uncollectible accounts. That does not necessarily mean that you should tell your debtor a joke or a hilarious story—you are not a stand-up comedian. But sometimes, *just by the way you present information,* you can draw attention to the humorous side of a situation or confrontation. Such an appeal to the funny bone may create a communication channel by inducing the otherwise unyielding debtor or attorney to drop his guard. Even the interjection of street methodology can be very persuasive. For example: The debtor might say, "I demand credit . . . The product is defective." Assuming you know for a fact that the debtor's allegations are false, you might respond with a humorous rebuttal, such as "Your fantastic allegation is as truthful as Saddam Hussein winning the Nobel Peace Prize!" This response is not only humorous but insulting. Make certain that the debtor's excuses are spurious before you defuse them with a street methodology response.

When to Inject Humor

There are no ironclad rules for determining when it is appropriate to interject humor. You can only learn by trial and error. But keep in mind that the purpose of humor in collections is not to entertain, but to eradicate psychological barriers to your getting paid. Whether humor is applicable in a given situation will depend on the feedback you get from the debtor and/or the attorney. You might test the waters by interjecting a phrase or a statement that would normally prompt a humorous reply. For example:

- "Mr. Debtor, as Harry Truman once said, 'The buck stops here.' Now, from what I understand, Mr. Debtor, you're the 'Harry Truman' at XYZ Corporation. The buck has 'stopped' at your desk, and we'd like to get paid!"

- "Mr. Debtor, I understand that this debt falls within your realm of responsibility, and I'm sure it's a thorn in your side as well as ours. May I remind you of Lord Chesterfield's words of wisdom? 'No idleness, no laziness, no procrastination; never put off till tomorrow what you can do today.' "

- "Harry Truman once said, 'If you can't stand the heat, get out of the kitchen.' Now, I'm not trying to create a heated debate, Mr. Pastdue, but . . ."

- "Since you're the only person who can get this paid, I'd better make this good!"

- "Tell me, Mr. Debtor, is it true that _____?" (Interject an element of humor that your debtor can relate to.)

Comment: These phrases and quotes may not seem humorous in themselves. The point is, it's not *what* you say that is important, it is *how* you say it. There are any number of juicy phrases and quotes that can lend an element of humor to a conversation when used properly. The trick to humor in collections is timing and delivery, and these can be mastered only by practice.

True story: I once represented a client who was owed in excess of $13,000. The debtor was a legitimate, well-respected company with a national reputation for quality merchandise. The matter involved a controversy over services rendered and had nothing to do with the ability or the inclination of the debtor to satisfy the debt. In my initial communication with the office manager, I was accorded a cold, perfunctory reception. Subsequently, the manager forwarded all the account documents to an in-house attorney, who was also perfunctory and belligerent. I did not want to pressure the debtor via normal collection procedure because my objective was not only to collect the debt, but also to salvage an ongoing business relationship.

I tried using humor to thaw out the office manager and, subsequently, the attorney, but that approach left them cold. The attorney put me off so many times that it became necessary to contact the president of the company. After several futile attempts to get through, I finally got a chance to speak with the chief executive. My approach was to treat the debt as a customer-service problem and, to maintain a cordial atmosphere, I interjected humor at the appropriate moment. My opening remarks went something like this:

"Mr. Chief Executive? My name is Michael Coleman, and my reason for wanting to speak to you is very important. I represent XYZ Credit Service. As Harry Truman once said, 'The buck stops here.' I can't get this problem resolved with your office manager or even with your corporate attorney. I'm taking my case directly to you, Mr. Chief Executive, because I know the buck stops at your desk . . ."

Now, the statement "As Harry Truman once said, 'The buck stops here' " does not sound funny in itself, but I uttered it in a joking manner to elicit a neutralizing response from the chief executive, who was curious about the problems I was having with his attorney and office manager. Continuing the conversation, I explained that the office manager was ignoring our invoices, and that when I brought the matter to the attorney's attention, the attorney was belligerent and refused to cooperate. *I did not criticize his employees.* I presented my case in such a way so as to give free rein to the CEO's imagination and let him draw the conclusion that maybe there was, in fact, a cancer within his organization.

In the end, the chief executive agreed with my position. He not only ordered the hostile office manager and attorney to pay the debt, but afterward resumed the business relationship with our client. Thus a profitable account was saved. There was a billing problem at the root of this controversy, but the hostile attitudes of the attorney and the office manager made it so difficult to get the debt paid. By taking the initiative and going to the top, and then by injecting humor to promote goodwill, the situation was resolved to everyone's satisfaction. Interestingly, it was only using the phrase quoting Harry Truman, which prompted a chuckle, that opened the door and paved the way to getting the debt resolved.

As a result of this incident I developed a rapport with the president of the debtor company, and he later confided to me that the office manager had an "attitude problem." (He was ultimately terminated.) The situation had snowballed because the attorney's belligerent attitude stemmed from inaccurate information provided by the office manager.

The important thing to remember is that when it comes to humor in collections, there are no set rules, guidelines, or criteria. Of course, this approach will not always work, but you should be aware that humor can be used to resolve difficult situations. Be ready to use it when opportunities present themselves in everyday situations. Learn to appreciate the value of humor. It will make you feel better, create a better work environment, and improve your collection ratio.

> *While there is infection, disease and sorrow, there is nothing in this world so contagious as laughter and humor.*
> —Harry Ward Beecher

"Bo Derek" Technique

We all remember Bo Derek in the movie *10*. In general conversation, how many times have you heard the phrase "on a scale of one to ten"? Ever since Bo Derek made movie history with *10*, we have become accustomed to rating things on the one-to-ten scale. Appropriately, this technique is included not in the chapter on strategy but in this section on humor, for every time I have used it, it has had a humorous ring, and it has often produced results.

Suppose you are engaged in a struggle to collect a debt. You are worn out and about ready to give up. Ask the debtor: "Ms. Pastdue, on a scale of one to ten, where are you in respect to getting this matter resolved?" (Note we did not use the terminology "getting this paid.")

Needless to say, you may or may not get an answer in numerical form, but this question will probably elicit a chuckle from the debtor. If the debtor responds that she is at "five," come back with another statement such as, "Well, Ms. Pastdue, how do we get to ten?" If the debtor responds that you are only at "two or three," then you know you have not sold the debtor and that you have a long way to go. If the debtor responds "five" or "six," she is only half sold. If the debtor responds "seven," "eight," or "nine," you know you are almost home.

Have you ever used a technique that allows you to gauge a debtor's temperature? That's exactly what this technique does, for it allows you to determine exactly where you stand. Many times I have used this strategy, not only with debtors, but also with their attorneys, and every time it immediately succeeds in arousing the other person's attention. Moreover, I estimate that 80% of the responses from debtors and attorneys have been positive, affirmative statements—sometimes made with a chuckle or in an equally humorous manner. What should you expect when employing the one-to-ten technique? Properly structured, most debtors will respond somewhere between seven and nine, indicating that your customer acknowledges liability. Five to six indicates you are at the halfway point, below four and a bell should ring—you need to resuscitate the patient!

Many of Hollywood's most noted productions are chock-full of quotes, metaphors, and melodrama, which can be creatively incorporated into the collection arena. Interject themes from famous TV sitcoms/commercials. This may seem far-fetched, even off-the-wall, but properly utilized, you can dramatically boost productivity.

The electronic gear to transmit recorded music and/or commercials is readily available. Purchase a CD player and amplifier from Radio Shack. Hello Direct in Seattle, Washington, sells the hardware. Their number is 800-435-5634. Next, obtain a catalog from TVT Records, 23 East 4th Street, NY, NY 10003, (212) 979-6410, and see how to make a $150 investment pay for itself many times over.

You are conversing with a debtor who will not budge. You are running out of options. Legal intervention is imminent. At the climactic moment, interject the famous *Perry Mason* or *Ironside* themes into your conversation with the debtor.

Example: Mr. Pastdue, we have a choice . . . we can either resolve this problem, or we can resort to the courts. (Interject *Perry Mason* theme into the conversation.) Our position is not to inundate you with a clutter of motions, notices to produce, subpoenas, interrogatories, depositions . . . all propounded within the paneled walls of the judicial theater, but unless we can arrive at a solution, your attorney is going to profit handsomely by his representing you.

In all likelihood, your nonpaying customer will be mesmerized by your theatrical presentation of the legendary *Perry Mason* legacy. Complement the theme with a humorous spiel, and you will position the collection call head and shoulders above this nonpaying customer's other creditors (chances are, this debtor is not paying other creditors).

Interjecting *Perry Mason* or *Ironside* themes into conversations is not restricted to debtors; it is also an effective persuasion strategy to use with an attorney. Remember, the debtor's attorney is not just an adversary—a debtor's counsel is also a salesperson commissioned with the power of influence over his client. Sell the attorney and you make the sale.

Hawaii Five-O

The famous cops and robbers *Hawaii Five-O* television series is not just making a spectacular comeback on cable TV's Family Channel—it's also produced substantial recoveries from Hawaiian debtors. Jokingly, when conversing with a Hawaiian debtor, I'll casually introduce:

> Nonresolution of your just and due debt will not only result in protracted legal intervention, but also a confrontation with the island's most infamous of detectives—Steve McGarrett ("Book 'em, Danno!").

The debtor, startled by this statement, responds favorably to the recognized *Hawaii Five-O* upbeat theme, paving the way to resolution.

TV themes most conducive to positive debtor responses are *Superman, Secret Agent, Mission Impossible, Paladin, 77 Sunset Strip,* and *Mannix.* Other sitcom themes I've also used in a more traditional persuasion strategy include *The Donna Reed Show, My Three Sons, Green Acres, Beverly Hillbillies,* and *Roy Rogers.*

Famous Commercials Are Also Powerful Persuasion Tactics

The utilization of TV themes into a debtor conversation is not the only persuasion device that has proven effective; I have also had tremendous success with commercials. Jokingly interjected into a humorous dialogue with debtors, I will flavor the conversation with, "We interrupt this receivable recovery for an important message from our sponsor . . .

- "Brill Cream—a little dab will do ya."
- "Winston tastes good like a cigarette should."
- "You can trust your car to a man who wears the star." (Texaco)
- "See the U.S.A. in your Chevrolet."
- "N-e-s-t-l-e-s, Nestle's makes the very best Cho-co-late!"

Any familiar commercial jingle is sufficient not only to entertain, but more important, to establish instant rapport. Overcome the logjam of debtor resistance, and recoveries that might not otherwise be possible are transitioned to dollars. Depending on what themes are used, the skill of the collector, and a debtor's response, a whopping 10% increase in recoveries is obtainable.

From a time perspective, this technique should yield the collection professional about an extra hour per day. (You will achieve your same daily quota in about one hour less time.) On average, you'll reduce downtime while adding at least 20 extra hours per month. Imagine, a whopping 10% boost in dollars because you've scorched your nonpaying customers speechless with a dazzling array of nostalgic reminiscence.

This strategy is not limited to direct debtor/attorney conversations. It is also effective for penetrating debtors who are shielded by voice-mail and/or answering machines. Imagine the euphoria when an evasive debtor (who is screening calls behind an answering machine) revels to the familiar *Superman* "It's a bird, it's a plane, no, it's your creditor trying to establish communication" spiel!

Sample Humorous Collection Letter

The following letter uses humor. Humor is a persuasive receivable management tool. This letter is brief and is intended to amuse and motivate customers to affirmative action. Consider that your slow-pays are being bombarded with a succession of boring, unenticing, conventional dunning notices. Conversely, this novel communication has yielded creditors more dollars with positive customer service a given.

> Dear _____:
>
> Your relationship with us is analogous to a Hollywood production! When we do business with you, *The Price is Right.*
>
> Engaging in protracted negotiations, we play Monte Hall—*Let's Make a Deal!*
>
> You sell our quality products—at a profit—a *Bonanza!*
>
> Sadly, however, our hearts are riven with pain, our souls tormented, for we, as partners in your success, wallow in a state of melancholy—crestfallen and disconsolate. Why? Because after our having extended credit, your obligation is unfulfilled.
>
> Only you can determine whether our Hollywood production will become a box office smash. If you bring your account current *immediately,* you'll hitch your wagon to ours and ride a profit trajectory to the *Twilight Zone.* With our products/services, your success is assured. And, with the money you'll make, you could be profiled on *Lifestyles of the Rich and Famous!*
>
> If you do not honor your obligation, however, the words of Arnold Schwarzenegger are applicable: "Big mistake." Then, instead of reveling in the wanderlust of "caviar dreams," as Robin Leach is fond of saying, we'll engage Dirty Harry, who will euphorically proclaim, "Make my day!"
>
> Your remittance will elicit a sunshine smile that will ripen bananas!
>
> P.S. Your mother carried you for only nine months; we've carried you longer!

The above letter may seem offbeat, even corny, but it does have its place in certain situations. Consider its application when you want to penetrate a hardened personality or where a dose of humor is appropriate.

Fact: Adding a P.S. to your letters will boost recovery. Why? Statistics prove that many debtors do not read a letter's content. They do, however, read the postscript.

Take the initiative and incorporate this powerful recovery strategy into your company's recovery efforts. Better yet, develop new and refreshing appeals that will motivate customers to keep their accounts current. Be the "leader of the pact."

Humorous Caricatures

Debt collection is serious business—an endeavor not usually associated with humor. Contrary to common belief, however, humor is a definitive tool, a valuable resource that in certain situations will aid the recovery effort.

Most accounts receivable problems are not intentional defaults but lethargy. Your cash-starved customers entered into the credit sale with every intention of paying you; the slow-pays are merely extending their financial problems to you. The solution is not one of psychologically badgering your slow-paying customers, but rather prioritizing their obligation to advance your invoice.

Humor is an effective tool—a device that will set you apart from your customers' other creditors, who like you, are competing for limited funds. Through implementation of humorous inducements, you gain customers' attention while isolating the transaction in debtors' minds. See Exhibit 2.1 for a sample humorous caricature you might want to try. It can be transmitted via e-mail or fax to greatly enhance your position.

The best advice is to experiment. Take advantage of the huge inventory of humor available in countless publications and on the Web. Augmenting these techniques with a conciliatory dialogue, you will squeeze more money from your receivables.

Telephone Techniques for Collectors

Regulate Speaking Speed

The human mind works at a rate of 600 to 800 words per minute. Yet we speak only 100 to 150 words per minute. Obviously, the mind works much faster than we can speak. But that does not mean you can "fast-talk" your way to receivable success. A good technique is to regulate your rate of speech to be consistent with your debtor's rate of speech. If you bombard a debtor with 150 to 200 words per minute, while the debtor is conversing at only 100 words per minute, you are speaking much too fast. You may overpower and intimidate the debtor. But will you make the collection? To be effective, you should throttle down to keep pace with your listener.

By the same token, a debtor who speaks too fast must be slowed down. Do not attempt to speed up your delivery to a fast-talking debtor. People who ramble on at an excessive rate of speed are likely to be dealing from emotion. You cannot reason with them in this state of mind. Tacitly reduce the debtor's speed of speech by intentionally regulating your own speaking rate. The debtor will not realize what you are doing. Remember, you are the architect of every collection call. You must take control and regulate voice, tone, volume, and speed.

Telecollecting

The telephone is much more than a communication channel between you and the outside world. It is a means to save time and boost productivity. It is the most important link between you and a bigger paycheck. Unfortunately, most collectors have had little or no training in effective telephone techniques. Attention to several key areas will enable you to utilize this marvelous instrument to the utmost.

First, it is important to recognize that people have an inherent fear of the telephone.

EXHIBIT 2.1   SAMPLE CARICATURE

TO:	FOR INFORMATION, CALL:
FROM:	AT:
PAGES (including cover sheet):	FAX NUMBER:

This is human nature. But over the last two decades, attitudes have shifted. The telephone has become firmly established as a penetrating marketing medium. Today, people are conditioned to telephone solicitations. No other tool in the collector's arsenal can generate more dollars. But certain techniques can make your calls more productive.

Use a Long Extension Cord

Most telephones come with a 3-foot cord between phone and receiver. This confines collectors to their desks, making them prisoners of their immediate work environments. Noted telemarketing expert Stan Billue has proven through extensive research that *we communicate better in an upright position*. So replace your current 3- or 4-foot phone cord with a 9- or 12-foot extension.

This does not mean that you should stand during every collection call, but you should be able to stand up and move freely around your desk when you feel the urge. The only difference is that you will be free to gesticulate. Body movements will affect the pitch and volume of your voice and be transmitted through the telephone line to your listener. Body language can be expressed through the telephone wire. This simple change in your office environment can work wonders—increasing productivity, minimizing boredom, and allowing better, more controlled communication. Extension cords are especially useful if you must work within a small cubicle. Anyone who is confined to a closed-in work area tends to burn out faster because of space constraints.

Use a Headset

Working on the telephone for long periods can create unhealthy habits. Normally, we hold the phone to our ear by pinning the device between our ear and shoulder. We get used to bending our heads to one side or the other. But this is a bad habit because it strains the neck muscles. Eventually, the resulting discomfort will decrease productivity.

The solution? Install a headset with an extended mouthpiece. This may not seem significant, but why do you think operators who handle large volumes of calls are so equipped? Headsets are expensive, but the added comfort will boost productivity and the equipment will more than pay for itself over the long haul. If you spend most of your time on the phone, you should consider the headset as a prudent investment.

Productive Posture

Slouching in your chair is another bad habit. Posture has a definite effect on the modulation, tone, and volume of your voice. You should sit erect, back flush to the chair, and focus your eyes either straight ahead or upward. If you use notes while on the telephone, glance down only occasionally to get the information you need, but do not continually lean over your desk with your neck bent. It is amazing what correct posture can accomplish. You will feel better and exert less effort. Invest in a good chair, and try on several for size and comfort.

Use "Echo" Phrases

Throughout your conversation, it is important to acknowledge the debtor's statements. Use such "echo" phrases as "Ahhh," "I see," "I understand," "Go on," to demonstrate not only that you are listening, but also that you are interested.

At the conclusion of a telephone conversation, are you normally first to place the receiver in its cradle? Often this can be detrimental. How many times has it happened to you? Just when you were about to terminate a call, some new idea came to mind. But before you could express your thought, the other person hung up. Debtors, too, have last-moment thoughts or questions. If you act first to terminate a conversation, you might lose valuable opportunities forever. Stay on the phone until you hear the debtor's phone go "click." Then you know the conversation is terminated and can safely hang up.

Delay preserves opportunities that might otherwise be lost, but even if this were not so, it would be rude to hang up first. If a debtor hears your phone go "click," who is to say how that "click" will be perceived? A very soft settling of the receiver in its cradle may at the other end sound harsh and abrupt. Why create a negative climate when it can be avoided? Do not slam down your receiver while the earpiece is still to the other person's ear. *Moral:* Always let the other person hang up first.

Tape Your Conversations and Learn from Your Mistakes

It might sound ridiculous to tape your conversations, but you can improve the quality of each collection call if you take time to analyze and improve your performance. With the help of an inexpensive earpiece and a cheap cassette recorder, you can record conversations at will. How you sound on the telephone is not as important as how you handle yourself.

It is amazing how much you can learn by playing back collection calls to analyze what you did right as well as what you did wrong. You can learn more from your mistakes than you can from your successes.

Remember the adage, "You can't see the forest for the trees"? That same principle holds true regarding your own speech. To see the whole forest, you would need a helicopter. To review your conversations, you need a tape recorder. Many mistakes of which you are not aware will unfold as you listen to yourself. The only way to become aware of the duds in your language arsenal is to continually review your conversations.

Get together with several other collectors. Each of you plays a different role to re-create actual collection calls. Record these conversations, then work as a group to analyze one another's strengths and weaknesses. This is an excellent training tool. Each collector can contribute ideas to benefit the whole group.

Most states have statutes governing the recording of telephone conversations. Generally, it is considered illegal to tape a conversation without the knowledge of the other party. If you want to record a call, inform the other party immediately that you are taping the conversation. If the person objects, turn off the tape recorder. Penalties for illegally taping a conversation can be stiff, so do not take chances. If you have questions, consult an attorney.

Pregnant Pause

Most people are so preoccupied with their own talking that they never stop to consider the importance of pausing to listen. Always pause at key intervals and allow the other person a chance to talk. Every time you ask a closing question or move for a close, you should pause. (See Chapter 4.) The pause will give you a chance to organize your thoughts, formulate strategy, and frame responses.

CHAPTER 3

Selling Psychology Applied to Collections

A professional collector must be as alert and well-informed as a salesperson. The similarity, however, between the collection and sales functions does not stop there. Collectors, like salespeople, require a working knowledge of body language, communication, and effective sales. They must also have something to offer if they are to bypass debtors' objections and change their base of thinking. In this chapter you will learn how the most creative selling strategies can be modified to be effective in collecting accounts receivable. The first part explains the vital difference between objections and conditions. It discusses ways to use empathetic statements to move a debtor from objection to negotiation—without alienating the debtor.

Recalcitrant debtors use excuse tools to evade payment. The effectiveness of collection communication often depends on your ability to defuse debtor stall tactics and create an atmosphere of urgency. In this section you will learn the assumptive tie-down, two-question closing, and the alternatives technique—innovative approaches that will help you isolate objections and convert them into recovery opportunities. Find out why it is important to "sell" debtors a choice.

Do you know what to say when a debtor breaks a promise or fails to adhere to a payment agreement? What should you do when a debtor tells you that he must refer the matter to somebody "higher up"? What do you do when a hard-core debtor challenges you with the statement, "Go ahead and sue"?

You will learn why it is important to evaluate a debtor's emotional state and get the debtor to slow down to increase the possibility of productive communication. You will learn how to ask leading questions, what to do when you get a negative response, and how to harness the power of silence. Sometimes in difficult situations you have to bite your tongue or risk letting debtors off the hook. This chapter offers pointers on how to confront debtors: how to overcome built-in objections, how to get debtors to respond favorably, and how to move debtors off dead center. You will learn how to beat debtors at their own game and laugh all the way to the bank.

Selling is the ability to lead a prospect to the persuasive decision you have already made (i.e., that the prospect should buy). It is a step-by-step mental process, an art form that skillfully combines body language, communication, negotiation, sales techniques, and some-times humor. *Collectors can learn much from professional salespeople.* Selling and closing tech-niques are applicable to all collection problems. After all, successful sales, like collections, are based on the following:

- An understanding of human psychology
- An understanding of strategy and negotiation techniques
- An ability to persuade and overcome objections
- A sixth sense knowing you are zeroing in on your debtor's hot button

The following advanced selling strategies have been modified to be most effective in the collection arena. These proven techniques should be learned and applied in every collec-tion protocol.

CHANGE THE DEBTOR'S BASE OF THINKING

Most credit transactions are initiated in good faith. At the origination of a credit sale, a debtor has every intention of meeting his obligation. Unfortunately, credit granting is risky business, and receivables often go down the tube. The result: Nonpayment. The applica-tion of psychology can go a long way toward converting a no-pay into a paid-in-full account. Changing a debtor's base of thinking will multiply your chances of success.

Basic law of success: You can help yourself only by helping others. People will not buy your line unless you have something of greater value than the dollars they will forfeit. Peo-ple who look only to benefit themselves are doomed to failure right from the start. The rewards go to people who search diligently for ways to help others.

FORMULA FOR HANDLING DEBTORS' OBJECTIONS

Debtors are likely to pose all kinds of imaginary excuses. View these obstacles not as stum-bling blocks but as opportunities. You can beat debtors at their own game by learning how to cash in on objections.

Objections are opportunities. When you move to collect an outstanding debt, you will usually get an objection. There is a formula for handling objections, but first you must understand the difference between an *objection* and a *condition*.

- *Objection.* Most collection problems stem from objections, which are the stated rea-sons for nonpayment. These arise from a debtor's personal misconceptions, priori-ties, or other subjective factors. Objections are often opportunities. They are nothing more than illusions in the debtor's mind that must be overcome.
- *Condition.* A condition is a reason for nonpayment that actually exists (i.e., the debtor has no money, is on the verge of bankruptcy, is going out of business). A merger or foreclosure could also be a condition.

A word of warning: What may appear to be a valid condition may in fact be an objection. Generally, you cannot overcome a condition, but you *can* overcome an objection. Here is how: *Bypass* the debtor's objection, but always acknowledge it.

Example: "Mr. Pastdue, I certainly understand why you feel the way you do. If I were in your position, I might feel the same way."

It is important to acknowledge an objection because, by doing so, you minimize the possibility that it will become solidified in the debtor's mind. Always bypass the objection with an empathy-building statement. Typically, a debtor will not bring up the same objection a second time. If he or she does repeat the original objection—no money, a billing error, a complaint about a product or service—you can be assured that the debtor believes the objection is valid. Here is the formula to overcome it.

Step 1. The objection.

> *Collector:* "As I understand it, Mr. Pastdue, your position is that you have a cash-flow problem and lack the necessary funds. Is that correct?"

If the debtor says Yes, go on to step 2.

Step 2. Answer the objection and sell the debtor on the idea of payment.

> *Collector:* "You know, Mr. Pastdue, I can certainly appreciate your position, and I'm sure that if you were financially able, you would satisfy the indebtedness you incurred. Isn't that correct?"

> *Debtor:* "Yes."

> *Collector:* "Mr. Pastdue, obviously you have other creditors and, like all businesses, you have such fixed expenses as rent, electricity, salaries, unemployment insurance, and taxes. If you didn't meet these fixed obligations, you wouldn't be in business. Isn't that correct?"

Note the use of the word "meet" as opposed to "pay."

> *Debtor:* "Yes, that's correct."

If the debtor says No, you must find out whether he is lying, or get the debtor to explain that response.

> *Collector:* "You know, I'm really glad that you are an honest person and took the time to share this information, Mr. Pastdue. I can certainly understand your dilemma. Mr. Pastdue, I am sure that at the time you incurred this debt you had every intention of doing the right thing."

Again, instead of the word "paying," use the phrase "doing the right thing."

> *Collector:* "Isn't that correct?"

Push for a "yes" response.

Collector: "Mr. Pastdue, that being the case, and in light of your reputation, I certainly would like to do everything I can to help you resolve this obligation and preserve your creditworthiness. Mr. Pastdue, can we work together to resolve this matter? Can you come to terms with your debt?"

Push for a "yes" response.

Step 3. Confirm the answer.

If the debtor says Yes, you have greatly increased your chances of success. Now you must probe for the debtor's hot button and move for a close. Entice the debtor to confirm a series of common-knowledge business expenses. Use these confirmations as trial closes, building toward your primary objective. Once you secure these minor acknowledgments, close immediately.

Collector: "You know, Mr. Pastdue, we have been in business for many years. We know people have problems, and we understand that fact. Our aim is to resolve this problem, not create a new one. We appreciate your willingness to cooperate, and I want to work with you. Tell me, can you process two checks, one dated for ____, and the balance dated ____?"

From this point, collection becomes a matter of negotiation. If you cannot secure payment in full, you can at least negotiate a settlement or installment.

Step 4. Question the debtor's objection.

If you have done a good job of flushing out the debtor's original objection, you should be able to frame an effective response and arrive at a commitment. If the debtor still refuses to budge, you should reexamine the original objection and probe the debtor's hot button.

Why should you question a debtor about something that has already been explained to you? Because one of these things is likely to happen:

- The debtor will repeat the original objection and, in doing so, hook himself even further.
- The debtor will pop the real, hidden objection.
- The debtor will repeat the original objection and possibly realize that the objection is invalid.

This is what you will accomplish by using this formula:

- You will learn whether the debtor's statement is an objection or a valid condition.
- When you show empathy and understanding, the debtor is likely to open up and convey the real reason for nonpayment.
- By listening to the debtor's response, you develop ammunition that will enable you to sell the debtor on his objections.
- You will confirm and bury the debtor's objection, so that the debtor cannot bring it up again.

Important principle: Never argue. Never prove a debtor wrong. Unfortunately, many collectors make this mistake and ruin viable opportunities. It is not your job to prove the debtor wrong (even though that person may be wrong). You will accomplish more if you prove the debtor right, so the debtor will want to pay you.

Consider two boxers squaring off in a ring. Knowing how to roll with the punches is just as important as knowing the right moves. A boxer who is about to receive a powerful right hook is not going to stick his chin out.

This principle holds true in human psychology. The natural instinct is to answer negative responses with an "I'll prove you wrong" attitude, but sharp, comeback answers will only alienate the debtor and foil collection efforts. There are times when arguing is appropriate, provided you are well-versed in transitioning the debacle into opportunity.

Perhaps 90% of a collector's arguing with a debtor is detrimental to receivable recovery, but there is a 10% margin when intimidation can achieve a favorable result. The trick is to know how to read and interpret the debtor, and then structure the debate into a recovery.

Hardened, sophisticated debtors are adept at evading bill collectors. Most are virtuosos at manipulating the legal system. In these instances, you can inundate your stubborn customers with customer service appeals and/or sell goodwill to infinitum—only to end up with zilch. In these dire situations, tact and ego massaging are useless. A compelling, vituperative dose of repartee, peppered with street methodology, might just move this antagonistic personality to a negotiable climate. There are just too many personality types that do not respond to conciliatory appeals: A virtuoso collector must know how to intimidate a wisenheimer debtor, sufficient to extract greenbacks, without yielding a lawsuit. The wherewithal to accomplish this feat can only be developed with experience. The more confrontational the debtor encounter is, the better equipped you must be to handle it.

Although the Federal Fair Debt Collection Practices Act prohibits collectors from harassing debtors, it falls short of defining exactly what is recoverable in terms of dollars. Does bombarding your opponent with street methodology constitute harassment? In order for a harassment suit to be successful, a plaintiff must prove damages. And if it does, can a debtor's allegations withstand the acid test of judicial scrutiny? Can your debtor prove damages? Ninety to one hundred percent of the time, threats of "harassment suits," are merely smoke screen excuses amounting to nothing more than intimidating the collector to retreat. The question is *not* whether a creditor will be sued for harassment, but rather to stay within legal limits. The real question is who is better at playing Monopoly—the collector or the debtor?

The truth is, super hard-core debtor types can only be dealt with effectively via the skillful application of street methodology. If you are uncomfortable with engaging in verbal combat with a hard-core debtor, then hire a collection agency or another collector who can play the good guy/bad guy routine. Recycling a difficult account will often produce money.

Bottom line? It's not arguing that magnifies recovery possibilities, but rather the application of street lingo, which, if directed on the weisenheimer-type debtor in such a manner as to strike the debtor's responsive card and result in payment, who cares? As Lenin said: "To make an omelette, sometimes you have to break a few eggs."

Trial Closing: The Assumptive Tie-Down Collection Technique

In the trial closing technique, simply ask positive, assumptive questions, such as the following:

- "Mr. Pastdue, you do have every intention of bringing your account current, don't you?"

- "Mr. Pastdue, if I can arrange to make it easier for you to resolve this, would you be willing to discuss a suitable arrangement?"

- "Mr. Pastdue, would you prefer that I contact your attorney with respect to your contemplated countersuit?"

- "Mr. Pastdue, am I right in assuming that you intend to get this resolved as soon as your cash position improves?"

- "Mr. Pastdue, you really don't relish damage to your credit reputation, do you?"

Two-Question Collecting

In the two-question collection strategy, you ask the debtor two questions: a major one, immediately followed by a minor one. For example:

"Mr. Pastdue, I have listened attentively to everything you said. I can assure you that I understand your situation entirely. However, it is in your best interest to resolve this matter as quickly as possible. I would like to have your check without any further delay. By the way, will you be mailing your check today, or would you prefer that I arrange for a courier to pick it up tomorrow?"

In other words, you pose the major question (Will you make payment in full as quickly as possible?), and then immediately follow it with a minor question (Shall I have a courier pick up your check?). If the debtor confirms the minor decision, the major decision is automatically carried. When you use this technique, pose the major question, but never give the debtor a chance to answer. Immediately follow with the minor question.

Debtor Callbacks

Callbacks represent yet another frustrating function in the collection process. Broken promises, failure to adhere to payment arrangements, stalls, delays, and the like test collectors' nerves, but they are all part of daily encounters with debtors. The first rule is not to rehash verbatim everything said in your previous call(s). Talk about something new, anything to rephrase the collection call. Color your presentation—be creative and seek new solutions that will appeal to the debtor. For example, suppose in a previous conversation the debtor agreed to make payments by the first day of every month. But the first payment is already several weeks late. You might start out by saying:

"Mr. Pastdue, you know that the last time we spoke, you agreed to make installments on a voluntary basis, to be received by my office on _____ (dates). I went out on a limb to convince our legal department not to retain local counsel to initiate a lawsuit. Needless to say, you embarrassed me. Your broken promises have made me look bad." (Sell the debtor a guilt trip.) "Mr. Pastdue, I would like to believe that your intentions are honorable. But at this stage, I must request your check for the full amount. I would like you to process a check made payable to _____. I will arrange courier pickup tomorrow morning, or would tomorrow afternoon be better for you?" (Give the debtor alternatives. It is easier to move a debtor toward the close if you offer a choice between something and something as opposed to a choice between something and nothing. Sell the debtor a choice.)

HANDLING THE "HIGHER AUTHORITY" OR "PASS THE BUCK" STALL

Frequently, when speaking to a debtor, a collector will hear statements such as the following:

"Let me talk it over with our _____, and I'll get back to you."

"Let me take this up with _____."

Many collectors have eaten of this sour fruit, but properly handled, a debtor's "higher authority" stall can be an opportunity. Sometimes such objections are valid, but most of the time they are not. In most instances, it is merely a stall tactic, another weapon in the arsenal used by recalcitrant debtors to evade payment.

The problem with this kind of objection is that:

- It is easy to let the debtor off the hook—without commitment.
- It buys the debtor more time.
- The debtor may in fact have authority to make a decision, but instead uses this ploy to throw you off track.

The collector must take an affirmative stand. Try to pin down the debtor's authority to make payment decisions. You might ask:

- "Ms. Pastdue, do you approve remittances to your suppliers and vendors?" (Note we substituted "remittance" for "payment.")
- "Are you a principal who is responsible for company obligations?"
- "Do you sign checks?"
- "Are you a corporate officer?"

If the contact responds Yes to any of these questions, then that person can make the decision to pay you also. If the contact responds No, then probe to determine the extent of the person's authority. Ascertain whether the contact is being sincere.

Next question: "Ms. Pastdue, may I ask what Mr. _____'s responsibilities are with your firm?"

The purpose of this inquiry is to determine who in the debtor company is responsible for payment. Once you know, zero in on that person:

Follow-up query: "Fine, is he there now?"

If the "higher authority" is in, get that person on the phone. The reason for this should be obvious. You cannot be sure that your initial contact will talk to the person responsible for the debt. It is in your best interest to arrange direct communication with the higher authority. Never allow an underling to speak for you.

If the initial contact is reluctant to let you go one-on-one with the higher authority, ask the person to arrange a conference call—between you, the first contact, and the higher authority—so that you can discuss the debt intelligently. If you still get a negative response, take the initiative and approach the higher authority directly with urgency and conviction. Some collectors telephone the responsible principal person-to-person to create an atmosphere of urgency.

OBJECTION: "I'LL THINK ABOUT IT"

The problem with the debtor response "I'll think about it" is that it is *not* an objection. It is intangible and should be construed to mean, "You haven't persuaded me to pay you."

The worst thing you can do is respond with an argumentative rebuttal. The debtor has said "I'll think about it" to throw you off. Do not let yourself be sidetracked. You must respond affirmatively.

Procedure: "Ms. Pastdue, that's fine." (No argument here.) "Obviously, you are telling me this for a reason. I'm sure you have a reason for feeling this way, so may I ask why you do not want to resolve this matter?" (Push for an affirmative answer.) "Ms. Pastdue, let's be aboveboard and put our cards on the table. Fair enough?" (Again, seeking a minor concession.) "When you did business with our company, did we tell you that we would 'think about' shipping the merchandise to you?" (Wait for answer.) "No. In the interest of good business, we promptly processed your order and saw to it that you received the merchandise in a timely manner. Now, Ms. Pastdue, don't you think it's a little unfair of you to tell me that you wish to 'think it over'? After all, you did incur a valid debt, a debt which you have a just, legal, and ethical responsibility to satisfy." (Proceed with normal collection sequence.)

OBJECTION: "GO AHEAD AND SUE!"

"Go ahead and sue me. You'll only be wasting your time. I'm judgment-proof!" When you get a response like this, you may be dealing with the capricious whims of a professional debtor who derives joy from beating creditors out of their money. This kind of hard-line response normally necessitates hard-line strategy. But try a softening statement first. If this does not work, then feel free to use a hard-line approach.

The risk of using a hard-line strategy right off the bat is that you will alienate the debtor and, if the hard-line approach fails, you might close the door for good. Here are two alternative approaches from opposite ends of the collection spectrum:

Boomerang Technique: The Soft Sell

"Mr. Pastdue, I appreciate your frankness. If I read you right, and I think I do, you are convinced that you would prevail were we to commence litigation or take other action. Mr. Pastdue, I appreciate your telling me this because I know you wouldn't make such a statement unless you had no intention of coming to grips with this problem. Would you extend me the courtesy of telling me why you feel this way?"

Even if debtors have already explained their position, you might ask them to repeat it. Why? Because people speak two or three times faster than normal when they become emotional. The worst thing you can do is match the speed and tone in a debtor's voice. You can only create a no-collection climate. To counter the debtor's objection, you must reduce your speed and monitor your tone of voice. Do not react emotionally to a debtor's threats.

Analysis: If a debtor who is in an emotional state of mind has made threats, ask the debtor to repeat his position. The debtor is likely to repeat the grievance with less thrust the second time. Show interest in the debtor's problem. Do not allow an outburst to stir your emotions. An empathetic, but dispassioned, approach may allow you to control the debtor psychologically.

What usually happens: When debtors reiterate their grievances, they hook themselves on those grievances and, in the process, create closing opportunities. Something said for the second time is usually said more slowly. If debtors are forced to slow down their rate of speaking, they may begin to see the invalidity of their own position and return to a more agreeable frame of mind. When this happens, productive communication is more likely.

What if you react to a debtor by cursing, threatening, and yelling? You will not only lower yourself to the debtor's level, but you might sever all communication entirely. The debtor, determined to have the last word, might even hang up. Then you will have accomplished nothing and will have lost all collection potential. If you can retain control and keep your head while the debtor is losing his, you will greatly increase your chances of success. There are some exceptions where debtors can only be motivated via street methodology. Use it with discretion.

Hard-Line Approach

Unlike the previous approach, which uses a reversing technique, the hard-line technique must be conveyed from a position of strength. Here is an example:

"Mr. Pastdue, I have listened attentively to everything you said. I have given you every opportunity to come to the table and resolve this matter. Moreover, my company has extended to you every degree of common courtesy. Apparently, you do not care to respond in kind, and it is evident to me that this matter must be resolved in a court of law. Unfortunately, this will necessitate the preparation and execution of legal papers. Mr. Pastdue, I find it reprehensible that an intelligent businessperson like you would take such a belligerent attitude. What if the shoe were on the other foot, Mr. Pastdue? How would you respond if someone were trying to beat you out of your money after you had extended credit in good faith?" (This last empathy-building statement conditions the debtor's mind by putting him or her in the creditor's situation.) "You wouldn't like it, would you? Of course not; nobody likes to get ripped off." (If the debtor responds favorably, the door is open to reestablish communication and possibly negotiate.)

TRIAL CLOSES

Professional salespeople gauge prospects' temperature by asking leading questions—questions that require favorable responses. If they receive negative responses, astute salespeople know that it would be a mistake to go on. They must back up, evaluate the reasoning behind their prospects' responses, and resolve the problems before continuing. The same psychology holds true in collecting. Collectors should also use a series of "trial closes," that is, the closing question technique.

What is a closing question? It is any question that will get the debtor to confirm that he will pay. After asking a closing question—SHUT UP! Why is this important? Because the first person who talks loses.

Whenever you ask a closing question, you are putting the debtor on the hook and exerting psychological pressure. If the debtor is slow to respond, you might be tempted to break the silence. But by interrupting, you let the debtor off the hook. The best strategy to exert pressure is to remain silent until the debtor speaks. There is no pressure greater than the pressure of silence.

You will get one of two reactions:

1. The debtor will go along with you.
2. The debtor will not go along with you.

As a collector, you can handle either one. If you get a negative response, you can handle that, can't you? But, once again, if you break the silence, you let the debtor off the hook. So always remember: Once you have asked a closing question, keep your mouth shut! The following are examples of closing questions:

- "You do intend to get this resolved, don't you?"
- "You value your credit and reputation, don't you?"
- "What can I do to help you resolve this?"
- "Will your check be processed today?"

ALTERNATIVES TECHNIQUE

Another good collection technique is to offer alternatives. For example:

- "Ms. Pastdue, will you send us a check for the full amount, or would you prefer to send two checks—one dated today, for half the amount due, and another dated next week, to cover the balance?"

- "Ms. Pastdue, our courier will arrive at your place of business to pick up your check tomorrow morning, or is the afternoon better for you?"

Storytelling can be used as a collections close. The principle behind storytelling is basically to "back up the hearse and let them smell the flowers." In other words, you tell the debtor a story that closely parallels his situation. The story ending should paint a clear picture contrasting the dire consequences that will result if the debtor refuses to honor the obligation against the relatively simple, painless solution you are offering. This type of close was originally developed, and is still used effectively, by the insurance industry. For example:

"You know, Mr. and Mrs. Prospect, I recently visited another home not far from here. The couple, to whom I was explaining the importance of life insurance, had a little girl. Oh, a real cute little kid—I would say about five or six years old. While I was trying to explain to the parents just how important insurance is, this little girl kept climbing onto her mother's lap. Well, you know what the mother did? She pushed her daughter off. Then the little girl climbed onto her father's lap, and he pushed her off. Then she came and sat on my lap, and her mother scolded her. I did not sell life insurance that evening. Just recently, I was reading the newspaper and I couldn't help but cry. For, you see, this couple was involved in a very serious automobile accident. The father was killed, and the mother remains in critical condition. All I could think of as I read this article was this adorable little girl who was so desperate for attention that she climbed onto the lap of a stranger . . ."

By telling this story, the insurance salesperson is obviously selling fear and emotion. Now, this same psychology can be applied to collect delinquent accounts. In storytelling, you describe *parallel situations* with which debtors can identify. For example, you might tell a story about a company that is similar to the debtor's business. This parallel business was also delinquent in paying its bills, but the company took positive steps to protect its good name. The company worked out equitable arrangements with its creditors and achieved a happy result. Talk about another debtor whom your particular debtor can identify with, a debtor who ended up looking good because he or she made the right decision—to pay you. Always tell stories that your debtors can relate to, preferably about actual, true-to-life situations. Build a collection of "stories" and use them to your advantage.

SOLVING BUILT-IN DEBTOR OBJECTIONS

Many products and services have built-in objections. These roadblocks to payment are generally obvious and, based on past experience, can be anticipated and forestalled. When your product or service has a built-in objection that is likely to be targeted in debtor complaints, brag about it first.

If the debtor brings up a built-in objection, such as "The price was too high," respond as follows:

"Mr. Pastdue, you are correct, our price is higher than our competitors' prices. As a manufacturer, we have two choices: (1) We can produce and service products cheaply, or (2) we can make that extra effort to produce quality products and provide quality service.

In servicing your account, Mr. Pastdue, we have strived to deliver the finest product and the best service. Naturally, it costs us more to provide that kind of quality, but you benefit because our products last longer, provide customer satisfaction, and reduce downtime. Isn't our commitment to service and quality worth a little extra?"

Get a commitment and proceed with the normal closing sequence.

INTERIM COLLECTION CLOSING

The interim closing technique is effective when you need to negotiate or when there is a time lag between delivery and collection. The first step is to move toward interim closing. Get together with the debtor to reaffirm your agreement. Take out a piece of paper and write down the names of people who are involved in the payment decision and all details of the transaction. For example:

> *Collector:* "Ms. Pastdue, I agreed that I would confer with our legal department on your behalf. I also agreed that we would prepare the necessary documentation in support of our agreement. I also agreed to make arrangements for your attorney to review these documents. Now, Ms. Pastdue, *you agreed* that you would . . ."

It is important to write down everything agreed upon by both you and the debtor. As you write it all down, you reaffirm your agreement. Now, take your completed notes, thank the debtor, and confirm the time when you will speak again and what the debtor will do.

FALSE CONCLUSION

In still another type of close, you state a false conclusion and lead the debtor to correct you. The point is that every time the debtor is free to correct you, that person is actually making a commitment. For example:

- *Collector:* "You've told me, Mr. Pastdue, that you can't satisfy your obligation. I assume you don't really care about your credit rating, do you?"
  Debtor: "Yes, I do." (The debtor has now committed himself.)
- *Collector:* "You never really intended to honor your debt, did you, Ms. Pastdue?"
  Debtor: "At the time I purchased the merchandise, I most certainly did."
- *Collector:* "I assume, Mr. Pastdue, that if we were to commence litigation over this matter, it wouldn't faze you one bit, would it?"
  Debtor: "It most certainly would! (or would not.)"

Remember: It is important to develop a rapport with your debtor as soon as possible. It does not matter how good your collection strategy is; if the debtor does not respond, the debtor will not pay. Rapport simply means that you establish good communication. Keep in mind that the more willing a debtor is to communicate, the greater your chance of success.

Consider these pointers when confronting debtors:

- Make the debtor like you. Sell yourself first. This is the sale before the sale. Remember, you never get a second chance to make a first impression.

- Listen attentively to what the debtor says. Never interrupt. Show that you are genuinely interested in this person's business and its problems. Talking is not so hard, listening sometimes is. But remember: Silence is selling!

- As you listen to the debtor, you will learn about that person, about the company, and about any problems. Listening has three primary advantages:

  1. First, the debtor may divulge some vital information that can be incorporated into your collection strategy. A debtor will almost always reveal *something* useful. Suppose, for example, you learn that a debtor has filed for a Small Business Association (SBA)-guaranteed loan. This information can be used to pressure the debtor. Obviously, the debtor cannot afford litigation or any detrimental public filing that might foil his chances of getting the loan. This places you in a strong negotiating position. Look for clues that will help you find the debtor's "hot button."

  2. By listening, you show an interest—and you buy time in which to frame a response.

  3. Last, but not least, avoid jumping to conclusions and saying things that might harm your collection effort.

Remember: Your success depends on how skillfully you isolate objections/conditions and convert them into collection opportunities.

Keep in step with your debtor. Never interrupt a debtor, assuming you know what he is going to say. Not only is it rude to interrupt, but you could guess wrong!

OF IGNORANCE AND INTELLECT: HOW VETERAN COLLECTORS OUTSMART THEMSELVES

When new collectors enter the field, they are generally given a brief orientation on their companies' procedures, products, and services and a crash course on collecting receivables. Lack of knowledge often makes new employees uncomfortable when they come into contact with debtors. The collectors are insecure, nonthreatening, and disinclined to contradict debtors' statements. Therefore, they do very little talking. The debtors usually talk 70% of the time and the collectors only 30%.

How the Negative Approach Overcomes Resistance

No one likes to be sold. We like to make our own decisions and resist the hard sell. Enter "negative selling." Negative selling gives prospects the feeling that salespeople are not trying to "sell" them, they are merely helping the prospects make their own decisions to buy.

Negative selling is a viable tool that can resolve potentially uncollectible accounts. This technique will often induce debtors to listen. By seemingly agreeing with debtors' thinking, you can get them to lower their guard. By letting a debtor take on an air of superiority, you encourage that person to talk.

Most debtors are hard to "sell" because they are suspicious of debt collectors, and they resist hard-line tactics. By giving debtors the impression that you are not going to high-pressure them into paying, you gain their confidence. When that happens, collection potential increases. The negative-selling approach reverses pressure back onto the debtor and stimulates productive conversation.

Negative Selling

The negative approach is not the best approach for every situation; however, it can be useful on many occasions. For instance, when debtors say they are too busy or give some other excuse for not paying, try the negative approach. For example:

Debtor: "I haven't been able to find the time to review this matter. I've been extremely busy putting together a major deal that involves a lot of money and commands all my time . . ."

Collector A: "Gee, that's impressive. You must really be successful. I know your time is very valuable, and I hate to bother you with such a trivial matter, but it's a known fact that if you want to get something done, you ask a busy person to do it." (Ego-building statements.) "Mr. Debtor, do you think it would be too much to request your personal attention in this matter? I know that if you personally take care of it, the matter will be resolved."

Collector B: "Mr. Debtor, your business has nothing to do with what you owe our company" (argumentative), "and, frankly, I don't see what this 'deal' has to do with your long-outstanding debt."

Interpretation: Collector B might succeed some of the time using the hard-line approach. This collector might very well prove the debtor wrong, but in doing so, more often than not the collector will destroy collection potential. It is not a collector's job to prove debtors wrong. Rather, you want to prove them right, so they will want to pay.

Conversely, Collector A appeals to the debtor's ego, encouraging the debtor to talk. Notice how Collector A "requested" the debtor's "personal" attention—applied psychology.

Waltz with the Debtor

Collectors usually take a hard, positive stance—taking control and being firm. In many cases this strategy would be correct, but not always. Some debtors cannot be backed against the wall. Take the wheeler-dealer debtor in the preceding example. This debtor maintains an air of superiority, and Collector A recognizes that this type of personality will not acquiesce to ultimatums or demands. Perhaps the collector appears weak, but the chance of success is greatly improved. What does it matter if a debtor feels superior to the collector if, in the end, the collector gets the check? *Getting paid* is what receivables management is all about.

Debtor: "I can't pay this account," or "I have no money."

Collector: "Gee, that's interesting. Is there a problem?"

Debtor: "I'm simply not in a position to do anything about this."

Collector: "It looks like we're not going to get paid, huh?"

Debtor: "No, I guess not."

Collector: "Well, let me ask you this. What do you think we should do about it?"

Your objective is to use the negative close until you psychologically alter the debtor's thinking and set the stage for the "kill."

Put the Pressure Back on the Debtor—Where It Belongs

The negative selling technique is a novel collection approach that removes pressure from the collector and puts it back on the debtor, where it belongs. The technique leads debtors to think they have won, when in fact the astute collector is maneuvering to get resistant debtors to drop their guard. When this occurs, you can maneuver the debtors to make the decision you want.

Why Less Is More

Ironically, many people who are new to the collector's profession use negative selling without even realizing it—and succeed. An interesting phenomenon takes place after novice collectors have achieved some degree of success. The collectors now reason that if they really knew the business, they would probably be even more successful.

Peter Principle: Eventually, with a little more experience under their belts and having had exposure to other collectors, novices graduate and become professionals—right? Wrong. Collecting accounts receivable, like any business, is a never-ending learning experience. Novice collectors who, reasoning that they have graduated from the university of hard knocks, erroneously believe that they now know everything about the business, have merely reached their "level of incompetence."

These "skilled" collectors graduate to higher levels in the collection department and are ready to show others the "right" way to collect. Experience is, in fact, the best teacher, but for most of us, selfish motives stand in the way of continued fulfillment and self-improvement. We reach a plateau and then burn out. We stop learning. Relying on past successes, we develop a know-it-all attitude. In short, learning stops as egos inflate.

These informed "collectors" now talk 70% of the time and, if they are lucky, the debtors talk just 30% of the time. The success ratios of the "experts" begin to decline. These once-astute collectors now find themselves caught up in a struggle for survival.

The proper implementation of negative selling lets debtors do most of the talking.

One Question Too Many

Professionals never ask a question unless they know the answer.

Trial attorneys use this technique. Consider the following scenario, in which an attorney cross-examines a hostile witness:

Attorney: "Did you witness a fight between ____ and ____?"

Witness: "Yes, I did."

Attorney: "But you really didn't see my client bite off his ear, did you?"

Witness: "Yes, I did."

Attorney: "How do you know that my client did it?"

Witness: "Because I saw him spit it out!"

In this illustration, the attorney asked one question too many. The attorney should have let the jury's imagination prevail. The same psychology applies in many collection situations. Asking one question too many can not only get you into trouble, but it can also destroy your potential for success. Know when to stop talking!

Boomerang Collection Technique

Does it make you feel uncomfortable or even unprofessional to remain quiet? Then consider your relationship with the family doctor. Doctors are among the greatest practitioners of the boomerang technique. When you arrive at your doctor's office, the doctor listens to your complaint and begins a series of probing questions. Typically, a doctor might ask: "How long have you been in pain? Where does it hurt? How do you feel now? Are you taking medication?" In short, the doctor prompts you, the patient, to talk.

The doctor does not rush in to solve your "problem" or begin a long dissertation on the anatomy. A doctor does not get clever with fancy words or cute medical terms. The doctor knows that at the end of your examination, he or she will prescribe treatment that will help relieve your pain. But before the "close," the doctor is going to have an accurate picture of your ailment. If a doctor acted any differently, you would certainly question this person's integrity, and you might even be looking for a new doctor.

Now, debtors do not come to you for medical advice, and certainly they are not suffering from any ailments that you can correct, but the principle remains the same: The more a debtor talks, and the more you listen, the more you will learn about the debtor and the more ammunition you will have for comeback answers. Still not convinced?

Key Phrases in Negative Selling

Negative selling is a surreptitious method of reversing the attitudes of hard-core debtors. You want to play on their egos and help them sell themselves on the idea of meeting their obligations. *Ask questions*—you want debtors to provide information you can use to collect.

Let debtors talk—you want them to talk themselves into settling their accounts. *Play the buffoon*—let them think you do not know anything about collecting accounts receivable. You want debtors to feel they are doing you a favor by answering your questions. Negative selling lures debtors into thinking that they are demonstrating their superiority by settling their obligations. Negative selling is one of the most potent collection tools. The following suggested phrases can be useful in employing this technique:

- "I can't figure out why . . ."
- "Can you let me know . . . ?"
- "Will you please tell me frankly . . . ?"
- "Will you do something for me?"
- "Do you think that . . . ?"
- "Do you mean what you said?"
- "Can you be more specific?"
- "How should we resolve this?"
- "Are you represented by counsel?"
- "Is this an ongoing problem?"
- "How do you fit into the scheme of things?"

Moral: The more debtors let down their guard, the more they will open up, and the more they will tell you. Give debtors enough rope to hang themselves.

The following are hard-and-fast rules that must be followed in using negative selling:

- Do not allow yourself to be intimidated.
- Do not allow a debtor to manipulate you into a box from which there is no escape.
- Know when to stop asking questions.
- Know how to manipulate the debtor by shifting the pressure from you, the collector, back to the debtor, where it belongs.
- Use negative phrases to encourage the debtor to talk.
- Do not put all of your eggs in one basket.
- Maintain a consistent collection strategy during each interview.
- Do not believe everything a debtor tells you. Remember to watch out for hidden meanings in conversations.
- Do not display emotion.
- Do not get personally involved in the debtor's problems or offer advice.

The negative approach is an advanced collection technique. It will take a great deal of practice before you become comfortable using it. But once you have mastered the technique, you will find it to be a viable and potent collection weapon. Remember, arguing and fighting with debtors will only cause resentment and could lead to legal problems as well. In most cases a little applied psychology will be more persuasive than antagonistic debate.

ART OF LISTENING

Collectors who want to improve their listening skills should try the following:

- Practice.
- Show a genuine interest.
- Understand the dynamics of effective listening. For example:
  - There is a difference between the speaking rate and the listening rate. We are capable of hearing almost four times faster than we can speak.
  - A 100% increase in speaking rate will not impair the ability to listen and comprehend.
- Remember that silence—not talking—is selling. Executives in the highest echelon of corporate management are more prone to listen than to talk.

There are three levels of listening ability you should be aware of:

1. Listening to remember
2. Listening for evaluation
3. Listening to understand and recognize the needs of the debtor

Improving your listening skills—listening for opportunities—can make you a better collector. Follow these steps as a guideline:

- *Pay close attention to your debtors' statements.* Debtors may ask probing questions. Use the negative approach to prompt debtors to speak. They may reveal their hot buttons. As a debtor speaks, you should construct a mental "word map" to use for rebuttals and counter-strategy.
- *Learn to recognize and correctly analyze hidden meanings in conversation.*
- *Acknowledge your understanding* with a series of encouraging grunts—"hmmm," "oh," or "I see." If debtors pause, say nothing. Remember the selling psychology; that is, after you ask a closing question, SHUT UP! When they pause, you do not want to interrupt their train of thought. Silence is selling; it is exerting pressure.
- *Do not evaluate what a debtor tells you.* Keep in mind that there are no absolutes. Statements should not be judged as good or bad, reasonable or unreasonable, or true or untrue.
- *Do not become emotionally involved.* Remember that most people are inclined to act out of emotion rather than logic.
- *Do not give debtors advice, even if they prompt you.* It is your job to collect debts, not to get involved with debtors' problems. Instead of getting involved, offer alternatives, and help debtors find their own creative solutions. The degree to which you help a debtor should be proportionate to the person's sincerity.

- *Display professional courtesy* by listening and acknowledging statements with empathetic responses.

- *Analyze the information debtors give you* from different perspectives and determine how that information might be applied to collect the debts.

- *"Build bridges" between you and your debtors.* Memorize many different collection techniques. When one does not work, "plug in" another.

- *Practice multiple collection techniques.* Most commonplace collectors practice only a handful of techniques. Conversely, a professional knows hundreds of techniques and which ones to use to achieve the desired result.

READING THE DEBTOR'S TEMPERATURE

The most astute collectors recognize how important it is to test a debtor's temperature throughout the collection process. Consider this example:

In tennis, the objective is to hit the ball over the net. The manner in which you serve the ball to your opponent will largely determine how the ball will be returned to you. The same principle holds true in communications that are bouncing back and forth between you and the debtor.

Your success as a professional collector is going to relate directly to the manner in which you accomplish the following tasks:

- Frame fact-finding questions.
- Use opening statements to stimulate attention and capture interest.
- Read, decipher, and understand debtor responses and detect hidden meanings in conversations.
- Negotiate with debtors.
- Collect information from debtor feedback.

Just as professional salespeople must consistently gauge and read their prospects' "buying temperature," you must read and correctly analyze debtors' buying temperature. Collection is a sale after the sale, and principles of professional sales apply.

DECIDING WHAT APPEALS TO USE

The information you gather about debtors as you seek to collect will help you formulate the most effective appeals. Look for clues in your data on debtors' income, lifestyles, community involvement, and the nature of their debts (purchases, business loans, or personal loans). If you talk to debtors, ask questions to gain more information. If debtors respond to your overtures by letter, examine those letters closely for clues to how to proceed most effectively.

Just as salespeople and advertising copywriters must size up prospects and come up with the right wording to get people to *buy,* you must decide on the most effective appeal to make people *pay.* Successful salespeople learn to listen and probe to find out what motivates their customers. When you speak to debtors, you should also try to strike the customers' hot buttons.

Copywriters use a variety of themes in ad campaigns to motivate would-be customers. Think along the same lines when you write appeal letters. If one hot button does not work, try another, each time stepping up the pressure.

Need for Self-Fulfillment

People like to think of themselves as moral, ethical, well-intentioned, sincere, honest, and, in some cases, religious. You can take advantage of this sense of inner self by appealing to debtors':

- Desire for success
- Desire to achieve personal goals and engage in creative expression
- Sympathy and concern for the well-being of others
- Feelings of guilt for unethical behavior

Debtors' Desires

Suggest to debtors that you can help them gain greater success if they pay their bills. This kind of approach works particularly well with the upwardly mobile. If you can convince such debtors that you can help them, you can win their respect and secure their cooperation. *A word of caution:* Do not let debtors keep you preoccupied with their problems.

For instance, here is a letter that appeals to a debtor's self-esteem:

> Dear Mr. Wrongdoer:
>
> A person like you appreciates the finer things in life. We understand that, and we want to do everything we can to help you maintain your lifestyle.
>
> We have been at your service, supplying you with the finest in quality products. But now your account balance of $600 is more than two months past due.
>
> We certainly want to go on helping you as we have in the past. Please send your remittance within the next few days, so we can continue to play a part in making your life pleasurable and successful.

MAINTAINING CONTROL IN TELEPHONE COLLECTION CALLS

Once you take the initiative to call debtors, you are in charge, but to successfully direct collection calls, you need goals. You have to know where you want the discussion to go and set the tone of the conversation.

You want to get paid as soon as possible and eliminate any barriers. Concentrate your energies on achieving that end. Should debtors try to deflect you with problems or statements that are unrelated to their debts, you must get the conversation back on track. Respond to debtors' appeals with empathy, then switch the conversation back to the matter at hand. In other words, acknowledge debtors' comments, but always shift back to the reason for the call. You have to be strong and maintain control.

One of the worst things you can do is jump to conclusions and act on unwarranted assumptions as to why debtors cannot or will not pay. You risk alienating debtors, which will reduce your chances of success. For example, consider the following conversation:

Debtor: "I wish I could pay you for the TV I bought. But I just don't have the money right now. I can barely pay the rent, and I've got lots of other bills."

Collector: "I'm sorry. I've waited long enough. I can't wait any longer."

Debtor: "But I already told you, I don't have the money . . ."

Obviously, the collector was not listening to what the debtor had to say. Instead of continuing to press an unproductive demand for payment, the collector should try to show understanding of the debtor's problem and indicate a willingness to help the debtor come up with some solution. For example, after the debtor has stated the problem, the discussion might run something like this:

Collector: "Well, I appreciate your concern. I know you want to do the right thing, and I realize you're having financial problems. Obviously, it's to our mutual advantage to maintain your account current, and I'd like to help you work out a solution. You know, you might consider a loan to consolidate your debts. That way, you could pay off all your debts and make smaller payments each month on the consolidation loan. If you were to take out a home equity loan, you could also realize some savings on your income taxes. Or maybe we can work out reasonable terms."

Use pauses: After responding to the debtor's objections, pause to give the debtor a chance to think and react. Silence—not talking—is selling! There is no pressure you can exert on debtors that is greater than the pressure of silence. If the debtor hesitates or responds uncertainly, you may be tempted to fill in the pauses and help out the debtor. Do not! Wait and listen. Let the debtor respond.

When you question a debtor, phrase your questions in a positive way to encourage the debtor to say Yes. The underlying theory is that once the debtor gets used to agreeing with you, he is more likely to continue to agree when you ask for payment and will be more receptive to your suggestions. In short, use questions to get debtors into a "yes" frame of mind.

Start off with a series of questions to which it would be hard to answer No. For example:

Collector: "You do think of yourself as a responsible person, don't you?"

Debtor: "Yes."

Collector: "And you do value your reputation in the community, don't you?"

Debtor: "Yes."

Collector: "Then, don't you agree that it is in your best interests to satisfy your obligation, so you can maintain your good credit record?"

Debtor: "Well, yes . . ."

As you ask these questions, assume the debtor will answer positively. Let your confidence shine through. Make it easy for the debtor to say Yes.

CHAPTER 4

Advanced Collection Techniques

Advanced collection techniques will empower you to outmaneuver debtors and circumvent broken promises. You will discover that while enthusiasm may be contagious, it can also be deadly to collection potential. Learn how to persuade the most stubborn debtors to pay. For example, how do you respond to a debtor's negative statements? What if a debtor starts haggling over price, long after the transaction has taken place? Capitalize on the debtor's objections, outthink and outmaneuver even the most difficult deadbeat.

Do you find that when debtors are located in a different geographical region, your efforts lose credibility? Many debtors feel they can thumb their noses at faraway creditors. This chapter will show you how to implement localization strategy to resolve remote accounts. You will also learn the importance of demarcation lines and when to make the decision to give up or proceed with legal action.

You may be painfully aware of the debtors' practice of filing spurious counterclaims to impede collections, but it is possible to beat debtors at their own game. Never again will you be victimized by this obstructionistic strategy.

You will learn how to use the implications behind the word "reputation" and how to shame debtors into paying. Get debtors to commit themselves psychologically. One useful trick is to get determined nonpayers to view the situation from a different perspective. You will be able to probe for debtors' hot buttons. This chapter also explains why it is important to let them talk and, in some cases, to feed their egos.

Have you ever run across a situation in which the responsible person will not come to the phone or avoids personal contact? You will learn how to counteract "the check is in the mail" (when it is not) syndrome. Learn how to respond and pin the debtor down. Sometimes you have to offer the debtor alternatives to push him over the goal line.

MOTIVATING TECHNIQUES: WITHDRAWAL METHOD

You can often bring the deep-dyed procrastinator to a Yes decision by appearing weak and nonchalant. Projecting a defeatist attitude may get debtors to feel superior, and when that happens, Mr. Pastdue is likely to take on an attitude of self-importance. This technique was born in professional selling. A good salesperson can sometimes rescue a lost account when the interview is over by packing up and preparing to leave. For example, a salesperson turns to the prospect, shakes his head wistfully, and says: "I appreciate the time you have given me. My only regret is that I have not fulfilled my obligation to you. At some future time, I'm sure another representative will visit you and cover the points I missed, and you will take advantage of _____."

If the sales pro looks defeated and *sincere,* the prospect is likely to come to the salesperson's defense and assure him that he did his job well—but the salesperson shakes his head again: "I guess I didn't demonstrate the built-in safety features that . . ."

"Yes, you did," the prospect replies, and, of course, the salesperson has his coat off again and the order book ready. A few more leading questions and the procrastinator has done a complete about-face and is ready to do business.

How to Use the Withdrawal Technique

The withdrawal technique has also proven effective in collections. Astute collectors who use this potent weapon let debtors think they can walk away from their obligations, but in reality the professional is cleverly preparing to move in and strike the jugular.

Consider the following example:

Debtor: "I'd like to pay you, and I am certainly going to try to resolve this matter." (Now meet Mr. or Ms. Super Collector.)

Collector: "That's great, Ms. Debtor, I really appreciate that. I guess that under the circumstances you can't satisfy this debt, right?"

As the collector proceeds into the call, it appears that the debtor, not the collector, is in control. The collector continues to respond passively, letting the debtor direct the conversation. Soon the collector will maneuver the debtor into the commitment mode. How many times have you reached the moment of truth, only to find that the debtor is beginning to have second thoughts? Even worse, some debtors go along with collectors simply to get rid of them. Debtors will say anything to get you off their backs. Beware: Debtors can be proficient liars.

All too often debtors sense that the collector is winning big and that they are being railroaded. It does not matter that at some point in the past a debtor incurred an obligation that is now past due. Some debtors do not look at it that way. All too frequently, collectors convey too much enthusiasm, and the debtors perceive that they are getting the short end of the stick.

Most collectors have been improperly trained. They have been told to push for the close, but they have not learned the art of putting debtors to work. The withdrawal maneuver uses psychology to shift pressure from you onto the debtors. Today's debtor is a wary creature. Many a time, an enthusiastic collector has gone for the close, only to have the debtor sense the hard sell and back off. Instead of getting paid, the collector ends up with promises—most of which never materialize. In such cases, the collector has been sold and sold hard, not the debtor.

The withdrawal technique is a reverse strategy, one that places the pressure back on the debtor (where it belongs). The key is to leave the debtor some slack and then gradually build toward a close. Do not show any enthusiasm or emotion. Plan your strategy and then casually make several trial closes.

Let the debtor have the stage; consider the following example:

Debtor: "I intend to send you a check."

Collector: "That's great! Can you mail it today?"

Analysis: The collector is too enthusiastic and has unwittingly conveyed a hidden meaning—that is, the collector wins, the debtor loses.

The following conversation is an example of the correct approach:

Debtor: "Can I send you a check at the end of the month?"

Collector: (Remaining calm, seemingly unenthusiastic, and showing no emotion) "Mr. Debtor, I appreciate the fact that you want to take care of this matter, and I know your intentions are good. (Empathy.) But tell me why you feel this can only be accomplished at the end of the month? Is there a reason we can't arrange for our courier to pick up a check today?"

Analysis: Backpedal—then reverse. If the debtor still will not budge, try asking why not. People tend to procrastinate, and debtors are no exception.

Key Your Approach to the Needs of the Debtor

A collector must use the withdrawal technique differently than salespeople would. In a selling situation, the astute salesperson can *continually* push the prospect, asking questions that encourage the prospect to talk about the benefits to be gained from the salesperson's product or service. The more the prospect talks about the advantages, the more the prospect believes what he is saying, until the prospect becomes the one who actually begins to close the sale.

In collection calls, on the other hand, this process must be greatly condensed. Be careful not to overdo it. Usually one or two reverses are sufficient to allow a debtor to believe he is making the right decision—to pay the debt.

What Is Most Likely to Influence Your Debtor?

Every now and then you will come up against customers who resist aggressive collector types. The more you try to pin them down, the greater their resistance. And if you persist in your efforts to collect, you may even find your contact terminated. What should you do?

The answer to this question depends on your answer to another: Are you mentally prepared to meet such a situation? If you are to handle recalcitrant debtors, you have to deal with them on their own turf.

Before you can persuade debtors to pay, you must win their confidence and respect. You must adjust your own thinking, words, and actions to those of the debtors. Next, you have to appear sincerely interested, flexible, and even-tempered.

Try to remain calm and cheerful. If debtors are rude and unpleasant when they resist your efforts, do not interpret their rebuffs as personal affronts. Try to control your own actions. Unless you do, you will never make the collection. You, not the debtor, must control the conversation—from beginning to end.

What does control mean? First, be clear on what it does *not* mean. It does not mean that you should do all the talking. Obviously, you will almost never collect a tough account if you do not let the debtor get in a word or two. But you must subtly take charge, always leading tactfully toward settling the obligation. The point is that if you are not in complete control at the end of your conversation, you will be in no position to ask for payment, much less get it.

Be Ready to Handle Any Type of Debtor

Debtors come in all types and personalities. Some are so talkative, they will sidetrack you if you are not careful. Others just sit there listening, saying nothing, offering no obvious clues to what their thoughts are. Some prospects appear nervous, uncertain, or undecided in words, manner, and actions.

Whatever type of prospect you encounter, one thing is certain: You must control yourself. Never get angry. Stick to the issue at hand—settling the debtor's obligation. Do not get involved with side issues. Above all, never let yourself win the argument and lose the collection.

Whatever the Type, Here Is What You Should Do

Do not take the debtor's behavior at face value because that behavior may not reflect the debtor's real nature. Even if it does, assume that what you are seeing is nothing but affectation. Perhaps it is a defense against paying, perhaps just a tactic intended to test your determination and negotiating skills. But do not think you can scowl at a debtor who disappoints you, then give the impression that you are sincere. Always act as if the person whose commitment you want is one of the most reasonable and intelligent people you have ever met. Whatever the debtor's behavior toward you, try to convince that person that you are there to help. If you can gain a debtor's trust, you will be persuasive—and walk out with the debtor's firm commitment to pay.

For example, you might say:

"Mr. Pastdue, I realize that this represents an important investment for you and your company, and I well understand your wanting to make a sound decision. Now let me assure you why making a remittance is the right one. By recognizing the opportunity to resolve this matter amicably . . ."

What do you accomplish when you use such an approach? Two things. First, you subtly ally yourself with the debtor, by apparently understanding and agreeing about the position he is in. At the same time, you create for yourself an opportunity to reemphasize all the benefits to the debtor of meeting his or her obligation.

Take time before each call to decide which elements of your knowledge are important to debtors. What are their hot buttons? Obviously, the choice you make depends on the particular situation. But you should try to estimate—as early as possible—which application of your information will be most convincing to your debtor.

This is the only way to make sure your conversation will be a logical explanation of crucial points—explaining why your debtors can solve their problems or satisfy their business needs by making a decision in your favor.

MORE ADVANCED COLLECTION TECHNIQUES

"It Costs Too Much"

Occasionally, you will confront debtors who challenge you about the price of your product or service, long after the fact. The debtors reason that they are in the stronger position, because they have the power to withhold payment. It is unfair, but debtors do strange things. A good comeback statement if you are challenged on price is:

Collector: "Mr. Pastdue, I'm really glad you brought that to my attention, and I can certainly appreciate how you feel." (Note the nonargumentative tone.) "Mr. Pastdue, our price is based on quality workmanship. Our product is among the best in the industry. Our published tariffs apply not only to smaller orders, such as yours, but also to large-volume purchases. I assume, Mr. Pastdue, that you sell a product or a service that has a built-in cost factor, including a profit margin. I am equally sure you don't go to your customers and arbitrarily cut the price, do you? (Trial closing.) Certainly, you would not take your product or service and sell it below your break-even cost, would you, Mr. Pastdue?"

(Boomerang technique: If the debtor gives you a favorable response to this question, you are putting the debtor in *your* position, and upon confirmation, you will have your collection made.)

Once debtors agree that they would not sell their products or services at a loss, you are in a position to close a commitment. By your empathetic response, you have put their thinking in line with yours. You can now close as follows:

Collector: "We feel the same way. Like any business, including your own, we have costs and expenses. Mr. Pastdue, you are a responsible businessperson, and you understand the situation. We extended credit to you in good faith, knowing that your intentions were good. May we have your check, Mr. Pastdue?"

Then proceed with a normal collection sequence.

Flip Side

In a creditors' quest for justice, some creditors will go to the mat with a customer who refuses payment as a result of a price dispute.

Case in point: Recently, a debtor refused to pay a $32,860 invoice citing unfair trade practices. He claimed that his competition was paying less for the same product. (This was true, except that the competitor was a registered dealer who had earned the discount.) The difference in price was approximately $3,800. The creditor refused to reduce the previously agreed price. The debtor refused to pay the $32,860 invoice. This dispute was resolved in the courts. The creditor won his $32,860 judgment after two years of exhaustive litigation. In terms of economics, however, the creditor recouped less than $20,000 (when attorney's fees were factored).

Worse, the debtor convinced the court to pay the judgment over two years. From complaint to resolution, the time period was four years. From an economic standpoint, the creditor was better off securing $28,000 or more at the outset (with a 20% collection expense) as opposed to a $32,860 recovery over an approximate four-year marathon, at a 33⅓% attorney's fee of $10,952. The point is that cash in hand today is always better than a promissory note tomorrow.

Bitter pill as it is, settlements are almost always in the creditor's best economic interests.

Mind Conditioning: Counterstrategy Statements

Another effective technique is a response to a negative statement. Try this the next time a debtor says something that is obstructive to your collection strategy.

Debtor: "I cannot make payments."

Collector: "Ms. Debtor, I appreciate what you're saying, and I assure you I am interested in the problem that is preventing you from making good on your just and due obligation. Could you tell me why you feel you can't get this resolved?"

Comment: Again, we are using the boomerang technique—putting pressure back on the debtor.

Debtor: "I am going to retain counsel and bring legal action against your company."

Collector: "That is interesting, Ms. Debtor. For I have just reviewed your file, and there is nothing to indicate that you were unhappy or displeased with our service. Obviously, you must have some reason to contemplate legal action. Would you mind sharing it with me?"

Comment: Try to get a debtor to talk, and listen attentively. Then use the problem-solving techniques in this manual. (See Chapter 1, "Problem-Solving Techniques.)

Location Objection

Often debtors will not make payments because the creditor is located in a different geographical region. These debtors believe that because they are far away, creditors will not take legal action. There are two resources that can help you deal with this problem:

1. Secure a copy of the *Sales Planning Atlas* (Hammond, Inc., Union, New Jersey), which lists counties throughout the United States. Cross-referencing is easy because this manual also lists cities, towns, and incorporated villages.

2. You should have at least one or perhaps two national law lists. (See Chapter 9, "Law Lists for Information.")

If you run into a location problem, the first step is to determine the debtor's intent. If you conclude that the debtor will not make payment, you should "localize" your collection strategy. Proceed as follows:

Strategy: Select the name of an attorney in the debtor's locale. In major cities you will have many law firms to choose from. In most cases, you will be able to find an attorney who has prior experience with your debtor. (Refer to Chapter 9: "Legal Recovery.") The attorney probably has received claims from other creditors and collection agencies. Experience with a particular debtor can be crucial in gauging the collectibility of your claim.

Select the name of an attorney whose office is close to your debtor. Then recontact your debtor and make the following statement:

Collector: "Mr. Debtor, I have done everything humanly possible to resolve this matter, but to no avail. Unfortunately, our legal department has prepared the necessary papers to commence protracted litigation. These papers will be forwarded to corresponding counsel, John Jones, Esq., with the law firm of _____ in _____" (name of debtor's city). "This drastic action seems necessary, Mr. Debtor. Unfortunately, you will be subjected to the cost of a legal defense. Furthermore, the fact that we had to go to court to collect this debt will become a matter of public record. This detrimental information will ultimately be processed through the national credit reporting system and will be reported to inquiring creditors for seven years, as mandated by federal law. Mr. Debtor" (make one last-ditch effort to stimulate payment), "maybe you are not concerned about ensuing legal action, but the public filings and the information transmitted to inquiring credit grantors can seriously undermine your creditworthiness, since you risk denial of credit in future transactions. I'm sure you agree that this would not be in your best interests. Aren't you concerned about these potential ramifications?"

The debtor will respond either positively or negatively. If the debtor is concerned about creditworthiness, then you have created leverage. If the debtor is not and remains adamant, then there is nothing more you can do. You should consider ending any further efforts to collect the account. You have reached a demarcation point, and it is time to discontinue further efforts (if uneconomical) or structure another approach (proceeding with legal action).

How to Thwart Spurious Counterclaims

Debtors often "manufacture" counterclaims as smoke screens to evade payment. The trick is to counter this ploy by beating the debtors at their own game. Not only will the debtors mire themselves in obstructive legal action, but they will also have to pay their attorneys to defend against your just claims. The debtors' attorneys, who are charging hourly fees to file spurious counterclaims, will be laughing all the way to the bank.

Assume that your debtor has threatened a frivolous counterclaim, one that you know to be ridiculous. This approach represents a blatant attempt to thwart your efforts.

What to do: Take a hard line. Call the debtor's bluff. Let the debtor know in no uncertain terms that you will not be intimidated. Then ask a leading question to pressure the debtor to concede that his newfound excuses for nonpayment are no more than a ploy to evade payment. Then tone down your approach to demonstrate that you are a reasonable person. That softening statement should be followed by a closing question.

Example: "Ms. Debtor, I am not buying icicles in the wintertime. If you are under the impression that your threats of litigation will induce us to drop this matter and allow you to walk away from your obligation, it will never happen. Let me assure you that I am prepared to counterattack your spurious action tooth and nail by vigorously pursuing substantial legal penetration. Keep in mind that you will be paying hard dollars to your attorney to try to finagle you out of paying for goods sold and delivered—an uncertain prospect at best. You will also be paying your attorney to try to prove legal enforcement of your counterclaim, which, ironically, never came up while you were using our product. You manufactured this excuse only when it came time to pay the piper. Now, tell me, Ms. Debtor, is it not a fact that this excuse is nothing more than a ploy on your part? It would be in everyone's best interest to eliminate the mudslinging and get down to brass tacks. Let's resolve this matter like decent human beings. After all, did we not extend you credit in good faith? You have an ethical as well as a legal obligation to satisfy your indebtedness. Can't we resolve this matter in an orderly fashion?"

Boomerang Technique

The collector now sets the stage to apply the negative selling technique to the debtor threatening a counterclaim.

> *Collector:* "Ms. Debtor, I've listened attentively to your arguments. Tell me, what is it that you want?"

Negative approach: The debtor will probably suggest that she will drop the counterclaim in exchange for a release from her debt to you. That being the case, you need to skillfully employ a little empathy.

> *Collector:* "Ms. Debtor, I understand where you are coming from, and I can even appreciate your frustration with external factors beyond our control that may have inconvenienced you. But, Ms. Debtor, we delivered this merchandise to you on open account and in good faith. At that time did you do business with us in good faith? I think it is unfair that we should become a risk-taker in your venture. Ms. Debtor, don't you think you owe it to the ethics of your profession and your personal integrity to resolve this matter?"

Note that the collector has asked two questions. Wait for the debtor to answer. These trial closes are intended to prompt a favorable response that will grease the way toward commitment.

> *Collector:* "I know of your reputation in the community, and I certainly would not expect that to change now. Would you kindly process your remittance so we can credit your account?"

The word "reputation" implies that you know something about the debtor. Immediately follow the reference to reputation with a closing question that prompts a commitment.

Problem: A debtor tells you, "We don't have any money."

When debtors tell you they "don't have the money," what they are really telling you is that although they probably have money to pay other bills, they do not have the money to pay *you*. Your job is to find out *why*.

Wrong approach: The rebuttal: "Mr. Debtor, I am not buying your bull. You certainly don't expect me to believe such a ridiculous statement (and so on)."

This hard-line approach will only put debtors on the defensive. They may hang up on you and refuse further communication. Here is a much better approach:

Trial closing technique: The empathetic statement: "Mr. Debtor, I understand your financial dilemma and your budget problems. Tell me, Mr. Debtor, at the time you incurred this debt, did you intend to honor it?"

This is a good strategy because it sets the stage to commit debtors psychologically. It pinpoints problems and puts the pressure back on the debtors, where it belongs. If they respond Yes to the question "Did you intend to honor your obligation?" you have successfully created a closing statement. Debtors might feel compelled to demonstrate their good intentions with positive commitments. If they say No, then at least you have the debtors' blatant admission that they never intended to pay.

Strategy: When debtors say No, they never intended to pay, the only strategy is to lead the debtors to view the situation from a different perspective. But be careful. Some debtors will not respond, although you would be surprised how many will. Here are your "lines":

> *Collector:* "In other words, Mr. Debtor, you incurred this debt with the intent to commit fraud? Your aim all along was to secure our merchandise and disregard your promise to fulfill the terms of our agreement?"

If the debtor is still hostile, continue: "You know, Mr. Debtor, I have to appreciate your truthfulness in making this statement, for I did a preliminary investigation of your company, and I was under the impression you were a reputable business—an honorable member of the business community. I can see now that you pay only suppliers with which you have to do business. When you enter into one-time transactions, you hide behind the corporate veil and leave your creditors vulnerable. I wonder how you would feel if your customers were to do the same to you?"

Some debtors are immune to collection efforts. Some even brag about how they have "beaten" their creditors. But most debtors have a hot button. Encourage them to talk. If debtors have inflated egos, feed them. There is always a chance they will drop a clue to their hot buttons. Often you can shame debtors into paying. If you can get debtors to talk about how *they* would react in *your* shoes, sometimes you can get them to commit themselves.

Problem: A responsible principal will not come to the phone, or avoids personal contact. Obviously, you cannot collect money unless you can communicate. The following are a few suggestions to gather information:

- Try calling the debtor at home, if you can obtain the number.

- Call a supplier, or solicit assistance from other sources. Be discreet. Make sure you are on firm legal ground before you divulge the nature of your call. (Generally, on commercial debts, you have a right to communicate with other creditors and reveal the nature of the inquiry. Consumer debts are more closely regulated, and you should not reveal to a third party that the debtor owes you money. Consult with your attorney concerning your rights and status under applicable laws.) Indicate that you have tried to contact Mr. _____, but he failed to return your calls. Tell the contact you understand it has a business relationship with the debtor, and say it is urgent that you contact the debtor.

- Obtain a national profile on your debtor from a national electronic search firm. Utilize the report to contact your subject. Refer to Chapter 8, "Skip Tracing and Asset Searches."

- Prompt employees of the debtor's suppliers or other business contacts to give you the debtor's address and/or recruit them to deliver your message. Be careful, however, not to reveal debt status if yours is a consumer transaction.

- Initiate a search of public records. (See Chapter 8, "Skip Tracing and Asset Searches.")

Problem: One of the oldest tricks confronting creditors is the line, "The check is in the mail," when in fact it is not. It is easier for debtors to lie than it is to explain why they cannot or will not pay. Lying is a tactic that makes it easier for debtors to buy time.

You should assume that debtors who use this excuse have no intention of mailing a check. Do not believe it when they tell you that their "intentions are good." Here is an effective response when a debtor feeds you the line, "The check is in the mail."

Collector: "Ms. Debtor, I understand that your intentions are good, and I believe you when you tell me that you have every intention of mailing a check. But I have to report to our legal department, which has instructed me to verify payment by dispatching a courier to pick up the check in person. Would you therefore arrange, Ms. Debtor, to process a check made payable to _____? I will arrange to have our courier there tomorrow morning."

The term "legal department" implies legal review and that your company is contemplating a lawsuit. If the debtor balks at this arrangement, find out why. Try offering an alternative. For example, "Ms. Debtor, would it be more convenient for you to have the check ready in the morning or in the afternoon?"

Note how skillfully the alternatives are offered. When given a choice, often that will be enough to push the debtor over the edge. A choice gives the debtor a sense that the debtor has gained control. But, of course, the important thing is not whether you pick up the check in the morning or the afternoon, but that the debtor has agreed to let your courier pick up a check at all. If a debtor will not agree to give a check to a courier, that debtor never intended to pay you.

POSTCOLLECTION CLOSE

Your job as a professional collector is to secure positive commitments from the debtor, but we all know that many commitments fall by the wayside. Debtors have a tendency to lie. Therefore, it is important to qualify your collection effort by making a *sale after the sale*. This can best be accomplished with qualifying statements. For example:

> *Collector:* "Mr. Debtor, I am glad you have chosen to resolve this matter in good faith. Mr. Debtor, it is necessary that I communicate this agreement to our legal department. I hope you would not make any commitment that you do not intend to keep. Do I have your assurance, Mr. Debtor, that your check will be received by our office no later than _____?"

Always try to pin a debtor down. Remember, a commitment is not enough; you cannot bank a commitment. You must secure bankable funds. *Always confirm your understanding with the debtor.*

Do not give up: Get a firm promise every time, and hold debtors to their promises. When a promise to pay is given over the phone, follow up with a letter confirming exact dates and amounts. Then call again if those dates and amounts are not met. For customers who cannot possibly pay their entire debts, work out an arrangement and document it with a promissory note, which will serve as evidence if you ever have to take them to court.

There is a tenuous line between overselling and underselling.

Overselling

When debtors fail to meet their commitments, it is generally a symptom of faulty selling. The probability is that you have failed somewhere in fulfilling your responsibilities as a collector. For example, there is always the temptation of pressuring your debtor into paying more than that person can really afford. Such a commitment may look good to you at the moment. But what is the point if it is to be rescinded at a later date?

Keep your demands realistic. This means several things:

- Study your debtor's actual situation.
- Examine past payment habits.
- Get a fairly precise idea of the debtor's budget.
- Ask pointed questions about who is going to make the payment(s), when, and how.

True, the information you gather may not be as promising as you would like. Still, it will suggest the dimensions of what really constitutes a reasonable commitment for each particular debtor.

Underselling

Always make sure that you are not too subtle in your selling approach. Underselling can be as unproductive as overselling. If customers are only mildly convinced that they should meet their obligations, they may decide to reverse their buying decision at a later date.

To assure yourself of having really sold a customer, take sufficient time to unearth—and answer—all of the customer's objections. Ignore one, or shrug it off, and the debtor is likely to brood over it after you have secured a commitment to pay.

The line between overselling and underselling is an extremely fine one. But once you learn to walk it, chances are you will probably see fewer commitments fall by the wayside.

How to Barter a Successful Collection

As a collector, you have been trained to collect the money or, failing that, to pursue legal remedies. Your goals and aspirations probably reflect that objective, but other opportunities go far beyond the recovery of dollars and cents. There exist many incredible opportunities to barter, or negotiating other arrangements with debtors to satisfy their obligations. You can barter for all kinds of merchandise and services. These opportunities often exist in otherwise uncollectible situations.

How to Recognize Barter Opportunities

Unfortunately, many collectors do not recognize that many uncollectible accounts have barter potential. Many debtors cannot pay their bills, and some are judgment-proof. This does not necessarily mean that these debtors are deadbeats. If a debtor lacks the resources to pay you, maybe you can trade for products or services. Situations where barter may be a possibility include the following:

- A merger, acquisition, or takeover has resulted from financial insolvency or other extenuating circumstances.
- The debtor is heavily liened and/or overextended.

- The debtor is contemplating bankruptcy.

- The debtor's business is seasonal.

- The debtor lacks necessary working capital.

- The debtor has more assets than available working capital.

- The debtor is prone to barter.

- The debtor has connections in the marketplace that might enable the debtor to trade its product and/or service (which you do not want) for that of something else (which you do want).

Case in point: A collection consultant was retained to liquidate an $8,050.30 obligation stemming from two full-page ads in a major magazine. Through vigorous research, it was determined that the debtor owned significant real estate, including a luxury condominium complex in Palm Springs, California. This complex sold condominiums to investors on a time-share plan, but the complex failed to reach anticipated sales goals, and foreclosure was imminent. All collection efforts proved fruitless. In fact, the debtor was nonresponsive and inaccessible. An investigation revealed that the debtor was heavily liened, and that numerous lawsuits were pending. Had the case proceeded into litigation, the creditor would have discovered that the debtor's bank and the county (because of unpaid real estate taxes) were secured creditors and that their claims far exceeded the value of the debtor's estate. Litigation would have been an exercise in futility. To add insult to injury, the backlog of cases in California was two to three years. It was a judgment-proof situation. A typical collection agency would probably recommend that the account be written off.

Alternate Avenues to Recovery

The collection consultant contacted the debtor's attorney, and an alternate collection strategy was developed. It could be assumed that the mortgage holders were anxious to foreclose on the property (having a vested interest), and would-be purchasers were anxious to secure the property at a bargain. This climate created tremendous negotiation leverage because, although a lawsuit would have been ineffective against the debtor, the creditor could challenge the validity of the sale (even though the creditor was unsecured) by applying to the court for an order to show cause and/or a preliminary injunction to block (at least temporarily) the sale. The motion for a preliminary injunction, claiming that the sale would prejudice the interests of the various creditors, would generally be filed in a court of equity. A temporary restraining order would throw a monkey wrench into the multimillion-dollar sale.

Obviously, a collector who commands this kind of information has leverage, but the information must be used correctly. In this actual case, the collector skillfully manipulated the debtor and the debtor's attorney (who was anxious to close the sale so that his client could salvage some money) into believing that any form of injunctive relief might upset the multimillion-dollar deal. The collector used the "iceberg" theory (i.e., you expand on a little bit of information—evidence—leading your adversary to believe you have much more than you really do). The debtor could not afford the risk that the transaction might be delayed. The sale was just too important.

How the Debtor's Attorney and Accountant Can Become Your Salespeople

The debtor's attorney or accountant can be your best friend. By using either or both of them as your center of influence, you can often find alternate ways of recovery. In the aforementioned case, a barter arrangement was the result. Under the terms, the debtor transferred "title" to a real property time-share unit on the condition that the creditor not pursue injunctive relief. The debtor signed over rights to one week every year at this luxurious resort for a total of 86 years.

What is even more interesting is that the new owners of the time-share unit have agreed to exchange time-share unit privileges with the owners of resorts in other locations, including Hawaii Kai, Florida, and the Bahamas. Imagine, free use of several exquisite resorts! The creditor can also swap time-share weeks with other owners of the unit at Palm Springs. (See Exhibit 4.1 for a sample Settlement of Debt Letter.)

EXHIBIT 4.1   SAMPLE SETTLEMENT OF DEBT LETTER

Dear Sir:

Pursuant to my conversation this date with a Mr. Gerald Michaels we agreed that your client, conditional on Mr. Michaels' conversation with our accountant, would settle our outstanding debt for exchange of an unencumbered deed to a prime season timeshare week at the Indian Wells Racquet Club in Palm Springs, California. The amount of the debt to be settled is totaled at $8,050.30. The Indian Wells Racquet Club is next door to the Indian Wells Golf Course, home of the Bob Hope Tournament.

As stated above, the week you are accepting is a prime week which this year occurs March 14 to 21. The week is referenced as

        CONTROL # 560 - 01 - 19/11MB
        Week # 11

This is the 11th week of every year always beginning and ending on Friday. Therefore the dates will change slightly depending on where Friday falls on the calendar.

I have attached an information package to explain more about the unit including reservation information. This is truly an exceptional location with excellent quality amenities.

Please send by return mail vesting information, i.e., name and address of whom you wish to hold title. I will then have my attorney prepare and send you the deed. Also please send us a conditional release from your client pending receipt of the deed to the Indian Wells property.

Value fo Barter

The value of such a trade? In this case, the retail price of a time-share on this property was $11,000—more than the original debt! Add to this the fact that the mark-up in advertising is about 200%. The creditor's true cost for providing was only $2,000. Think of it: a net investment of $2,000 leveraged into $11,000.

Bartering Is Limited Only by the Imagination

It pays to know a debtor's business. It is often easier to persuade the debtor to satisfy an obligation with goods or services than it is to collect money. Collection consultants have successfully secured for their clients such amenities as luxurious vacation trips, personal computers, electric typewriters, cameras, television sets and VCRs, home improvements, wardrobes, expensive china, office supplies, telephone systems, and even luxurious automobiles. On one occasion, a collection consultant negotiated to accept the use of an elegant motor home worth $62,000 for three months in satisfaction of the client's $1,700 debt. The debtor ultimately went bankrupt and no other creditor got so much as a dime, but the consultant's client had one heck of a vacation! (Incidentally, the use of the motor home was not considered a "preferential payment" under the Bankruptcy Code.)

How to Detect Barter Opportunities

There are no hard-and-fast rules to determine where lucrative barter opportunities exist. You must be perceptive and creative and look for opportunities. But do not propose a settlement by barter too quickly. Maybe the debtor will pay you the money. If you give in too easily, you might have to settle for less than full value. Always weigh the amount owed against the potential value of the barter. Determine what other avenues are open to you and then make your decision based on the economics of the situation (i.e., value received). If you apply the collections-by-barter technique, your collection ratio will improve, and you will reap many goodies that otherwise would have been unavailable to you.

PAY IT WITH ROSES

Clearly, money is not the only means available to satisfy bad debts. There may be good reason to push for merchandise or services to satisfy an obligation in lieu of hard cash. Consider the following actual case history—another successful collection that was resolved via the innovative barter system.

A particular collection consultant's client, Halsey Advertising, contracted to sell display advertising in an in-flight magazine to a company, Rose Royce, which sells long-stemmed roses by mail order. Rose Royce is unlike a conventional florist in that it selects only top-quality roses and sends them in an elaborate decorative package. Under the terms of the advertising contract, the debtor (Rose Royce) was obligated to pay the client (Halsey Advertising) $15,111.65, which included a 15% agency discount—contingent upon payment in full in 30 days. If the debtor did not honor the contract, 15% was to be added to the $15,111.65 net.

But the debtor did not meet the $15,111.65 obligation despite repeated efforts by both Halsey Advertising and the field representative who sold the insertion order. The delinquent obligation was subsequently placed with the consultant for collection.

The consultant immediately rolled up his sleeves and went to work. Unfortunately, numerous contacts with the debtor did not yield a check, and it became necessary to employ advanced collection techniques that prompted the debtor to retain legal counsel. The consultant had verified that the debtor was a new business that had overextended itself in a number of advertising campaigns. The advertisements not only bombed, they also depleted the company's cash reserves. In a typically creative move, the consultant used the debtor's law firm as a selling agent and negotiated a payment arrangement that called for part of the obligation to be satisfied with $2,000 worth of roses!

Because the debtor did not satisfy the $15,111.65 principal amount, let alone the 15% discount, the consultant told the debtor's attorney that he would not accept payment of just the principal amount. He pointed out that the 15% represented an advertising agency discount, which Halsey Advertising passed on directly to Rose Royce contingent upon payment in full within 30 days. Since Rose Royce did not honor its commitment to pay promptly, it was not entitled to the 15% discount.

A heated debate erupted with the attorney over this 15%. The debtor's position was that it would pay the principal, but not the 15%. Most creditors would back off at this stage and accept the principal amount, but not this particular collection consultant. Years of experience as a collector and negotiator drove him to hang in there and press for the additional 15%. The reasoning? If continued hard bargaining proved fruitless, he could still settle for the principal amount. But if the consultant stood his ground and fought for the close, the debtor might back down, and he could collect the whole amount. (See Exhibit 4.2 for a sample settlement letter.)

Credit Grantor's Errors

When creditors become frustrated with debtors, they immediately give in at the first sign of money and settle for terms that are less than they could get if they were to hang in there and fight a little harder. As the letter from the debtor's law firm (in Exhibit 4.2) substantiates, the debtor's attorney did in fact act as the collection consultant's salesperson. He was able to convince the attorney that he was legally entitled to an additional 15% by pointing out that he was already being forced to settle, accepting a payout without interest, and that his client was not going to sit by and allow the debtor to further benefit to the tune of approximately $2,000. The consultant was able to persuade the debtor's attorney to persuade his client to provide $2,000 worth of long-stemmed roses to settle the difference. He pointed out to the debtor's attorney that this $2,000 would cost the debtor only around $1,000, calculating the debtor's markup to be 100%. Thus, the amount the debtor was giving up was actually less than the 15% discount. But since advertising is

EXHIBIT 4.2   ROSE ROYCE/HALSEY ADVERTISING SETTLEMENT
LETTER

Dear Sir:

This letter will confirm our telephone conversation of Tuesday, December 8, 20__, during which we agreed to the following in settlement of the above-referenced matter:

1.   Our client, Rose Royce, will agree to pay your client, Halsey Advertising, the sum of Fifteen Thousand One Hundred Eleven and 65/100 Dollars ($15,111.65), to be paid as follows:

(a)   Initial Downpayment of Four Thousand Dollars ($4,000.00), to be paid One Thousand Five Hundred Dollars ($1,500.00) immediately (our client's check in that amount is enclosed herewith); and payment of Two Thousand Five Hundred Dollars ($2,500.00) on or before January 8, 20__;

(b)   Payment of the balance of Eleven Thousand One Hundred Eleven and 65/100 Dollars ($11,111.65) in consecutive monthly installments of Six Hundred Dollars ($600.00) each, to be paid commencing January 15, 20__.

2.   The fifteen percent (15%) agency discount previously received by Rose Royce will be exchanged for Two Thousand Dollars' ($2,000.00) worth of services from Rose Royce.   The services to be offered by Rose Royce will be offered during the period January 1, 20__ through and including March 30, 20__ and will consist of delivery of long-stemmed roses overnight at a base retail price of Fifty-Nine Dollars ($59.00) per dozen, except during the period from February 1, 20__ through and including February 14, 20__, at which time the base retail price for this service will be Seventy-Five Dollars ($75.00) per dozen.

Please review the foregoing carefully and, if you agree with same, kindly execute the enclosed copy of this letter and return it to the undersigned in the enclosed self-addressed, stamped envelope.   If the foregoing does not accurately reflect your understanding of our agreement, please contact the undersigned or Karyn Mounsey immediately.

Thank you for your courtesy and cooperation in bringing this matter to a quick resolution.

marked up substantially more than long-stemmed roses, the client benefited from the barter agreement.

You will note in paragraph one of the attorney's letter that a total of $4,000 was to be paid in two installments of $1,500 and $2,500. The debtor did honor this commitment, and the balance of the $15,111.65 principal was to be paid in monthly installments of $600 each.

The success of this transaction further proves the awesome power of barter. Applied to collections, it can resolve disputes that otherwise might end up in the courts.

In every collection call there are opportunities that go beyond dollars and cents. Before you give up in disgust, writing off the account or placing it with an attorney, evaluate the debtor's business and determine whether its services or products might be used to offset the obligation.

The moral: Before you jump the gun and sue your debtor, stop! Take a step back, reevaluate the problem, and explore other opportunities.

Using Barter Organizations

You can take your service or product to a professional bartering organization, such as the National Commerce Exchange, which has offices throughout the United States. These organizations have computer banks filled with people interested in bartering. You can always trade with other members for whatever you need. Keep in mind, however, that bartering organizations charge a fee based on the value of merchandise or services exchanged. You are also required to report such transactions on your federal tax return.

"Good Guy, Bad Guy" Approach

You undoubtedly recall some "cops and robbers" movie in which a suspect was hauled into the local precinct and interrogated about a crime. In this scenario two detectives play the roles of "good cop, bad cop." This is a harrowing psychological technique with devastating consequences to the suspect. The first detective, playing the "bad guy," conducts a brutal interrogation—badgering the suspect with contempt, declaring that the police know that this person committed the crime, threatening the suspect with dire consequences, and perhaps even roughing up the accused. The suspect is manipulated into believing that he is headed for "the chair" unless the police get a confession. The second detective provides a stark contrast, taking the suspect's "side" and expressing understanding of and sympathy for the suspect's situation. This scenario continues until at some point the bad guy (first detective) leaves the interrogation room. The suspect is now alone with the "good guy" (second detective). This detective now gains the confidence of the distraught, unsuspecting accused, who has been thoroughly beaten and battered psychologically. The second detective plies the suspect with consolation and sympathy, assuring the suspect that everything will be all right. The second detective promises to help the suspect if the suspect will just "come clean." Eventually, the suspect lets down his guard and confesses to the crime.

Did the police get their confession solely from the bad guy's interrogation? No. Was the criminal's confession prompted solely by the empathy displayed by the good guy? No. This was a two-tiered approach. The bad guy played on the suspect's worst fears until the suspect was ready to break down. Then the bad guy exited the room, leaving Mr. Nice Guy to secure the confession. An overwhelming majority of confessions have resulted from this little act of deception. Now, how does the "good guy, bad guy" approach apply to collections?

Adapted for Receivables Recovery

This novel approach can be implemented by one collector acting out the roles in two entirely different conversations, or it can be implemented by two collectors, one playing the bad guy, the other the good guy. There are many actual case histories in which stubborn debtors have been induced to resolve their obligations through the use of this tactic. The approach works because a debtor subjected to the bad guy is put under immense pressure. When the debtor is subsequently confronted by the gentle, empathetic, good-guy approach, he is moved from a hostile state toward a more agreeable frame of mind. Some debtors come across out of a sense of relief that the bad guys will not call again, or simply to avoid further confrontations. Other debtors who satisfy their obligations with the good guys actually feel that by paying the good guys they are somehow "getting back" at the bad guy. Sometimes this approach is more effective in reverse (i.e., starting out with the good guy, and then escalating to the bad-guy mode).

For example, a scrap dealer owed the client of a collection consultant more than $45,000. The client had already attempted the bad-guy approach before turning over the account. Evidently, that approach was not effective because the client's efforts were unsuccessful.

Enter the Good-Guy Collector

Partly as a result of the client's attempts to browbeat the debtor into payment, the debtor was extremely hostile and recalcitrant. Thus, the consultant decided not to enter the recalcitrant fray with all guns blazing. Her strategy was to defuse the debtor's hostility and grab his attention by offering an attractive incentive to liquidate the debt. The debtor in this case was one of several scrap dealers competing for the client's scrap metal. In the consultant's initial contact, she baited the debtor with the possibility that his company might be "awarded contracts to do additional business," and that she could help the company "win a lucrative bid." The consultant told him that a new bid list was coming out in a few weeks and, *providing the outstanding debt was paid,* she might be able to arrange for her client to sell the debtor a substantial volume of scrap iron at a favorable price. As a result of this conversation, the outstanding balance was paid, and the new transaction was completed C.O.D. The consultant knew the scrap dealer was hungry to buy the scrap metal for resale, and she appealed to that greed.

The collection consultant reminded the debtor that her client intended to sell the scrap on a competitive-bid basis. She estimated that the bids were submitted and assured the debtor that if he submitted a bid just $100 over that of the next highest bidder, his company would receive the lucrative contract. The debtor immediately paid half the debt in cash and arranged a letter of credit to cover the balance. The consultant followed through with her commitment, and the net result was that everyone benefited. The debtor submitted the right bid and profited from the transaction. The client got paid, avoided a litigious situation, and disposed of tons of scrap iron at an additional profit. In fact, the debtor's attorney even helped conclude the deal. Everybody walked away with a sense of accomplishment. This was a perfect example of the "good guy, bad guy" approach in actual practice, although it was carried out in reverse: "bad guy, good guy."

Remember the "good guy, bad guy" approach. It will produce financial miracles.

COLLECTION BY DRAFT

Collection by draft is an uncommon remedy, but it does have its place in the collection fraternity. Simply prepare a bank draft. Forms are available from law blank publishers, including Blumberg, Inc., at 62 White Street, New York, NY 10013 (visit *www.blumberg .com* to access forms online).

- Have the debtor read his or her account number to you over the telephone.
- Fill in the account number, amount, and other information.
- Send the original draft to your debtor.
- Send a copy with a cover letter (see Exhibit 4.3) to the debtor's bank—together with any necessary bank fee—for presentment to the debtor. (You may get better results if you have your bank forward the draft to the debtor's bank, which is more apt to act expeditiously for another bank than for you directly.)

The debtor's bank will present the draft to the debtor for the debtor's signature. (Naturally, you cannot sign the draft because you are not a signatory on the debtor's account.) If the debtor approves the draft, the funds will be transmitted to your bank. If the draft is not paid, you will get it back unsigned.

Collection by draft is an intimidation tactic that puts the bank on notice that you intend to collect the debt. The success of this little-known technique stems from the fact that a

---

EXHIBIT 4.3   SAMPLE COVER LETTER*

ATTENTION: Collection Department

Enclosed please find our draft no. _____ in the amount of $_____, made payable to Good Faith Creditor, drawn on _____ _____ to be placed for collection, and drawn on the _____ _____.

This draft is being drawn relevant to the annexed invoices _____ _____ for whom which monies are due.

If draft is not accepted, please protest for nonpayment. If it is still rejected, please return, so that we may take legal action as appropriate.

Tnank you in advance for your cooperation.

---

*This format is for commercial debts only.

Warning: Creditors should not exercise this remedy against a consumer.

bank draft has psychological impact. A bank will not pay a draft without the debtor's approval, but many debtors, knowing that their bank has been notified of the draft, will be embarrassed into making payment. In essence, the influence of the debtor's bank is what makes a draft work. Of course, this tactic should not be used if you intend to do further business with the debtor because it causes embarrassment to the debtor and may damage his or her credit standing.

Note on legality: When you send a draft to the bank, you should not make any reference to the debtor's indebtedness that could be construed as libel or slander. Do not indicate that the account is past due if the debt is consumer related or make any accusations. Note that the language in the letter (Exhibit 4.3) references amount owed, invoice numbers, and so on.

An additional remedy: If a draft is not honored, you might wish to *protest for nonpayment.* Not all banks will cooperate in processing such a transaction, but certain collection consultants have had limited success with the technique in appropriate circumstances.

To: Customer's Bank	Account No:
Subject: Pre-legal criteria	Creditor:
Bank Customer (Debtor)	Amount:

Enclosed—Site Draft and Support Documentation

Pursuant to the provisions of the Uniform Commercial Code, we have enclosed a site draft drawn on the above referenced account, for monies owed by your customer that remains unpaid.

Despite repeated demands and/or broken promises for remittance, your customer has ignored its legally incurred obligation.

The Uniform Commercial Code directs that you contact your customer (the debtor) and inquire whether the signatory and/or a responsible principal will authorize and sign the enclosed site draft. Provided restitution is made to the creditor for the full amount, then the debtor (your customer) will be discharged from any and all liability. Documentation in support of the creditor's claim is enclosed.

If your customer (the debtor) refuses to honor the enclosed site draft, you are required to return this site draft "UNPAID," including the reasons thereof. A self-addressed, stamped envelope is provided for your convenience.

On large debts, and where appropriate, the creditor may exhibit the unpaid site draft as criterion in support of an involuntary bankruptcy petition.

You are required to process this draft in conformity with the Uniform Commercial Code.

A copy of a similar documentary collection pursuant to the Uniform Rules for Collection of Commercial Paper Publication 522 of the U.C.C. is enclosed.

Thank you for your anticipated courtesy.

This is an attempt to collect a debt. Any information obtained will be used for that purpose.

Note: Creditors are encouraged to obtain a copy of commercial credit laws published by the National Association of Credit Management (*www.nacm.org*).

The site draft technique is effective in situations where a nonpaying customer maintains a borrowing relationship with his bank. A debtor often does not disclose to his bank his defaults with vendors. The result is that your embarrassed debtor could ruin an otherwise productive lending relationship; sometimes a debtor's banker will intervene and collect the debt.

Depositing a Creditor-Prepared Check Drawn on the Debtor's Bank Account

Warning: Consult with an attorney before employing this payment remedy.

Imagine if you could just deposit a check, drawn on the debtor's bank account, and presto, you have a paid-in-full receivable. Wherein a site draft is discretionary, the presentation of a check is legal tender, which will be debited from the debtor's bank account.

I first learned of this novel approach from Gold's Gym, a subscription health club franchise. Customers sign an enrollment agreement that authorizes monthly debits from the customer's checking account, either via check or electronically. The customer can terminate the debits via notification to his bank.

Adapting this technique to receivable recoveries, I established an account with service provider MCA of Virginia: P.O. Box 35228, Richmond, Virginia 23235 (Tel: 804-272-8515). MCA prepares checks, which are forwarded to the creditor. The drafts are then deposited just like regular checks drawn against the debtor's bank account.

For legal reasons, great discretion must be exercised to draw checks against the debtor account only where a debtor had specifically authorized the draft.

Because the creditor is depositing a negotiable instrument drawn against the debtor's bank account—without due process (i.e., execution of judgment)—be very cautious.

In addition, be careful not to casually implement this practice unless you have authorization from the debtor. The strategy is extremely effective, but only under the most controlled of circumstances.

Western Union Draft

Another version of the site draft, check depositing strategy is offered by Western Union—albeit with a difference. In this strategy, the debtor provides bank account information to the collector, which is processed by Western Union as a check drawn on the account. A cancelled check is returned to the debtor with his statement, providing a receipt. Contact Western Union for particulars (*www.westernunion.com*).

POINT OF DIMINISHING RETURNS

Accuracy, timing, and positioning are crucial to any collection strategy. Perhaps one of the most important qualities a professional collector can possess is the ability to recognize demarcation lines in the collection cycle. A demarcation line is that point at which continued or increased efforts to collect an account fail to produce a proportionate increase in the probability of success.

Persistence is an admirable quality, but inevitably you will reach a point of diminishing returns. Continued effort will produce no definite result. Unfortunately, collectors often become involved in pursuing a hopeless case when they could be investing their time more productively. Successful collectors recognize demarcation lines. They know where to direct their attention to yield maximum results *and* when it is time to terminate their efforts.

By the time you have made your second phone call, you should have a pretty good idea of which way the account will go. Conventional wisdom suggests that repetition of the facts at this point will be useless and wasteful. Not true!

Repetition is often necessary to get your money. Sometimes even the best collectors succeed only after several attempts. In selling, it is understood that most sales are made on the fifth closing attempt. Why should collections be any different? This does not mean that you should make voluminous phone calls to collect a $200 account. The economics would not justify it. If it costs you $500 in time and effort to collect a $200 debt, you have won the battle, but lost the war; however, where economically feasible, depending on the balance due and debtor feedback, you should consider continued pursuit. A different approach or even mere persistence will frequently pay off and salvage an otherwise uncollectible bad debt.

Know when you reach a demarcation point (the point of diminishing returns).

DEBTOR LOCALIZATION

Does geographic distance between creditor and debtor affect collectability? Would communications from a California-based creditor seem insignificant to a debtor in Iowa? In some cases, yes. But generally speaking, distance is of secondary importance compared to the quality of communication. Geography need not be a barrier *if* you are a proficient communicator. Nonetheless, from a legal standpoint, local influence definitely adds credibility. So what is a creditor to do to spur a distant debtor to satisfy his indebtedness? The answer is that the creditor should localize its strategy by conditioning the debtor to believe that severe legal consequences are about to come to fruition. Here is how:

- Invest in a state-by-state county map directory (e.g., *Sales Planning Atlas,* Hammond, Inc., Union, New Jersey; or *Business Control Atlas of the United States,* American Map Corporation, Maspeth, New York).

- Select the names of attorneys or collection agencies in the debtor's county and use this information to localize the debt.

Caution: Some collectors resort to subterfuge, impersonating marshals, sheriffs, or other law enforcement officials from the debtor's county. This practice is illegal; however, you can use local collection agencies, credit bureaus, or law firms to zero in on the debtor and establish instant credibility.

Every collector should have a county directory. Armed with this valuable tool, you can look up a debtor's town or city in the index, quickly reference the county, and then, in your communication, make reference to the local law firm or agency that will pursue the account. References to the debtor's county create a localized effect and strengthen your position.

Important legal note: You should not threaten to enlist local law firms or collection agencies without their permission. Also, you should not threaten such action unless you intend to follow through. The federal Fair Debt Collection Practices Act (FDCPA) makes it illegal for third-party collectors *collecting consumer debts* to threaten action that is illegal or that they have no intention of actually pursuing. Generally, FDCPA restrictions are relaxed for commercial claims; however, commercial collectors are regulated by the Federal Trade Commission Act, and some states have enacted legislation that imposes additional restrictions on collection activities by creditors and/or agencies.

The legal forwarding system recommended in this book (see Chapter 9) is an excellent method to achieve the following:

- Gain the advantage of the local influence factor.
- Protect yourself legally by enlisting attorneys or agencies familiar with local law. Localizing collections is an effective weapon in the collections arsenal—use it wisely!

MIXING-BOWL CONCEPT

Collection management is an inexact, multifaceted science. Collection techniques could be compared to seven-digit telephone numbers: Almost limitless combinations are possible. Similarly, although the alphabet contains only 26 letters, we can create hundreds of thousands of words with those 26 letters. The point is, by combining a variety of collection techniques, you can always come up with another approach. The practitioner of accounts receivable management is the architect of the collection strategy, who has at his disposal virtually limitless possibilities to motivate debtors to pay.

Numerous collection devices have never appeared in print, were never taught in a collection seminar, and have never been used by the collection agency industry. These devices exist only in your imagination. For example, another new technique that can greatly magnify your possibilities for success is the charitable contribution collection strategy. This approach has already proved to be one of the most effective collection devices. It enables the collector to literally collect the uncollectible, resolve the unresolvable, and make the impossible possible. (See Exhibit 4.4 for a sample Contribution Receipt Letter.)

Mission Impossible

We all remember the noted TV series *Mission Impossible,* in which highly innovative techniques implemented by trained agents achieved seemingly impossible results. Each episode was prefaced with a strategy session in which the agents discussed their game plan. Following this brainstorming session, the agents made the impossible possible and brought

EXHIBIT 4.4 SAMPLE CONTRIBUTION RECEIPT LETTER

Contingent upon receipt of bankable funds of $2,343.18 by ____ ____, 20____, we agree to make a $100.00 contribution to Bryan's House for Aids Related Illness.

In the alternative, you may deduct $100.00 from $2,343.18 owed and forward a copy of the donation to us.

This offer is in a spirit of goodwill and to convert a negative situation into a positive result.

Please advise.

dire emergencies to successful resolutions. Usually this entailed a brilliantly conceived and executed "sting," incorporating creativity, imagination, and cunning. All the episodes of *Mission Impossible* had one thing in common: The key ingredient in the agents' success was their effective use of *creativity* and *imagination*.

Suppose that the dire threats to national security depicted in *Mission Impossible* were addressed with conventional methods (e.g., legal processes, international debates, resolutions, negotiations, political pressure). What would be the outcome? Certainly the "bad guys" would quickly grasp the game plan and take immediate steps to counteract it. Second, conventional methods would be extremely time-consuming and in the end might actually do more harm than good. The time element would further undermine the efforts of the "good guys" to achieve their critically important objectives.

The comparison: Now consider the business of collection in light of our analysis of *Mission Impossible*. If we subscribe to conventional dialogue, our inclination is to follow these steps:

1. Exhaust our own internal efforts.
2. Place the account with a collection agency.
3. Prosecute the claim in court via litigation.

Our deeply held convictions dictate that the legal system is the last resort that will achieve our objectives. But will it? Let us explore this myth. Is litigation a viable remedy? Is the judicial process a guarantee that justice will be forthcoming? Are we likely to intimidate the debtor through expensive litigation? In most cases, the answer is a resounding No!

One irrefutable fact: All litigation creates an adversarial environment.

What is wrong with our legal system: Seeking redress in a court is a win/lose proposition; that is, someone wins and someone loses. Because you, the creditor, are initiating the lawsuit, the debtor perceives that you are out to take his assets, forcibly and at great expense. It does not matter that the debtor incurred a legitimate debt, nor does the fact that you are entitled to justice carry any weight. The naked truth is that justice is not cheap, and the average debtor defending a lawsuit will perceive you as a villain out to take his chips. Now the climate has changed to the win/lose scenario; that is, you win and the debtor loses.

Bitter Truth

In some situations the mere threat of litigation will be enough to motivate upright debtors to pay, but from *most debtors* such threats elicit just the opposite reaction. Let us not mince words. Your attorney is out for one thing and one thing only—to collect the money. Although you are legally correct and are entitled to resort to litigation, a proficient debtor can throw numerous roadblocks in the way of legal recovery. Putting a debtor up against the wall will accentuate your differences and often make matters worse. Lawsuits are expensive, time-consuming, and very ugly. In most cases, the attorneys benefit from protracted litigation, not you, the litigant.

Attorneys Are Not Salespeople

A great deal of respect is due the legal profession, and we are certainly entitled to our day in court. But personal experience involving many litigious situations has firmly convinced me that most lawsuits can be avoided, settled, or otherwise resolved amicably.

Unfortunately, attorneys are not sales oriented and many lack communication skills. Experience has taught me that many legal practitioners have tunnel vision. They see only one route to resolve a dispute—the courts. In truth, the attorney who is most successful on behalf of the client is not one who has exhausted every perceivable *legal* recourse—encompassing voluminous motions, memorandums of law, and lengthy trial proceedings—but one who can resolve the matter as quickly and as fairly as possible by *minimizing* litigation and maximizing communication. If your attorney can get a problem resolved without going through the expense of litigation, then that attorney has succeeded where the legal system might very well have failed.

How to Collect from a Hard-Core, Judgment-Proof Debtor

Imagine this scenario: Your company is owed $45,000 by a corporation that will cease to exist in a few months. Worse, the debtor allegedly has ties to organized crime and was recently indicted for possession of stolen property, transporting illegal aliens into this country, trafficking in drugs, and other offenses. You might place the claim with your collection agency, but if the agency strikes out, you end up with nothing. You then expend several thousand dollars in up-front legal fees to commence legal proceedings. Shortly thereafter you learn that Hardcore Debtor has more than $1.8 million in pending litigation, including a $200,000 federal tax lien, more than $900,000 in secured obligations to a bank, and a multiplicity of other lawsuits by creditors representing an additional $700,000. Despite aggressive dunning initiated by several collection agencies and dozens of lawsuits representing hundreds of thousands of dollars and involving more than a dozen law firms, not one creditor has recovered a single penny.

Such a debtor was placed with a collection consulting firm, which ran into the same difficulties that were encountered by its counterparts. Conventional collection approaches were doomed to fail. The debtor would not communicate with creditors, thumbed his nose at the legal system, and devoured attorneys for lunch. As the collection consultant delved into this interesting case, they learned that the Federal Bureau of Investigation (FBI), Internal Revenue Service (IRS), Department of Taxation, Department of Labor, Environmental Protection Agency (EPA), and the district attorney's office had the debtor under investigation and constant surveillance. This proficient, hard-core debtor was well-versed in collection terminology and quite capable of frustrating the enforcement of a money judgment. The consultants discussed the case with several attorneys who were embroiled in court actions against the debtor. They learned much, but the inescapable conclusion was that conventional methods would not work. The debtor was, in fact, judgment-proof. No creditor collected so much as a dime—except one. This consulting firm's client got paid the full $45,000 worth of the obligation. (Note: The same firm subsequently represented the former Conrail when that corporation's attorney failed in efforts to collect a $16,000 judgment against the same debtor and was successful in that instance as well.) How? The firm was able to probe the debtor's hot button and utilized the information to structure a unique strategy.

The following steps provide a diary of a collection strategy in the aforementioned case.

1. *Establish communication.* Creditor places a $45,000 claim with a collection consulting firm. Conventional collection procedures are begun, but the debtor refuses to communicate. Collection efforts are intensified, but the debtor still will not communicate.

2. *Develop information.* The consulting firm commences an independent investigation, including a search of public records. It is determined that the debtor is being sued for hundreds of thousands of dollars in unpaid obligations. The debtor is also subject to an unsatisfied tax lien and a $1.8 million money judgment. The firm communicates with other vendors, creditors, and governmental agencies to develop further information (horizontal debtor pursuit).

   Research includes interviewing attorneys who are currently prosecuting claims or involved in postjudgment proceedings against the debtor. None has collected any money.

   At this point the collection consultants learn that the debtor is under investigation by the FBI, the district attorney's office, and other government agencies, including the IRS, for criminal improprieties.

   Eventually, the debtor's business is raided by federal agents, the state police, the EPA, and federal customs and immigration officials. The debtor and other responsible principals are arrested for illegally hiring aliens, possession of stolen merchandise, tax evasion, and drug trafficking. A case is prepared for presentation to a grand jury. Indictments are imminent.

   From communications with law enforcement officials, the consulting firm learns that the debtor allegedly has ties with organized crime figures and that the government is building a substantial criminal case against the debtor. The case achieves national publicity, appearing on the front page of a national newspaper, and receives extensive coverage on radio and television.

The debtor immediately begins to liquidate all holdings, converting his assets to cash with the intent to defraud creditors. The situation has reached a critical stage as the debtor intends to file for bankruptcy under Chapter 7 (liquidation). Prospects are bleak.

3. *Probe for the hot button.* The collection consulting firm implements a hard-line approach, attempting to intimidate the debtor by cooperating with government and law-enforcement agencies. It becomes involved in the proceedings in an attempt to create leverage with the debtor and the debtor's attorney, offering to disassociate the firm from the proceedings if the debtor will pay the $45,000 debt to its client. But the debtor is not moved by this approach and ignores all efforts to negotiate a settlement.

Another strategy is then initiated, this time the good guy/bad guy approach, wherein the consulting firm persuades clients to continue to sell the debtor on C.O.D. or letter-of-credit terms if the debtor will agree to pay a 20% surcharge on each order—that amount to be applied toward paying off existing obligations. Thus the firm baits the debtor with additional business opportunities. The firm sells the debtor and his attorney hard, but the debtor still does not respond.

The consultants then try putting pressure on the debtor via other creditors with an involuntary bankruptcy approach. They start organizing creditors and judgment creditors to put the debtor's assets (which are substantial) under control and scrutiny of the federal bankruptcy court. This approach also fails when other creditors are unresponsive. In the meantime, the debtor is rapidly selling off assets. The consulting firm probes for additional information and ultimately learns that the debtor, belying his criminal character and alleged ties to organized crime, is an ongoing contributor and benefactor of the Boy Scouts of America and other charitable organizations. This information is developed by the consulting firm for use in a different kind of collection strategy.

4. *Develop interest.* At this juncture, the firm advises its client that it would cost a minimum of $2,500 to commence legal proceedings against the debtor and that such action would in all probability be fruitless. Digging deep into its bag of techniques, the consulting firm then initiates another highly innovative approach. It communicates directly with the debtor's business associates and family, conveying the message that the client is willing to donate the $2,500 that would normally be used for litigation purposes to the Boy Scouts of America and give credit for the donation to the debtor.

Legal note: Third-party communications may be improper in certain situations, when collecting consumer debts, for example. Familiarize yourself with the Fair Debt Collection Practices Act and consult with your attorney before commencing third-party contact.

5. *Use sales strategies.* Finally, the debtor returns the consulting firm's call and a productive conversation ensues. A consultant points out that becoming deadlocked in litigation would accomplish nothing more than enrich the lawyers and compound the debtor's already prodigious legal problems. The consultant stresses the intrinsic public relations value of contributing the legal fees to the debtor's favorite charity, the Boy Scouts of America. To highlight the event, the consultant suggests that the client write a press release, publicizing the good deed and goodwill of the debtor, who was buried in an avalanche of adverse publicity. The debtor for the first time begins to bend and show signs of cooperation, but he still does not commit. Continuing to sell, the collection consulting firm then offers to donate part of the collection agency commission to another charity of interest to the debtor. An emotional conversation ensues, and all obstacles to settlement are removed. The debtor now shifts from a belligerent attitude to one of agreement and cooperation. Communication is now established, and so, with the use of applied psychology and a Herculean uphill sales approach, the debtor is slowly moved to commit to pay the $45,000 debt with certified funds in five business days. In return, the consulting firm agrees to make two donations—representing the legal budget and part of the collection agency proceeds—to charitable organizations designated by the debtor.

6. *Follow up.* To ensure that the debtor cannot back out of his commitment, which was made in an emotional state of mind, the consulting firm confirms the transaction in writing by immediately documenting the pledge with the Boy Scouts of America and the Heart Association, indicating the amounts of the donations, which are contingent upon Mr. Hardcore Debtor's honoring of his commitment to satisfy the $45,000 obligation. To further confirm the verbal agreement, it notifies the newspapers that have previously written derogatory articles concerning the debtor's indictments that the debtor will make a sizable contribution to the Boy Scouts of America at his place of business. It then formally invites Troop 440 to participate in the festivities along with the local and national news media. The collection consulting firm carefully solidifies the transaction, making it virtually impossible for the debtor to back out of the commitment. It subsequently calls Mr. Hardcore Debtor to reaffirm the agreement: "Mr. Debtor, you certainly wouldn't let down the kids who are depending so much on this donation to buy new tents for the local troops." The debtor confirms he will have the money in five business days and feels good about paying the debt. To further psychologically commit the debtor, we ask the debtor to notify the charities of his intent in writing.

   A few days, later the collection consulting firm, on behalf of and as agent for its client, receives $45,000 for the primary client and $16,000 for Conrail. Not only did it collect on behalf of both creditors, but the debtor chartered an airplane to deliver the checks. He met the principal consultant at the airport and presented them in person. (Remember that this same debtor was resisting all legal maneuvers. Not a single lawsuit resulted in collection.)

The impossible mission has been successfully completed. Had the firm's client commenced legal proceedings against the debtor, it would in all likelihood have ended up with an uncollectible judgment—a worthless piece of paper. There were more than a dozen attorneys pursuing creditors' claims in court, and not one successfully collected a client's claim. Why? Because not one of the attorneys probed for the debtor's hot button. Were the attorneys or the legal system at fault? No. The fault lies in our perceptions about resolving potentially legal issues. Instead of locking horns with a hard-core, judgment-proof debtor via expensive, time-consuming litigation, create a positive climate around the negative situation.

A note regarding attorneys: The point is that an attorney should be a salesperson first and a lawyer second. The best attorney for collecting accounts receivable is not necessarily the one who has best mastered legal practice. The best attorney is the one who is a virtuoso communicator and negotiator.

Before you shell out your hard-earned dollars on legal fees, take the initiative to learn more about your adversary. What are the debtor's interests, hobbies, and so forth? To what fraternal organizations does he belong? Make it your business to find out what appeals to the debtor. Armed with this knowledge, communicate with the debtor and *be creative.* Touching a "soft spot" may motivate the debtor and enable you to accomplish the mission impossible.

CHARITABLE DONATIONS

Every day we are exposed to endless solicitations by charitable organizations, every one of which extols the virtues of a worthy cause. In all likelihood you maintain a favorite charity, whether it be cancer research, the American Red Cross, or a less conventional purpose such as the preservation of Galapagos turtles. In all probability, your nonpaying customers have a favorite charity, too. Even if they do not, it is likely that they favor one cause over another. Our charitable preferences never enter into the debt collection arena, yet it is one of the most powerful inducements to resolve a debt. Creditors forfeit the awesome potential of merging a collection strategy with a request for a donation in lieu of legal fees. Before explaining how it works, you must first recognize that all debt recovery entails expenses. This is especially true when a creditor sues his customer for monies owed representing attorney's fees and disbursements applicable for both creditor and debtor. The costs of prosecuting and defending a lawsuit provide negotiation leverage. A shrewd creditor can work both ends against the middle; that is, utilizing collection and litigation expenses as an inducement to maneuver nonpaying customers to the bargaining table.

For example, suppose your customer owes you $5,000 together with contract liability interest calculated at 1.5% per month on the unpaid balance. For simplicity, assume your terms are net 30 and the account is 12 months past due. At this juncture, your customer would owe you $5,900 ($5,000 principal, plus $900 interest). Also assume that you are on the threshold of suing your customer. Your estimated litigation and out-of-pocket costs are as follows:

Attorney's noncontingent fee	$500.00
Disbursements	$300.00
Total attorney's fees	$800.00
Principal amount of debt	$5,000.00
One year's interest at 1.5% per month	$900.00
Creditor's actual loss/exposure	$6,700.00

In this hypothetical example, two creditor areas represent negotiation leverage: the $800 estimated attorney's fees and the $900 interest, for a total of $1,700. From the debtor's perspective, estimated legal fees to defend the creditor's lawsuit would be at least $1,000. Altogether, there is $2,700 in negotiating leverage. Even if we deduct the $900 interest, there is still $1,800 in litigation costs—monies that both sides will incur.

The joint creditor/debtor financial posture to sue/defend is only part of the underlying components to reckon with; *time* and *emotion* are also factors. Assuming the debt proceeds into litigation, the element of time must also be considered. There are also the intangibles, such as the emotional drain and the hostilities between creditor and debtor. A creditor should consider all of these factors. How much is your time worth? A settlement of *X* dollars now may be worth more than a worthless civil judgment in the future.

A Donation to Charity in Lieu of Legal Fees

Consider if we could divert our hostilities and legal expenses into a productive resolution, which would not only resolve the debt, but also benefit a worthy cause. Wouldn't this make economic sense? Here's how a creditor would approach a potentially litigious situation:

> *Collector:* "Mr. Pastdue, we've come to a crossroads. Your $5,900 obligation is ripe for judicial intervention and an executable judgment. Surely a protracted legal confrontation serves neither of us. We both have to pay attorney's fees albeit our attorney represents our interests on a contingency. From your perspective, it's likely you'll have to pay your attorney an hourly fee offset from a retainer. It's estimated that our combined legal expenditures will be approximately $1,800, a sum that enriches our lawyers. Eventually, our litigation will conclude, and when that happens, one of us will win and the other will lose. Wouldn't it be more productive if we transitioned our joint legal fees and settled our differences with a donation to charity?"

Chances are, you will elicit a favorable response to this question. If your nonpaying customer responds in the negative, continue as follows:

> *Collector:* "Mr. Pastdue, I can appreciate that donating monies to charity has nothing to do with your debt. I am merely suggesting a sensible alternative. The fact is your debt must reach a conclusion—either by negotiation or confrontation—the latter of which costs us both time and money. I am asking you to set aside your animosity and work with me to a mutual solution."

The collector/creditor should make several convincing verbal attempts probing for the debtor's hot button. Ask revealing questions such as "If you could benefit any charity, who would it be?" You may have to dig deep, but somewhere within the psyche of your debtor there must be a soft spot. Once you find it, zero in on it, offering to donate a representative portion of the legal fees, waive the interest, or make another concession, but utilize a portion of your estimated expenses as leverage to consummate a settlement. Your defaulting customer must recognize the monetary value of your joint legal fees before this technique will work. The greater your debtor's exposure to paying legal fees, the greater your chances of success.

In our hypothetical situation, the creditor has $1,700 in negotiating flexibility and the debtor has an estimated $1,000 expenditure for legal fees. Once the debtor tacitly signals being receptive, propose an alternate solution to the debt such as the following: Waive the interest of $900 and provide the debtor with *your check* made payable to *his* favorite charity. If necessary, add to this sum by offsetting a portion of your estimated legal fees. Combine both the creditor's and the debtor's estimated legal fees as an inducement or any combination thereof. However you divvy it up, make absolutely certain that you document the transaction immediately. For example, if your debtor agrees to pay you $5,000, in exchange for your $900 donation to his favorite charity, confirm it in writing. You must exchange mutual written confirmations. Never make the donation until you are in possession of bankable funds for the entire debt, and *never* reference the donation to the charity as relevant to settlement of a debt. Revealing a contingent payment of a debt in exchange for a donation could violate the FDCPA, especially if the debtor is a consumer. As far as the receiving charity is concerned, the donation was made as a result of a business transaction. You might consider locking in the donation by faxing or e-mailing the charity with a communication setting forth that if a transaction ensues, a $900 donation will ensue. This will psychologically commit the debtor and make it more difficult for him to renege on the deal. See Exhibit 4.5 for a sample letter resolving a debt via a donation to charity.

Finally, there is one more economic factor to consider. If you are a creditor initiating this technique, you have even greater leverage than if you placed the account for collection. In that event, you would pay an agency 25%, or $1,250, on the recovery of the $5,000 principal. If you sued the debtor, you would likely pay a lawyer 33.33%, or $1,666.50. The bottom line is that any time you transition a representative portion of your collection/litigation expenses to charity in exchange for payment of a debt, you are ahead not only financially, but also saving valuable time and energy. Your debtor also benefits, as does the charitable cause. To sweeten the deal, you could discount the debt and agree to the offset being paid direct to the charity. In some instances, if the debtor makes the contribution from his resources, he would also derive the tax benefit. There are many ways to structure a donation to charity in lieu of legal fees, interest, or other contract liability. The key is to probe for the debtor's hot button, and once discovered, to sell this remedy as a practical solution. Donating monies to charity in lieu of paying collection or attorney's fees makes economic sense. It's a win/win opportunity.

EXHIBIT 4.5   RESOLUTION OF DEBT VIA DONATION TO CHARITY: SAMPLE LETTER

Dear Mr. Coleman:

I have received your letter of (*date*), in which you memorialized the terms of the settlement that has been reached between your client, ABC Jewelers ("ABC"), and my clients, Mary and John Smith ("Mr. and Mrs. Smith").

ABC claims that XYZ Company ("XYZ") owes it $19,764.50 in principal and interest and that, in addition thereto, an additional $6,581 in collection fees would be incurred if ABC pursues its claims against XYZ. ABC claims that Mr. and Mrs. Smith have personally guaranteed XYZ's indebtedness to ABC and that, as such, Mr. and Mrs. Smith are indebted to ABC for the amount of XYZ's indebtedness to ABC.

Without conceding the validity of ABC's guaranty claims, Mr. and Mrs. Smith have agreed to compromise and settle ABC's claims against them on the following terms:

1. Upon their receipt of a copy of this letter, Mr. and Mrs. Smith will remit $3,000 to ABC.
2. On or before (*specific date*), Mr. and Mrs. Smith will remit $9,000 to ABC.
3. On or before (*specific date*), Mr. and Mrs. Smith will make a $250 donation to Please Help Charity.
4. Upon ABC's receipt of the above described payments, any and all claims ABC holds against Mr. and Mrs. Smith will be deemed to be fully satisfied.

All of the above described payments, including the $250 donation, will be sent to you for distribution to "ABC" and "Please Help Charity" respectively. The $3,000 and the $9,000 payments to ABC will be made payable to ABC Jewelry. The $250 donation will be made payable to Please Help Charity.

Thank you for your cooperation in resolving this matter without the need of litigation.

HOW TO ESTABLISH YOUR OWN IN-HOUSE COLLECTION AGENCY

It is a proven fact that the mere threat of collection agency intervention often stimulates payment in situations where creditors' collection efforts have failed. Why are collection agencies more successful than creditors at recovering receivables? Collection agencies would like you to believe that you cannot do what they do, but the truth is you can accomplish the same results at a fraction of the cost. With a little ingenuity, a dash of imagination, and an ounce of creativity, a creditor can create an effective internal collection agency and never pay a fee again. There are, however, some disadvantages to in-house collection agencies, and you must carefully consider the alternatives.

An in-house agency would save your company the contingency fees charged by third-party collectors. The average commercial collection agency charges 25% of collected receivables. Collectors of consumer debts charge 33.33% or more. The fee may be even higher if an account proceeds into litigation or is more than one year old. High fees and the fear that customer goodwill may be destroyed make many creditors reluctant to place problem accounts with collection agencies, but agency fees tend to be high because of a collectibility factor—by holding on to their receivables longer, creditors make the accounts harder to collect. The longer a creditor maintains the receivable, the less collectible it becomes.

This problem does not exist if your company has its own internal collection agency. You do not have to worry about high collection agency fees, so you can establish the best cut-off point (when accounts are transferred to your internal recovery system—perhaps after 90 days), from a *collections* standpoint.

The advantages of maintaining an internal collection agency are as follows:

- You have complete control over receivables.
- You never pay a fee to a third party or worry that someone else is earning interest on your money.

Important legal note: An in-house collection agency is considered under federal law to be a third-party debt collector subject to the Fair Debt Collection Practices Act, which specifically limits and prohibits what debt collectors may and may not do in the collection process. The Act prohibits harassment or abuse in the collection process, and the use of false or misleading information. The Act also proscribes the following:

- Defines unfair collection practices.
- Provides procedures to validate debts.
- Defines permissible actions regarding multiple debts.
- Defines actions to be taken by a debt collector bringing legal action against a debtor.

Many states also have statutes that regulate debt collections, including requirements that collection agencies be *licensed* with the state banking commission or some other state office. They may be required to post a bond as surety. Note that where conflicts exist between state and federal statutes, the rule is this: *The tougher law governs.*

Before you decide to set up an in-house collection agency, carefully review federal, state, and local statutes and regulatory requirements. Discuss the pros and cons of the proposed in-house agency with your local attorney. Both civil and criminal penalties are possible under state statutes and/or the federal Fair Debt Collection Practices Act. Obviously, these laws should not be taken lightly.

What to do: If you elect to go the internal collection agency route, here is what to do:

The first step is to create a separate, legal entity with a name that clearly denotes "collection agency." A corporation is probably your best bet because that would shelter you from personal liability. Meet with a local attorney to explore all the legal ramifications. You could, of course, set up a sole proprietorship or partnership, but that is not recommended because both leave you vulnerable to personal liability.

Select a name for your in-house collection agency that will convey all the influence of a third-party debt collector. The following are examples:

Credit Adjustment Bureau	Credit Corporation of America
American Recovery Corp.	Receivable Management Corp.
National Fiscal Corp.	Associated Adjustment Corp.

Series of Dunning Letters

Compose a series of dunning letters. In the 1970s, a new breed of collection agency came into being—letter-writing services. These agencies sell a series of dunning letters for an up-front, fixed fee. The industry has gained tremendous momentum. Of course, certain accounts should be handled by a professional collector, but letter-writing services handle hundreds of thousands of accounts and are competitive with contingency agencies, which only earn a fee if they collect.

Computers enable a letter-writing service to send a prearranged series of letters, sometimes even more cheaply than the creditors could do it themselves. Typically, these services charge $8 to $15 per account. Creditors receive real value from these services. In fact, it really does not cost creditors anything because the small fee is offset by the savings on expenses they would have incurred by sending out letters themselves. Money collected by a letter-writing service goes directly to the creditor; the agency does not deposit collected funds. Furthermore, letters are cheap, and accounts that are placed when they go 60 to 90 days past due should yield a 70% to 90% recovery rate. There are many excellent programs available. Many combine letters with regular-interval e-mail. Some offer computer call dunning. Chances are, the outside collection agency you have been using offers a letter service. If not, some of the large firms that specialize in e-mail letter dunning include the following:

Transworld Systems (GreenFlag Profit Recovery)
5880 Commerce Boulevard
Rohnert Park, CA 94928-1651
(707) 584-4225
www.transworldsystems.com

National Revenue Corp.
4000 East Fifth Avenue
Columbus, OH 43219
(877) 827-5672
www.nationalrevenue.com

OSI
5626 Frantz Road
Dublin, OH 43017
(614) 766-0803
www.osioutsourcing.com

Create a Collection Letter Package

A tremendous variety of letters are available from these services. A client can select from this multitude of letters to create a customized package that meets its own particular needs. Exhibit 4.6 provides two of the many letters available from a collection-letter package.

EXHIBIT 4.6   SAMPLE COLLECTION LETTERS

"BROKEN PROMISE" #1

(date)

(Name and address of debtor)

PAST-DUE BALANCE: ($000.00)

(Salutation)

When you promised to mail your check, we accepted your word without a second thought. Yet . . . today . . . we find that your check was not received. The above balance is delinquent. And you did promise to clear that balance. Today. Please, do mail your promised check.

(END)

"BROKEN PROMISE" #2

(date)

(Name and address of debtor)

PAST-DUE BALANCE: ($000.00)

(Salutation)

Please give careful attention to this most serious matter. Consider the following:

1. You promised to mail a check to clear your past-due account. That promise was not kept.
2. Even though we reminded you of your commitment, you did not mail the check.

The serious delinquent stage of your account requires that you clear your account now. Today . . . please process . . . your check for the above amount.

(END)

Third-Party Influence

A small personal computer can be used to set up an in-house letter service. Your PC would have to be programmed to automatically prepare dunning notices at predetermined intervals. A series of letters, ranging from mild letters with a customer service slant all the way to hard, final-notice letters, should be customized to suit your client base.

You must, at the outset, determine how frequently dunning letters should be sent. This can be accomplished only with testing. There are many theories on the timing of follow-up letters—recommended intervals range from 10 to 30 days. Test various intervals within this time frame to determine what kind of timing gets you the best results. E-mail also has established a place in debtor communications.

Now you are ready to reap the harvest of your efforts. You will be amazed at the results you get solely from the third-party influence. Agency letters will always be more influential than your correspondence. You must decide in the beginning whether you wish to put a telephone number on your letterhead. If so, you must be prepared to handle incoming calls. If you wish, you can indicate a phone number in the body of the letter requesting that debtors communicate with your customer service department. Test your communications *with* and *without* a phone number. Generally, phone numbers can be a problem if balances are small (i.e., less than $75).

Remittances and Payments

Stress in your letter that all payments should be made directly to your company (the creditor) but remitted to a post office box set up exclusively for the in-house collection agency. Because checks will be made out directly to your company, you can deposit payments either in a special trust account (which would require separate bookkeeping and added expense) or to the company account. It is recommended that, initially at least, you deposit all collected funds monies in your primary banking account and use your internal collection agency only to influence payment. If, however, you maintain a respectable volume, you may wish to establish a trust account organized as a separate entity.

Cost Versus Profit

Letters are the cheapest and quickest form of communication. Properly executed letters should achieve a significant ratio of recovery at minimum cost; however, dunning letters will not solve all of your receivable problems. There comes a time when you must take more positive action, but you must carefully weigh the economics of continued pursuit by manual dunning or attorney intervention. It is unprofitable to call on past-due balances less than $100. Such small balances generally should be dunned by letter. There are, however, some exceptions:

You *should* call small-balance debtors if the following conditions exist:

- Your customer base does not include hard-core debtors or mail-order accounts.
- Telephone numbers are programmed into statements or invoices or somewhere else where they can be easily retrieved.
- You have minimum-wage labor for follow-up.
- You maintain a customer service department trained to handle small-business balances and service problems.
- You keep telephone calls to a minimum and maximize the use of dunning letters.
- You use telephone contacts to develop rapport and enhance future business.

According to the American Collectors Association, the cost of calling a debtor—including labor, time, and other factors relating to overhead—averages more than $17.00 each. You must amortize this cost over your entire receivables portfolio to determine costs versus profit.

$250 to $500 receivables: Often referred to in the industry as "borderline receivables," these amounts represent a dual-edged sword. You should be conscious of cost versus benefit, as in the small-balance area, but you can go a little further to pursue the larger balances. Remember that time and money work against the creditor in effectuating small-balance recoveries. The economics may not justify pursuit.

ATTORNEY LETTER INFLUENCE

An attorney's letter often has the greatest impact. Arrange with your corporate counsel to use his name in your letter series.

The attorney's letter must be strong and straightforward. The letter could suggest legal implications if your debtor does not pay (except small balances). Many mail-order companies achieve a whopping 40% average recovery solely through attorney letters. Your attorney's name should appear on the letterhead with an address different from your company address, but with *no telephone number.* You do not want your debtors to contact your attorney directly. The letter should state that all calls must be directed to your company or agency.

Never pay your attorney a percentage of collections from the attorney letters. You will only create additional bookkeeping costs and inflate recovery expenses. Why should your attorney get a commission simply for allowing the use of his name? If you are already paying a retainer, you should ask your attorney to provide this service as an accommodation in exchange for any accounts that ultimately do require legal intervention. The attorney benefits because he or she will get the opportunity to pursue all legal accounts. Most corporate attorneys who are on a retainer basis are usually receptive. (Chances are, your corporate attorney is not a collection attorney and would not want to handle commercial claims.) If necessary, you can offer additional inducement (e.g., more business or a fixed fee payable on an annual basis). If your attorney does not go along with this arrangement, find another attorney.

Warning: Never make the mistake of assuming that a letter-writing service will achieve optimum results. One major disadvantage of dunning letters is the time it takes to process the letter series. That lost time can be a big disadvantage. For example, what happens if three months later you try to call an account that did not respond to the letter series only to find that the debtor's telephone has been disconnected? Perhaps if you had communicated with the debtor early in the game, the account could have been salvaged. Moral: Use letter-writing services with discretion.

Assignments

Another creditor option is to assign a receivable to a willing buyer. The assignee then becomes the owner. Be careful that a receivable is not assigned on a contingency basis because this will likely be interpreted as an illegal means to collect a debt. Generally, for an assignment to be legally enforceable, the assignee must pay for it, usually at a substantial discount. Assignments apply to investors who purchase receivables at a discount. The advantage of selling your receivables is that you generate instant cash. The disadvantage is that you will pay a premium. Factoring organizations specialize in receivable finance and can be a valuable resource. One factor specializing in financing commercial receivables is Paragon Financial Group, Inc. (Tel: (800) 897-5431, Web site: *www.paragonfinancial.net*).

CHAPTER 5

Small-Balance Collection

Collection of small balances poses a unique set of problems. A large part of your accounts receivable may consist of balances less than $500, yet the economics of these receivables create a built-in hindrance to your efforts. In this chapter you will learn why collection agencies may not be the best alternative to collect small balances and how to proceed effectively to collect those stubborn accounts.

You will learn when to initiate collection calls—and pitfalls you should avoid. The fact is, small-balance collection techniques have not kept pace with changing times. Hard-line tactics no longer work. Bluffing is not an effective technique against debtors in today's litigious society. You will learn why tact, skill, and psychological persuasion are the remedies in modern small-balance collection, together with a small claims strategy. (See Chapter 6: Suing in Small Claims Court.)

This chapter will tell you how to avoid actions that destroy recovery potential. Are you aware of the most devastating weapon available to collectors? You will discover how to structure credible arguments that vividly illustrate the direct connection between non-payment and poor credit ratings. You will learn to take your debtors on a journey into the future to show them why it makes good business sense for them to satisfy their obligations.

This chapter gives a graphic illustration of the processes involved in the pursuit and collection of small receivables. You will see how the experts use information gathered from debtors to find the debtors' "hot buttons" and initiate the most effective collection approach. Do you know when to terminate pursuit or how to choose an agency to collect small balances?

You will also learn how to minimize expensive, time-consuming collection calls on small-balance debtors, and how to use a one-shot approach to penetrate and overcome problems. In addition, this chapter provides samples of high-impact collection letters—from a personalized reminder letter to form letters, compelling follow-up letters, stamps, mailgrams, and telegrams. Gain a psychological edge from the way you frame your collection letters. Discover valuable tips for writing money-producing collection letters, emphasizing the importance of the "you" factor.

EFFECTIVE TECHNIQUES TO COLLECT RECEIVABLES LESS THAN $500

The recovery of small balances is radically different from collecting larger receivables. Surprisingly, the least effective collector in this area is the collection agency industry. Most collection agencies work on a "no collection, no fee" basis. The problem is that large-balance collectors are spoiled, preferring to work the larger, more profitable claims. When they are forced to work smaller claims, prejudice is the result. To the dismay of small creditors, small receivables get much less attention than larger claims. Many collectors will use large-balance collection techniques against small-balance debtors. Others might not call on small-balance debtors at all. Most collection agencies are guilty of limiting pursuit to dunning notices and/or minimal phone contact.

Economics of Small-Balance Collection

The first question: How many calls and/or letters can be invested in a small delinquent account before collection becomes unprofitable? A good rule of thumb is to separate small balances, using $500 as the line of demarcation. Accounts less than $500 are classified as small balance. Accounts more than $500 are intermediate and/or larger receivables. From an economic standpoint, accounts less than $500 are never profitable to litigate and usually cost more than they are worth to pursue by other means.

Psychology of Small-Balance Collection

The first and foremost rule: When you initiate small-balance collection calls, *never threaten litigation*, except in a small claims court context. Legal-style letters and/or threatening attorney intervention are only believable in a small claims action. Why? Because the small claims forum is an accepted and expeditious forum. We live in a litigation-oriented society. Today's debtor is simply too clever, well-educated, and astute to be intimidated by frivolous threats of litigation. Many debtors have had experience with collection agencies or attorneys. They know all the tricks. Debtors know how much it costs to initiate a lawsuit—the expense of producing witnesses, the cost in terms of your time and attorneys' fees. Usually the debtor will call your bluff. The opposite is true with small claims court. Judge Joseph A. Wapner, Judge Judy, and the *People's Court* have done much to change public perception.

Times Have Changed

Twenty or thirty years ago, debtors were more honorable. They respected their obligations. Not so today. Unfortunately, collection techniques have not kept pace with changing times. It is very common for collectors to engage in psychological warfare with debtors, threatening all kinds of horrible legal consequences, challenging the debtors on every front. This usually ends with the debtors hanging up their phones and terminating all communication. The situation becomes even worse when collectors attempt to reestablish communication because the debtors are now in control. The collectors have lost all credibility and have ruined what might have been collection opportunities. Their actions destroyed recovery potential.

Important legal note: Professional collectors, including attorneys, who collect consumer debts are regulated under the federal Fair Debt Collection Practices Act. All creditors must also comply with the Federal Trade Commission Act and various state statutes. Any, or all, of these laws may severely restrict your collection activity. Consult with your attorney if you are uncertain of what actions are prohibited in your jurisdiction.

An Effective Way to Recover Small Balances

Tact, skill, and psychological persuasion are the most effective means of persuading debtors to pay. This is true whether balances are large or small. To quote an old saying: "You can catch more flies with honey than you can with vinegar." One negotiating tool available to collectors is to point out the ramifications of nonpayment in terms of adverse credit reports. Suggest (do not threaten) that the debtors' valuable credit might be affected if negative credit information is reported to the national debtor database. Change debtors' "base of thinking," taking them on a journey into the future—to a time when they will be denied credit or will be otherwise inconvenienced because they neglected these small obligations.

A good selling job will convince debtors that they risk damage to their creditability, their ability to get credit in the future. Collectors can expand on the ramifications of the Fair Credit Reporting Act and explain how adverse credit reports can harm debtors' power to purchase on credit. It is not enough to tell debtors their credit will be affected. The collector should employ a time and space technique to ambush their small-balance debtors. That means collectors should do the following:

- Let the debtors think they are *off the hook* by admitting the validity of their objections.
- When the debtors think they have won, pull the rug out from under them by negatively stressing the benefits they will lose by refusing to settle their obligations.

It is imperative that you change the debtors' base of thinking. The time and space technique is a powerful collection tool—use it!

How to Implement the Time and Space Technique

Debtor: "We're not going to pay this debt. Go ahead and sue us!"

Collector: "Mr. Debtor, we have no intention of commencing a lawsuit against you. It's not likely we will confront you on the steps of the courthouse. As I'm sure you can appreciate, Mr. Debtor, the very economics of the matter would not justify legal action."

Important note: It sounds as if the collector is giving up. But in reality, the collector is lowering the debtor's resistance. Now the collector employs a negative change of pace to get the debtor to decide that it is in his best interest to pay.

Collector: "Mr. Debtor, even though our company's policy does not mandate litigation in such trivial matters, let me ask you something. How important is it for you, as a reputable firm, to continue to do business on credit for the next seven years?"

Notice: The collector uses the word "reputation" to imply credibility and expands on the seven-year limit on reports of adverse credit information to inquiring credit grantors.

Collector: "Mr. Debtor, this will be the last time I speak with you." (Again the collector implies that he or she is letting the debtor off the hook.) "But let me assure you, Mr. Debtor, that you will sustain potential damage, inconvenience, and actual monetary loss that far exceed the cost of a lawsuit or the amount of this unpaid debt. Mr. Debtor, we interface vital credit data to several credit-reporting bureaus, including trade associations in your industry. As mandated by federal law, this information will be reported to inquiring credit grantors for a period of seven long years. Now, let me ask you, Mr. Debtor, as a reputable and ethical business firm that depends on credit from its suppliers, can you afford to have a credit decision denied because you failed to satisfy this small, long-overdue obligation?"

Important: Wait for an answer. Do not interrupt.

Collector (responding to debtor's response): "You see, Mr. Debtor, six months from now, when you are denied credit, the chances are better than 90% that such adverse action will occur because of your past credit history. You can't afford to let this happen. Now let me ask you, Mr. Debtor, is it really worth the embarrassment, the added expense, and the inconvenience of having a major credit decision, which might otherwise be favorable, go against you, simply because the person making the decision assumes you are not a good credit risk?"

Important: Pause, wait for the debtor's response.

Collector: "Unfortunately, Mr. Debtor, federal law mandates that this information be recorded and made available to any inquiring credit grantor for seven long years." (Make seven years sound like a long time.) "Mr. Debtor, do you really want these potential consequences hanging over your head for the sake of a couple of hundred dollars?" (The collector belittles the amount owed by the debtor.)

As you can see, the time and space technique takes the debtor on a journey in time, *to change the debtor's base of thinking* by perceiving a consequence in the future, resulting in credit denial. We use applied psychology to present credible arguments that illustrate the direct connection between nonpayment and debtors' credit ratings.

When the debtor reaches a decision on a minor point, that mindset carries over. In effect, the debtor is also making the major decision to pay you. For example, consider the questions posed by the collector in the preceding illustration:

- How important is it for you, as a reputable firm, to continue to do business on credit during the next seven years?
- Can you afford to have a credit decision denied because you failed to satisfy this small, long-overdue obligation?
- Mr. Debtor, do you really want these potential consequences hanging over your head for the sake of a couple of hundred dollars?

Remember, debtors have the advantage over you. You must turn the tables. These questions change the debtors' base of thinking. They prod debtors into giving the answers you want and reaching the conclusion you want them to reach—that it makes good business sense for them to come to terms with their obligations.

If you cannot motivate debtors with this approach, the chances are minimal that you will succeed with a hard line. Years ago, 70% to 80% of debtors might have responded to hard-line tactics, but small-balance debtors are not swayed by such tactics.

You have to change your approach to be consistent with the current climate. The credit ramification/small claims techniques have proven to be a viable formula to motivate small-balance debtors. Collection agencies and individual collectors who have perfected this technique report significant results. Learn to employ a time and space/localized small claims court approach.

Use your clout: You have a right to report adverse credit information about your debtors to mercantile credit-reporting agencies or credit interchange bureaus. Many industries exchange credit information. If you use credit bureau reports, you can also input information.

Know when to quit: There comes a point when you must let go and terminate pursuit. If you cannot succeed with a minimum of effort, you should weigh the economics of continued pursuit. You must consider what your time is worth. Know when to terminate an unresponsive account. Time is money. Let go, and invest your valuable time in something more productive.

CHOOSING AN AGENCY TO COLLECT SMALL BALANCES

Another alternative is to turn over stubborn small balances to a collection agency. If so, choose an agency that is geared to handle small-balance receivables. Most collection agencies are not. They tend to "legislate the cream"; that is, they devote their time to the larger, more profitable receivables and deemphasize the smaller ones. For example, most agencies do not make phone calls to collect small claims. You might be better off with an inexpensive letter-writing service.

Exhibit 5.1 shows detailed procedures and remedies to collect small balances. The diagram

EXHIBIT 5.1   NATIONAL SMALL-BALANCE ADMINISTRATION:
                   INTEGRATED RECOVERY SYSTEMS

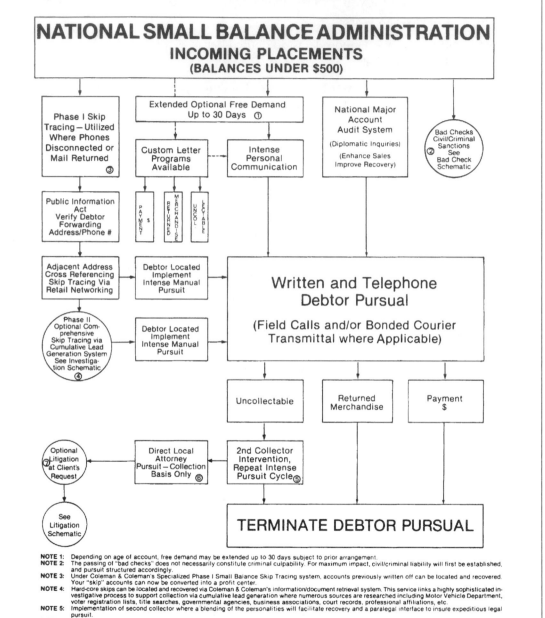

NATIONAL SMALL BALANCE ADMINISTRATION
INCOMING PLACEMENTS
(BALANCES UNDER $500)

NOTE 1: Depending on age of account, free demand may be extended up to 30 days subject to prior arrangement.
NOTE 2: The passing of "bad checks" does not necessarily constitute criminal culpability. For maximum impact, civil/criminal liability will first be established, and pursuit structured accordingly.
NOTE 3: Under Coleman & Coleman's Specialized Phase I Small Balance Skip Tracing system, accounts previously written off can be located and recovered. Your "skip" accounts can now be converted into a profit center.
NOTE 4: Hard-core skips can be located and recovered via Coleman & Coleman's information/document retrieval system. This service links a highly sophisticated investigative process to support collection via cumulative lead generation where numerous sources are researched including Motor Vehicle Department, voter registration lists, title searches, governmental agencies, business associations, court records, professional affiliations, etc.
NOTE 5: Implementation of second collector where a blending of the personalities will facilitate recovery and a paralegal interface to insure expeditious legal pursuit.
NOTE 6: Direct local attorney-to-debtor contact is initiated on a "contingency collection basis" only. Counsel now becomes an extension of Coleman & Coleman's own collection efforts, creating a local influence factor.
NOTE 7: Subject to client's request, commencement of a protracted lawsuit may be prosecuted against your debtor.

illustrates the role the collection agency should play to gain maximum thrust to convert the small-balance debt into a bank deposit.

Unfortunately, from a collection agency's standpoint, it is not economical to pursue small-balance accounts. This becomes evident when you consider that in most cases these troublesome receivables were already subjected to intense written dunning and heavy telephone contacts before they were ever referred to a third-party collector. The collection agency can do little more than the creditor has done already to collect the account. A certain collection consulting firm was able to carry third-party intervention one step further by forwarding unresponsive accounts to attorneys for *collection* (not *litigation*). In this process, an attorney is retained not to commence litigation against the small-balance debtor, but as an additional source of influence, acting as an extension of the collection consultants' own internal efforts. This forwarding system is the closest you can get to utopia in small-balance administration. But although some debtors are intimidated by contacts from professional debt collectors and/or attorneys, the recovery ratio and profit margin is generally not high enough to make it worthwhile to aggressively pursue debts less than $500. The bottom line: It is usually not feasible for most collection agencies to pursue small-balance receivables manually. Many collection agencies take great pains to implement small-balance procedures only to learn the hard and brutal fact that it often does not pay. Some have given up in disgust. Many of the larger national collection agencies actually discourage their clients from turning over small-balance accounts.

If you have a substantial number of low-dollar claims and want to pursue those accounts through third parties, find an agency that will work the accounts vigorously. Many retail collection agencies maintain a small-balance desk for accounts of $100 or less. Ask the agency for references. Get the names of two or three clients and find out what kind of results you can expect from the agency. Generally, it is to a creditor's advantage to subscribe to a letter-writing service on a fixed-fee basis. Such a package will bombard the debtor with computer-generated letters at strategic intervals.

The ever-increasing limits on plaintiffs who can sue in small claims courts, without hiring an attorney, has greatly increased a creditor's recourse. Remember, 50% of the time you will not have to endure the time/expense of trying your case in the "People's Court"; a summons/complaint applicable to your debtor's jurisdiction and a fax communication will yield substantial results.

Tip: Nolo Press, located in California (*www.nolo.com*), and Americans for Legal Reform in Washington, DC (*www.americans4legalreform.com*) publish do-it-yourself books on pro se litigation. Both publish books on small claims courts. Creditors should invest in publications offered by Nolo Press and Americans for Legal Reform.

The latter has been instrumental in increasing statutory limits per what creditors can sue for. The goal of Americans for Legal Reform is to eliminate costly attorney's fees while streamlining procedures with a $50,000 small claims jurisdiction.

The irony of small-balance collections is that there is no panacea, and the economics will never justify the means. So save yourself a lot of expense and aggravation. Subscribe to a letter service, pay a fixed fee, and forget about small balances. Going to the *n*th degree with phone calls and follow-ups is simply too labor- and cost-intensive. No one wants to write off an outstanding account, but often it is the only logical alternative.

Psychology and Framing of Effective Collection Letters

Be diplomatic when you communicate with debtors. Avoid words that have negative connotations (e.g., "delinquent"). Instead, substitute the phrase with "past due." Of course, as collection efforts drag on and you shift into a more aggressive mode, you will resort to stronger phraseology, but initial collection letters should be mild and incorporate some degree of courtesy. This is especially true if there is a possibility you will continue to do business with the debtor or if you know the debtor is not a deadbeat—that there may be compelling reasons for nonpayment. The following are tips for writing good collection letters:

- *Construct your letters from the debtor's point of view.* Your goal is to motivate the debtor to pay. Avoid such personal pronouns as I, we, my, our. Incorporate the *YOU* factor. Always relate to the debtor in terms of your customer's business. Remember, your debtor is tuned in to radio station WIIFM—What's in it for me!

- *Keep your letters short and concise.* Most collection letters should be kept to one page. Generally speaking, long letters should not be used because people tend to put them aside and forget about them. If for some reason a letter must go on to a second page, never begin the second page with a new paragraph. Continue a paragraph from the first page onto the second, so that the reader must continue reading.

- *Use high-impact picture words and motivating phrases to convey feeling and emotion.* Construct your letters the same way copywriters prepare advertisements. Avoid dull, rambling sentences. Use words with *punch* to deliver your message. Refer to the collector's vocabulary section in Chapter 2 for a glossary of high-impact terms.

- *Give letters a unique style and eye appeal.* Make it easy for debtors to read them and respond.

- *Keep paragraphs and sentences short,* and always start off with your strongest point.

- *Emphasize the first words and the last words in your letters.* Those are the words that people tend to remember. Always start with your strongest points to gain your debtors' immediate interest. It is also important to close with attention-grabbing statements.

- *Proportion your letters properly.* Leave plenty of white space. Use large margins, generally 1 inch to 1.5 inches on either side. This makes your letters attractive and easy to read.

- *Test different formats.* Gauge what approach produces the best results. Some experts prefer concise, easy-to-read words and simple phrases. This may be appropriate if most of your debtors are consumers, but you can be a little more creative with commercial debtors. The point is to select phraseology that will have the greatest impact on your typical customer. Use "people" language.

EXHIBIT 5.2 TIPS ON IMPROVING COLLECTION LETTERS

TEN DEADLY SINS OF COLLECTION LETTERS

1. Give the debtor a reason not to read.
2. Use headlines that whisper sweet nothings.
3. Use words that do not paint mental pictures.
4. Leave your debtors dangling.
5. Fail to exercise creativity.
6. Use lots of fancy words.
7. Use all kinds of clever-sounding language.
8. Use pat techniques instead of original ideas.
9. Insult the debtor's intelligence.
10. Make threats you cannot fulfill.

FIFTEEN WAYS TO IMPROVE COLLECTION LETTERS

1. Use attention-getting headlines (the words in large letters).
2. Write compelling reasons to pay.
3. Omit introductory statements.
4. Use only necessary words.
5. Always ask for action.
6. Use good judgment.
7. Read aloud.
8. Encourage a response.
9. Use a "P.S." and emphasize your strongest points.
10. Test pastel-colored envelopes to stand out from other mail.
11. Write letters as a copywriter would design an ad.
12. Establish credibility.
13. Enclose a self-addressed business reply envelope.
14. Do an evaluation test with different scripts and analyze results.
15. Choose the best after-test strategy.

- *Never begin a sentence with* I, We, My, *or* Our. Remember, your first words set the tone and must be attention grabbers. Incorporate the "you" factor by using such words as "you" and "your."
- *Use a "P.S." at the end of your letters to summarize the main theme.* People will usually read the P.S. first, so make certain that it presents your strongest points in two or three short sentences. You can also use a "P.P.S." (See Exhibit 5.2 for additional tips on collecting and improving collection letters.)

How to Structure Your Letter

A collection letter has two primary purposes:

1. To capture and retain the debtor's attention
2. To motivate the debtor to act

The question technique is dynamite when you want to gain a debtor's attention. Properly worded questions can motivate more quickly than statements. For example:

- Did you take care of our invoice for $550, dated June 5?
- What can we do to help you meet this obligation?
- Do you value your credit?
- Is there a problem?
- What can we do to resolve this problem?

Delivering Ultimatums

There are several schools of thought about the efficacy of ultimatums. Generally speaking, ultimatums tend to prompt the debtor to do just the opposite of what is demanded. Before the Fair Collection Practices Act of the early 1970s, debtors were more responsive, and the term "collection agency" had impact. Ultimatums lent credibility. Today's debtors are more keenly educated. They know the various collection laws and that your threats are not likely to be carried out. Nowadays, ultimatums are credible only if they come from attorneys, and even then they lose credibility if they are sent via form or computer letters. Studies indicate that only 30% of commercial debtors are motivated by ultimatums. Seventy percent, or more than two-thirds, are less inclined to act. Ultimatums are far more effective when delivered to debtors orally, except when the threat of litigation is showcased via a copy of a threatened summons.

Backfire: Avoid such redundant or noncompelling statements as the following:

- Looking over our records, we discover that your account is . . .
- It has recently been called to our attention that you are . . .
- We have been advised that your account is now seriously past due and . . .

Mundane statements are a waste of space. They contribute nothing to your overall strategy.

Who, What, and When

Letters are the cheapest means of communication and are an intrinsic part of the debt collection process. Your letters should always prompt debtors to do *what you want them to do;* that is, come to terms with their obligations to you. Indicate a time frame, but do not state: "This is the last notice you will receive" or the like. Debtors are thrilled when you tell them you will not contact them again. Be careful about your wording when you suggest payment schedules. Indicate how the debtor should pay. You might want to suggest an overnight bonded courier, or wire transfer, explaining that you will absorb the transportation charges.

Sample Collection Letters

The following sample letters range from personal to form letters.

Dear Mr. Pastdue:

You probably overlooked your long-overdue account for $500 from June. It is still overdue. We sent you a notice 10 days ago.

Can you please forward your check so that we can credit your account? If your check is already in the mail, please excuse this notice.

The preceding is a personal letter. Basically, it tells the debtor: *This is a reminder, your account is overdue, please forward your remittance.*

The following samples are obviously form letters because you fill in the blanks with the appropriate amounts.

Dear _____:

A friendly reminder to let you know your account #_____ for $_____ is now overdue.

You may have overlooked our previous notice to you, so here's a second notice for your convenience.

Can you please put your check in the mail today?

★★★

(Date)
(Name and address of debtor)

PAST-DUE BALANCE: $_____

Dear _____:

Our statement was sent to you, showing your recent past-due balance. It may have merely been overlooked, so . . . here is another copy.

Please do mail in your check today, so that we may keep your account the way you want it to be: current.

Thank you.

★★★

Debtor: Creditor:

Acct. No:
Amount Due: $

Pursuant to Public Law 90-321, Title VI 91-508, Title VI, 601, 84 Stat. 1136, more commonly known as the Federal Fair Credit Reporting Act (FCRA), your Creditor has the right to report your delinquent payment history.

Section 1681 (c) (4) of the FCRA mandates that your delinquent status be reported to inquiring credit grantors for seven years. Failure to honor your contractual obligation may result in the following:

- Credit denial and/or aggressive collection action, including other vendors who may deem you uncreditworthy or sell to you only on C.O.D., together with other ramifications:

- Protracted litigation, where warranted
- Forfeiture of special discounts and/or incentives
- Rejection of credit and/or less favorable terms

Section 606 of the FCRA authorizes you to obtain a free copy of your profile *only* if you are denied credit. Otherwise, you may obtain a copy of your credit report at minimal charge.

By remitting your full balance *now*, you will not only enhance your credit reputation but also prevent legal intervention.

You may elect to satisfy your contract obligation via wire transfer as designated:

Good Faith Creditor
c/o Good Faith Bank
Attn: Wire Dept.
100 Main Street
Camp Hill, PA 17001
(717) 123-4567

Please fax a copy of your transmittal to (717) 555-1234 so that your account may be credited together with preventing credit ramifications.

TAKE FURTHER NOTICE that the FCRA permits you to obtain a free copy of your credit report *provided* you are rejected for credit. In that event, you must provide a written copy of the rejection to the undersigned within 30 days. A copy of the report that resulted in credit denial will be provided.

Commercial Debts:
The above referenced creditor has interfaced your default to inquiring commercial credit grantors, including D&B, NACM, Data Link, and various trade associations. As a result, you may be denied commercial credit. The FCRA *does not* govern commercial transactions, nor are you entitled to a free report. Copies of your credit-reported commercial defaults may be obtained by sending $100 together with a stamped 9" by 12" envelope with $.83 postage affixed *stamps only* (postal idesia not acceptable) to the above address.

STAMPED REMINDER OR PRINTED STICKER

Another approach is to send debtors copies of your invoices stamped with a "past due" notification. This approach conveys a greater sense of urgency than the initial notification and serves as a follow-up reminder. The following are examples of this type of reminder:

- PAST DUE!
- PLEASE REMIT TODAY!

- A FRIENDLY REMINDER: YOUR ACCOUNT IS OVERDUE.
- WE'VE BEEN EXPECTING YOUR CHECK. WON'T YOU PLEASE SEND IT TODAY?
- WE DIDN'T GET YOUR EXPECTED REMITTANCE LAST MONTH. WON'T YOU PLEASE SEND IT TODAY?
- YOUR ACCOUNT IS OVERDUE, AND WE WOULD LIKE TO HEAR FROM YOU—VIA YOUR CHECK!

Preprinted stickers are available in commercial stationery stores, or you can have them made up with your own message.

USE OF MAILGRAMS OR TELEGRAMS

Mailgrams and telegrams have an advantage in that they convey more urgency than personal letters. They are particularly good if substantial amounts of money are at stake. If you use telegrams or mailgrams, keep them short and to the point.

Western Union offers the following suggested texts for collection telegrams:

- PLEASE ADVISE IF CHECK COVERING YOUR ACCOUNT NOW DUE HAS BEEN MAILED.
- YOU HAVE APPARENTLY OVERLOOKED YOUR JUNE REMITTANCE. MAY WE PLEASE HAVE YOUR CHECK PROMPTLY?
- TODAY IS THE LAST DAY YOU CAN TAKE ADVANTAGE OF DISCOUNT.
- ONLY IMMEDIATE COMPLIANCE WITH OUR LETTER BY JULY 15 WILL PRESERVE YOUR CREDIT.
- URGE YOU WIRE YOUR INTENTIONS ON YOUR ACCOUNT IMMEDIATELY TO PROTECT YOUR FUTURE CREDIT RATING.
- MUST WITHHOLD SHIPMENT OF ORDER RECEIVED TODAY UNTIL ACCOUNT BROUGHT CURRENT. WIRE REMITTANCE IMMEDIATELY TO ENSURE PROMPT DELIVERY.
- URGENT WE RECEIVE REMITTANCE. WE VALUE YOUR BUSINESS TOO MUCH TO BE COMPELLED TO RESORT TO LEGAL ACTION.
- IMPERATIVE REMITTANCE ON YOUR ACCOUNT SENT IMMEDIATELY TO AVOID ACTION BY OUR LAWYERS.
- WIRE FULL BALANCE DUE BY JULY 30 AND WE WILL INSTRUCT ATTORNEY TO WITHHOLD ACTION. FAILURE TO SEND WILL LEAVE US NO CHOICE BUT TO PROCEED IMMEDIATELY.
- REMITTANCE MUST BE RECEIVED IMMEDIATELY TO PREVENT REPOSSESSION OF ITEMS CHARGED YOUR ACCOUNT OF MAY 10.

CHAPTER 6

Suing in Small Claims Court

Subjecting your nonpaying customer to a "Judge Judy" attitude adjustment is as easy as ABC. The ongoing drama of TV lawsuits has instilled in the public's imagination quick resolution of civil disputes. It began during the 1980s when Judge Joseph A. Wapner administered instant justice for everything from a dog groomer who cut a poodle's hair too short to a disgruntled fiancé who wanted his engagement ring back. By the 1990s Judge Judy emerged as a tough, no-holds-barred administrator of justice gaining prominence on national television. Under her tutelage, Judge Judy reprimanded countless litigants—much to the delight of her audience. Unbeknownst, however, from the daily diet of TV courtroom drama, are the accomplishments of a nonprofit organization known as Americans for Legal Reform (AFLR). This lobbying group spearheaded the small claims movement, campaigning vigorously for do-it-yourself justice. The AFLR has a mission—to dramatically increase jurisdictional amounts, while simplifying discovery, all with an eye on judicial economy. The association has succeeded, for its lobbying efforts having upped the ante of what plaintiffs can sue for. Today, litigants owe a heartfelt vote of thanks to the AFLR for their arduous pursuit of affordable justice.

Only a decade ago, small claims jurisdictions were typically less than $5,000, with many jurisdictions less than $3,000. Today, however, plaintiffs can sue pro se for sums heretofore not possible.

With ever-increasing limits, small claims court is an *expeditious* forum—a creditor's gold mine of unparalleled economic benefit—the ultimate quick fix to cure most receivables defaults.

How to Utilize the Small Claims Court System

Contrary to common belief, small claims justice is available to creditors at a fraction of the cost of hiring a lawyer. Suppose, for example, that you are based in Omaha, Nebraska, but your debtor is in Los Angeles, California—no problem! Obtain the small claims forms either by calling, writing, or in many cases, online. Although small claims jurisdictions vary, two criteria are universal: (1) The summons (the petition that orders your adversary to appear before

"Judge Judy" and (2) The complaint. Your dispute and damages are incorporated into user-friendly forms and served upon your adversary, together with an expeditious trial.

Small claims court provides speedy resolution of your claim (i.e., "Instant Justice"). Unlike a conventional lawsuit, which is bogged down with discovery, protracted delays, and technicalities, small claims offers a quick fix. In relation to delinquent receivables, the creditor needs only to prove the following:

- Legal entity of defendants (e.g., corporation, partnership, or sole proprietorship)
- Defendant contracted with plaintiff for merchandise and/or services
- Plaintiff delivered merchandise and/or performed service
- Default by defendant (debtor)
- Damages (e.g., nonpayment of debt)

Rarely does a small claims trial consume more than 15 minutes. If the creditor amply documented the transaction and assuming the nonpaying customer does not have a valid defense, the creditor will certainly prevail. This chapter contains several specimens on how to construct a small claims civil complaint. You will note that the verbiage is the same for preparing a complaint in New Jersey as it is in Alaska. The only difference is jurisdictional amount and service of process. Before you sue your nonpaying customer, however, you can employ a few techniques to improve your chances of success.

First, you may not actually have to sue your debtor. It is often sufficient to prepare a summons and complaint and either fax or e-mail it to your adversary (*Warning:* Third-party debt collectors are prohibited by the FDCPA from threatening litigation without actually filing a lawsuit), together with a cover letter that you intend to file suit in your adversary's jurisdiction. *Advantage:* Your nonpaying customer is more likely to respond positively once in receipt of the official-looking summons and complaint. In addition, a local influence factor (i.e., proximity to a court in your debtor's locale) is very persuasive.

By intimidating your adversary with your proposed lawsuit, you accomplish the following:

- A visual legal consequence within your adversary's locale
- Expense and aggravation—having to appear before "Judge Judy"
- An eyeball-to-eyeball confrontation
- Potential damage to creditworthiness
- Possible embarrassment and inconvenience
- If your debtor is a *corporation*, possible attorney representation expenses

HOW TO SUE IN SMALL CLAIMS COURT

There are approximately 8,000 collection agencies in the United States catering to diversified interests. Retail or consumer collection agencies make up the bulk, with commercial debt collectors specializing in business obligations. Trade collection agencies represent special interests, while the medical field has its own representation. Regardless of their demographic profile, collection agencies universally forward claims to attorneys for collection and/or litigation.

Most of these claims are small balances. By definition, a small balance is one that can be economically litigated, usually without attorney representation. For the creditor, small claims represent the most economical and expeditious method of converting a no-pay into paid status. Small claims courts are user friendly, providing instant Judge Judy–style justice. For creditors, they are a bonanza.

With small claims courts constantly increasing their jurisdictional limits, a major portion of collection agency representation can be eliminated. Creditors would be wise to utilize the small claims forum as an extension of their accounts receivable recovery effort. In most situations, creditors can utilize these forums pro se (i.e., self-representation), without retaining an attorney. To utilize the system, a creditor must possess the following:

- A basic knowledge of contract law. The elements of sustaining a contract action are set forth within this chapter.
- An inventory of Small Claims Summons and Complaint forms relevant to your debtor's jurisdiction. Obtain these on a case-by-case basis, gradually building a library relevant to your customer base.
- Verification of the debtor's legal entity (e.g., partnership, corporation, or proprietorship)
- A properly prepared Summons and Complaint, combined with the fortitude to use them as psychological persuasion—a coming attraction of the contemplated action
- A bonded law list to recruit an attorney to appear on your behalf in the event you have to try the case (about 50% probability) and/or if the jurisdiction requires corporate plaintiffs to be represented by counsel

The following sections analyze each element and demonstrate how to incorporate them into an accounts receivable success strategy.

The first criteria is that you must have a valid contract with your nonpaying customer to sustain an action. It is not sufficient that you shipped merchandise or rendered a service; a meeting of the minds is a prerequisite, combined with consideration, default, and provable damages. A transaction initiated by the "seat of the pants" may provide your debtor with a legal loophole to escape liability. A credit application, purchase order, or check (even one returned as non-negotiable) constitutes basic contract law. The Latin legal term referred to is *quantum meriut*, meaning goods sold or services provided and not paid for. Refer to the elements of contract law elsewhere in this chapter, making certain that your complaint alleges each criteria in short, simple language.

As each account proceeds to nonpayment, determine the county in which your debtor is located. Call the Small Claims Court within your debtor's jurisdiction, and request copies of Summons and Complaint forms, together with an information brochure. Many county courts maintain Web sites, and their forms can be downloaded. Most will mail forms, while others require a letter and a self-addressed envelope. Create a file of Small Claims forms or photocopy originals for future use.

Ascertaining Jurisdictional Amounts

You can only sue per each jurisdiction's limit. If a debtor owes you $6,000, and the limit is $3,000, Small Claims is not the correct forum; however, if your debtor owes you $4,300, and the jurisdiction amount is $5,000, you can utilize Small Claims. *Tip:* If your debtor owes you $5,300 and the jurisdictional limit is $5,000, you cannot sue in Small Claims unless you *waive* the $300 difference and sue for $5,000. *Make certain* that you note in your complaint: "Plaintiff has been damaged in the sum of $5,300, but waives $300 and sues for $5,000." Your suit must be within each court's jurisdiction, or it will be dismissed.

Another tactic is to separate invoices and commence more than one suit. For example, in the $5,300 hypothetical example, if your $5,300 claim is represented by two or more invoices created over time, you can sue separately, although their total ($5,300) exceeds the jurisdictional $5,000 limit.

Verify Your Debtor's Legal Status

If you sue your debtor as an individual or sole proprietorship, and the entity is a corporation, you risk your case being dismissed. Your suit can only survive if you sue the proper entity. Many search firms and Web sites publicize relevant information. D & B Credit Reports are also reliable for ascertaining the correct legal entity. *Always* make certain that you sue the correct legal entity (e.g., corporation, partnership, or proprietorship).

Prepare Your Summons and Complaint Properly

The Summons and Complaint are two documents that commence and maintain the action. The Summons is the petition that orders your defendant/debtor to appear in court at a designated time and place, while the Complaint is a mirror image of your contract dispute that must specify the following:

- Yours and your debtor's legal entity (i.e., plaintiff and defendant)

- The circumstances creating the contract liability (e.g., purchase order, invoice, non-negotiable check)

- Default

- Damages

When drafting your complaint, adhere to the KISS formula: Keep It Simple, Simon!

Small claims complaints should never be lengthy. They should be short, concise, and to the point. Generally, between 5 to 10 short sentences are sufficient. See Exhibits 6.1, 6.2, and 6.3 for sample Small Claims Complaint forms for three different states.

Judge Judy Bluff

One technique that works about 50% of the time is faxing or e-mailing your proposed Summons and Complaint to your adversary. (*Warning:* Third-party collectors cannot legally threaten litigation that a creditor does not intend to initiate.) Usually, when a nonpaying customer sees a Summons and Complaint augmented with the local influence factor (i.e.,

---

EXHIBIT 6.1   SAMPLE SMALL CLAIMS COMPLAINT—VERMONT

STATE OF VERMONT
COMPLAINT IN SMALL CLAIMS COURT

Fill in information on yourself here

Plaintiff's Name

Address

City, State, Zip Code

Residence Telephone No. | Business Telephone No.

Fill in information on the Defendant, the person you are suing, here.

Defendant's Name

Address

City, State, Zip Code

To be completed by Court Personnel

Date Complaint Filed | Docket Number

Plaintiff's attorney, if any (IN THIS CASE)

Name of Plaintiff's Attorney

Address

City, State, Zip Code

PLEASE TYPE
OR
PRINT, USING
BALLPOINT PEN.
PRESS DOWN HARD.

Fill in the amount of your claim here.

Amount of Claim

Court Costs*
$

Total

*$25.00 for $500.00 or less
$35.00 for more than $500.00

Briefly explain your complaint:

Signature of Plaintiff | Date

TO BE COMPLETED BY COURT PERSONNEL.   DO NOT WRITE BELOW THIS LINE.

SUMMONS IN SMALL CLAIMS COURT

TO THE DEFENDANT NAMED ABOVE:

YOU ARE HEREBY SUMMONED TO ANSWER THE ENCLOSED COMPLAINT OF THE PLAINTIFF. YOU MUST ANSWER THIS SUMMONS WITHIN TWENTY (20) DAYS OF THE DATE OF SERVICE BY COMPLETING AND MAILING IN THE ENCLOSED ANSWER.

Be sure to read the instructions and information printed on the back carefully before completing the Answer.

District Court Clerk | Date

YOU ARE BEING SUED IN SMALL CLAIMS COURT.
READ THE INSTRUCTIONS ON BACK OF THIS
SUMMONS.

COURT'S COPY

EXHIBIT 6.2   SAMPLE SMALL CLAIMS COMPLAINT—PENNSYLVANIA

COMMONWEALTH OF PENNSYLVANIA

CIVIL COMPLAINT

Magisterial District Number   —   —

DJ Name: Hon.

Address:

Telephone No.   (   )

PLAINTIFF:

Name
Address

COMPLAINT NUMBER: **CV**

DATE FILED:

DEFENDANT(S):   VS.

	AMOUNT	DATE PAID
FILING COSTS	$	
SERVICE COSTS	$	
J.C.P.	$	**1.50**

TOTAL $

D-1   Name
Address

D-2   Name
Address

TO THE DEFENDANT: The above named plaintiff(s) asks judgment against you for $ _____ together with costs upon the following claim (Civil Fines must include citation of the statute or ordinance violated):

I, _____ verify that the facts set forth in this complaint are true and correct to the best of my knowledge, information, and belief. This statement is made subject to the penalties of Section 4904 of the Crimes Code (18 Pa. C.S.A. § 4904) related to unsworn falsification to authorities.

_____
(Signature of Plaintiff or Authorized Agent)

Plaintiff's
Attorney:

Address: Telephone:

HEARING IS SCHEDULED BY DISTRICT JUSTICE AS FOLLOWS:

Location   Date   Time

IF YOU INTEND TO ENTER A DEFENSE TO THIS COMPLAINT, NOTIFY THIS OFFICE IMMEDIATELY AT THE ABOVE TELEPHONE NUMBER. YOU MUST APPEAR AT THE HEARING AND PRESENT YOUR DEFENSE. UNLESS YOU DO, JUDGMENT WILL BE ENTERED AGAINST YOU BY DEFAULT.

IF YOU HAVE A CLAIM against the plaintiff which is within district justice jurisdiction and which you intend to assert at the hearing, you must file it on a complaint form at this office at least five (5) days before the date set for the hearing. If you have a claim against the plaintiff which is not within district justice jurisdiction, you may request information from this office as to the procedures you may follow.

Service of Process

D1 D2
☐ ☐ Registered/Certified Mail

D1 D2
☐ ☐ Returned Receipt Attached

D1 D2
☐ ☐ Proof of Service Attached

☐ D1 Date Served _____

☐ D2 Date Served _____

D1 D2
☐ ☐ Not Served

☐ D1 Reason _____

☐ D2 Reason _____

AOPC 308 - 90   **DISTRICT JUSTICE   PERMANENT COPY**

appearing before Judge Judy within their neighborhood), resolution or settlement often ensues. If you have properly prepared your Summons and Complaint, you not only localize the debt within your debtor's jurisdiction, but you also bring the matter to a head quickly. If your customer does not favorably respond, then you know you may either have to proceed to trial or write off the debt. *Tip:* A properly prepared Summons and Complaint is crucial. Your adversary will often consult with an attorney. Your objective is to present a convincing

EXHIBIT 6.3   SAMPLE SMALL CLAIMS COMPLAINT—OHIO

Original—to court   Blue—to defendant   Lilienthal/Southeastern Printing, Cambridge, OH.
Duplicate—for return of service   Pink—to plaintiff   48986

SMALL CLAIM COMPLAINT

_____   _____Municipal Court

_____   )   _____County   Court

_____   Zip Code

Phone No. _____ Plaintiff_____,)   _____Area _____District

_____   }

_____   _____, Ohio

_____   Zip Code   Case No. _____

Phone No._____ Defendant_____

TO THE CLERK:
    Please take notice that a claim is hereby filed against the above defendant(s) and request that he (they) be
summoned to appear in Court to answer same.

                    STATEMENT OF CLAIM
□ ACCOUNT—EXHIBIT A ATTACHED AND MADE A PART HEREOF □ WAGES_____

□ OTHER _____

_____

_____

    Wherefore plaintiff prays judgment against defendant in the sum of $_____, plus interest

from the _____ day of_____,20_____, at the rate of _____% and costs.

STATE OF OHIO   )
COUNTY OF _____)ss.   **AFFIDAVIT OF COMPLAINANT'S CLAIM**

_____, being first duly sworn, on oath states that ,_____   the Plain-
tiff ____ in the above entitled cause, that the said cause is for the payment of money that the nature of plaintiff's
demand is as stated, and that there is due to plaintiff from the defendant the amount stated above; defendant(s)
(is are) not now in the military or naval service of the United States.

                                    _____

    Subscribed and sworn to before me this _____ day of _____,20_____.

                                    _____
                                    Clerk, Deputy Clerk, Notary Public

            NOTICE AND SUMMONS IN ACTION FOR MONEY ONLY

To: (1) _____   (2) _____ _____
            Defendant   Defendant

    _____   _____
        Street and Number   Street and Number

    _____   _____
            City   City

_____ ask (s) judgment in this court against you for

_____dollars ($_____), plus interest from the _____

day of _____,20_____ at the rate of _____/and costs, upon the following claim: _____

_____

    The court will hold trial on this claim in the Small Claims Division located at _____

_____ at   _ o'clock _____. M. on_____,

the _____ day of _____, 20_____.

    If you do not appear at the trial, judgment may be entered against you by default, and your earnings may be
subjected to garnishment or your property may be attached to satisfy the judgment. If your defense is supported
by witnesses, account books, receipts, or other documents, you must produce them at the trial. Subpoenas for
witnesses, if requested by a party, will be issued by the clerk.
    If you admit the claim but desire time to pay, you may make such a request at the trial. IF YOU BELIEVE
YOU HAVE A CLAIM AGAINST THE PLAINTIFF, YOU MUST FILE A COUNTERCLAIM WITH THE COURT AND MUST
SERVE THE PLAINTIFF AND ALL OTHER PARTIES WITH A COPY OF THE COUNTERCLAIM AT LEAST SEVEN
DAYS PRIOR TO THE DATE OF THE TRIAL OF THE PLAINTIFF'S CLAIM."

                                    _____
                                        Clerk — Deputy Clerk
1. he is, she is, they are   Small Claims Division

legal consequence for damages that is not only correct but also persuasive. Your debtor's attorney can be a valuable resource, recommending that the threatened suit be resolved.

Once you prepare your summons and complaint, fax or e-mail it to your adversary with a short cover letter as follows:

Dear Mr. Pastdue:

You are in default per the annexed contractually due invoices in the sum of $3,641.97. We would prefer resolution in lieu of confrontation. However, unless you are prepared to make restitution, we will have no alternative but to secure an executable judgment relevant to your contract liability, together with your being summoned to appear before "Judge Judy."

Upon issuance of an index number, your default will be recorded in public records and interfaced to inquiring credit grantors. Notwithstanding potential credit denial and/or legal repercussions, you may sustain other consequences, including sheriff intervention, levy of attachable assets, embarrassment, and additional execution expenses. Your remittance of $3,641.97 will alleviate this drastic action. Your voluntary remittance is requested.

This letter is not lengthy, but it is persuasive. Note that the wording is intended not only to instill legal consequences, but also to allude to future credit rejection, including a negative industry reputation. Overall, a properly prepared complaint combined with a psychologically intimidating bluff (i.e., your threatened lawsuit) will motivate most nonpaying customers to satisfy their debts.

Half Will Pay, But the Other Half Will Require a Judge Judy Attitude Adjustment

The other half of nonpaying customers *will not* respond favorably to your threatened lawsuit, and will either refer you to their attorney or assume a drop-dead attitude. If your customer does not grab the bait, the next step is filing your complaint. At this juncture, you have two alternatives:

1.   File your Summons and Complaint pro se (i.e., *without a lawyer*).
2.   Retain a lawyer to file your Summons and Complaint.

A creative credit manager can squeeze more legal bang for the buck by filing the complaint pro se and permitting the court to effectuate service upon your debtor/defendant, and if required, hiring an attorney on the eve of trial. Generally, there is a window of time between service of legal papers and its trial, typically several weeks to a few months. Because of the efficiency of the small claims forum, plaintiffs do not have to wait long before obtaining their day in court.

A Clever Tactic

One tactic that is routinely employed against hardened defendants is requesting an adjournment a day or two before the scheduled trial date. A letter is faxed to the court requesting an adjournment on the grounds of providing an out-of-state witness who must travel to testify during trial. Courts always grant at least one adjournment. Conversely, the adjournment request is mailed to the debtor/defendant—a process that takes at best two days. The result? Inconvenience! By exercising this strategy, in all likelihood, Mr. Pastdue will appear before Judge Judy, only to learn that the case for trial has been adjourned to a future date. The result is that your deadbeat customer makes a nonproductive trip to the courthouse.

This can be especially aggravating in larger cities where the volume of cases necessitates a bifurcated calendar call, consuming an entire morning or afternoon. The net effect is that you can rob your nonpaying customer of time while still preserving your day in court. This strategy also screens the collectability of your receivable because your defending debtor is more likely to negotiate settlement if he does not have to appear in court a second time. Another benefit is that this technique gives you additional time to retain a lawyer to represent your interests, in the event you choose attorney representation.

Transitioning From Bluff to Economical Legal Representation

So you have represented yourself pro se—without legal counsel. You have showcased the Summons and Complaint, filed it, secured a trial date, and obtained an adjournment. Eventually, you will have to appear for trial. This can be expensive if you have to travel, especially if the claim is out of state. Suppose your company is in New Jersey and your debtor defendant is in Los Angeles. In lieu of a roundtrip to L.A., it could be far more economical to retain local counsel to represent you. Because you have done all the paperwork, your case is turnkey (i.e., all the lawyer has to do is present your case in person). At this juncture, legal representation would be dirt-cheap—about $200 offset with a contingent commission is fair compensation. Here is how your case would unravel:

- Contact several collection attorneys derived from a law list. (We recommend *The Forwarders List*: 40 Windsor Corporate Center, 50 Millstone Road, Suite 200, East Windsor, NJ 08520, phone: (609) 371-7860 or 1-800-638-9200, which publishes the names, addresses, and service areas for attorneys throughout the United States. There are no fewer than a dozen law firms that routinely handle receivable litigation within Los Angeles.)

- Fax or e-mail your complaint to a local firm with a cover letter offering $200 offset against a contingent commission of 25%.

Guaranteed, you will likely receive offers from most collection attorneys because this is easy money. Using our example, suppose your $5,300 lawsuit, filed for $5,000, is settled for the full amount. Your attorneys recovered $5,000 and earned 25%, or $1,250. Offset from the $200 noncontingent retainer, your lawyer earned $1,050 for what amounts to a few hours' work. (Chances are, if you choose a firm in your debtor's locale, they may already have several cases and/or experience with your debtor.) Therefore, their appearance costs are negligible because they are amortized over several creditors. This is especially likely to occur in larger cities.

Eliminating Collection Agencies

Utilizing this technique nationwide will require experience in several jurisdictions. Eventually, however, you will become a wizard, turning out small claims suits throughout the country. As you hone these skills, you will become proficient, even learning how to execute money judgments, which in itself is an inexact science.

Once perfected, you will maintain the legal muscle to intimidate—and recover—virtually any receivable nationwide, all turnkey and with great economy. Your overall ratio of recovery should exceed 75% (50% without actually filing suit in Small Claims Court, and 25% factored for hardened types with whom you will have to proceed to trial). About one-quarter of your cases will be unsolvable.

Even more compelling is that of the 50% who pay *without* filing suit, these will yield you a 100%, noncommissionable recovery. Stated another way, you will virtually eliminate collection agencies and accelerate recoveries while transitioning the lion's share of your monies to your bottom line.

GENERAL INFORMATION ABOUT UTILIZING SMALL CLAIMS COURT

What the court can do:

- Explain and answer questions about how the court works.
- Advise you what the requirements are to have your case considered by the court.
- Provide information relevant to your file.
- Provide you with samples of court forms where applicable.
- Provide you with guidance on how to fill out forms.
- Answer questions about court deadlines.

What the court *cannot* do:

- Give you legal advice. Only your lawyer can give you legal advice.
- Tell you whether you should bring your case to court.
- Give you an opinion about what will happen if you bring your case to court.
- Recommend a lawyer, but they can usually refer you to a local lawyer referral service.
- Talk to the judge for you about what will happen in your case.
- Let you talk to the judge outside of court.
- Change an order issued by a judge.

Common Legal Terms and Definitions

Adversary: Party whose interests are opposed to or opposite the interests of another party.

Defendant: Person (party) against whom the court action (complaint) was filed.

Docket or Index Number: Number the court assigned to this case when the complaint was filed. The docket number is listed on the summons complaint and all pleadings.

File: To file means to give the appropriate forms and fee to the court to begin the court's consideration of your request.

Judgment: Official decision of a court in a case.

Judgment Creditor: Party to whom money is owed.

Judgment Debtor: Party who owes money.

Levy: Obtaining money by legal process by seizing the judgment debtor's property, which is taken to secure or satisfy a judgment.

Motion: Written request in which you ask the court to issue an order or to change an order it has already issued.

On Submission: Nonoral legal argument decided on the supporting papers.

Oral Argument: Personally appearing in court in an attempt to convince the court to do what you want it to do.

Order to Turn Over Funds: Signed document from the judge commanding someone—usually the garnishee—that funds have been attached, and it will be remitted to the judgment creditor.

Party: Person, business, or governmental agency involved in a court action.

Plaintiff: Person (party) who commenced the court action by filing the complaint.

Return Date: Date plaintiff and defendant are ordered to appear in court.

Service: Mailing or delivering copies of your papers to the lawyer for the other party or to the other party if there is no lawyer.

How to Commence a Small Claims Action

Types of small claims:

- Breach of a written or oral contract
- Return of money used as a down payment
- Property damage caused by a motor vehicle accident
- Damage to or loss of property

- Consumer complaints for defective merchandise or faulty workmanship
- Payment for work performed
- Claims based on bad checks
- Return of a tenant's security deposit
- Claims arising from professional malpractice (e.g., alleged malpractice by a doctor, dentist, or lawyer)

Remember that if you believe you are entitled to damages greater than the jurisdiction amount, and you sue in small claims court, you give up the right to recover damages over that amount. If your dentist used defective material for a filling, and the cost of professional services was $165, the small claims court is an appropriate forum; however, if the surgeon slipped with the scalpel, severed a nerve, and you became an invalid as a result of the malpractice, small claims would not be the court in which to try your case. The additional damages cannot be claimed later in a separate lawsuit. In many instances, however, the money and time saved by waiving the difference makes economic sense to utilize the small claims process. If the amount in controversy is $2,500, and jurisdiction is only $2,000, the $500 difference is worth quick adjudication of your claim.

Filing the Complaint

Small claims actions are usually initiated in the county where the defendant resides. In some jurisdictions, the claim can be filed where the tort (civil wrong) took place. Check with the clerk of the court.

The clerk of the small claims court will advise you where and how to file your claim, but the clerk cannot render legal advice. In some jurisdictions, claims must be filed in person, whereas in others the claim can be mailed. When filing your claim, make certain that if you are the plaintiff, you do the following:

- Give your full name, address, and telephone number.
- To ensure proper service of the complaint, give the correct name(s) and address(es) of the person(s) named as the defendant(s) in the complaint. It is important that the defendant be properly identified as an individual, a sole proprietorship, a partnership, or a corporation. You may have to perform a search of public records to ascertain the correct legal entity.
- State the exact amount of money for which you are suing. Avoid rounding it off.
- State the reason why the defendant owes you money, but be brief.
- State whether there is at this time another case involving both you and the other party(ies) and, if so, the name of the court.
- Sign the completed form.
- Pay the correct filing and service fees where applicable.

PREPARATION FOR TRIAL

Interrogatories

Some small claims courts provide for an exchange of information by the litigants. Whether you are the plaintiff or the defendant, questions from the opposing party, called "interrogatories," must be answered within a statutory time frame.

Plaintiff

If you are the plaintiff, you must prove your case. Arrange to have any witnesses and/or records you need to prove your case at trial. *A written statement, even if made under oath, cannot be used in court.* Only actual testimony in court of what the witness(es) heard or saw will be allowed. Prepare your questions in advance and rehearse them. You must provide an expert witness because the defendant has a right to cross-examine. A defendant cannot cross-examine a piece of paper.

Bring to court records of any transactions that may help prove your case. Such records may include the following:

- Canceled checks, money orders, sales receipts, purchase orders, bill heads, and so on
- Bills, contracts, estimates, leases, credit card charge slips, and so on
- Letters
- Photographs
- Other documents proving your claim

Defendant

If you are the defendant, you should prepare your side of the case as the plaintiff prepared his case. Bring all necessary witnesses and documents to court with you on the scheduled trial date.

You must come to court at the time and date shown on the trial notice. If you do not, a default judgment may be entered against you and you may have to pay the money the plaintiff says you owe. Generally, one adjournment is almost always permitted to each side for a valid reason.

Day of the Trial

The defendant and the plaintiff must come to court at the time and date stated on the trial notice, unless otherwise notified by the court. Bring all witnesses and evidence needed to present your case.

On the day scheduled for trial, the court may help you settle your case through mediation by a trained mediator. The mediator will try to help the plaintiff and the defendant reach a satisfactory agreement, but the mediator is not a judge. If a settlement cannot be reached, every effort will be made to have your case tried by the judge on the same day. Some cases are assigned to arbitrators, who have the power to adjudicate the dispute and render a final judgment; however, because no court record is made of a trial that is settled before an arbitrator, there is no right of appeal.

If you win your case, consult with the clerk for information on how to collect your judgment.

How to Prepare and File a Civil Suit

The next court after small claims is filing a lawsuit in district, county, or supreme courts. Every state has different procedures, but most have streamlined short-form Summons and Complaints (obtained from the court or through a stationery store).

Initiating a lawsuit in courts of higher jurisdiction is simple when the form is used. In New York State, for example, filing a lawsuit in district court (maximum jurisdictional limit is $15,000) is easily accomplished with a combined summons and endorsed complaint. The summons (top portion of the form) is the magic document that commands the defendant(s) to answer the charges brought on by the plaintiff. The endorsed complaint (bottom portion) is the cause of action for which damages are sought. Note that the paragraphs in the following case are short and to the point.

The following is a hypothetical short-form Summons and Complaint to sue a defendant who borrowed $500 to pay his electric bill:

Paragraph 1:	Brief statement of where plaintiff resides. *Note:* Must be a resident of locale and within the jurisdiction of the court.
Paragraph 2:	Indication of defendant's domicile (town, county, and state where the person lives or business is located), which *must* be within the jurisdiction of the court. If suing a business, it must maintain at least one office within the court's jurisdiction.
Paragraph 3:	Brief statement as to events leading to a contractual arrangement ($500 loan to a friend, the defendant, to pay his electric bill and the legal basis for a contract).
Paragraph 4:	Brief statement that defendant promised to pay back the $500 (contract).
Paragraph 5:	Failure to pay back the $500—breach of contract/damages. Should indicate that request for payback was made, the form it was made in (writing, verbal), and when request was made. (Attach a copy of document if request was made in writing.)
Last paragraph:	Relief sought: "Wherefore, plaintiff demands judgment against defendant in the sum of $500 together with interest from September 1, 2002 (the date of the loan), together with the disbursements of

this action." (Disbursements include index number fee, process service fee, transcript and docketing fees—to make the judgment stick against defendant, as well as fees for Sheriff's execution if necessary.)

Five elements are necessary to prosecute a contract action:

1. *"Meeting of Minds."* Wherein two or more entities consummate an understanding (in writing or orally)

2. *The ability to perform the bargain.* Contracting with Luciano Pavarotti, the famous opera singer, to repair a chainlink fence is radically divergent from his expertise and would probably be unenforceable; however, a contract with a carpenter to add an extension to a house is within the realm of the contracting party's expertise and is enforceable.

3. *Remuneration.* Compensation—the bargain and financial arrangement for performing the service

4. *Breach.* The willful and intentional failure to live up to the terms agreed

5. *Damages.* The loss sustained by the aggrieved party(ies)

CHAPTER 7

Making Your Debtors an Offer They Can't Refuse

Don Corleone, the ruthless Godfather known for such memorable quotes as: "I made him an offer he couldn't refuse" and "Either your brains or signature will be on this contract" and Dirty Harry's proclamation: "Go ahead, make my day" are ingrained in the public's imagination. For vindictive creditors, these quotes strike a responsive cord—retribution! Vigilante justice! Getting even!

When an account defaults, creditors engage in an internal recovery effort, typically exhausting protocol until a demarcation is reached (i.e., placing the receivable for collection and/or litigation). The pursuit of deadbeat customers is usually intertwined with the collector's job description. Some debtors, however, tend to push emotional hot buttons, mustering our resources in a vitriolic endeavor to collect our monies. Emotion overtakes business sense transitioning into a personal vendetta.

Sometimes we become so consumed when a nonpaying customer selfishly profits from our services or products that we set out on a vindictive crusade to not only secure our monies but also to teach the debtor a lesson. A feeling of street justice ensues as you visualize making your debtor "an offer he can't refuse." Yet for all your imaginary aspirations of obtaining instant restitution, you know that you cannot resort to such barbaric behavior. Neither can you imprison your nonpaying customer because debtor's prison became extinct during the American Revolution. A sense of victimhood ensues as that helpless feeling overtakes you, for you know that you have only two legal options: (1) placing the account for collection or (2) suing. A lawsuit, however, is a time-intensive, expensive (putting good money after bad), and frustrating experience.

Ever since the release of *Collection Management: The Art of Getting Paid* Second Edition (1998), coupled with presenting accounts receivable seminars throughout the United States, practitioners of credit management have asked me if I had additional tricks up my sleeve—other maneuvers to extract monies from hardened deadbeats. The answer is yes! Over the years I have painstakingly perfected many techniques to extract monies from impossible situations. These techniques will subdue even the most formidable debtors, maneuvering them into checkmate. What follows is a crash course in a "Mission Impossible" accomplishment—

a blueprint that takes debt recovery to the max. I have perfected these techniques not only to secure monies from hardened—and usually judgment-proof debtors—but also for delivering my own brand of street justice. *A word of warning:* Implementing these techniques requires the practitioner to be on solid legal ground. What follows is legal but cannot be threatened without actually filing suit. *The FDCPA prohibits frivolous threats of litigation.* Before illustrating actual case histories, there is yet another requirement. You *must possess* the legal knowledge to not only present it within the framework of a threatened lawsuit, but you must also be able to sell the consequences to the debtor and his attorney.

Implementation of these techniques will most assuredly prompt negative debtor response, usually in the form of a threatened lawsuit or counterclaim. People by nature (and especially criminal-minded debtors who procured the debt with an intent to defraud) are of a mind-set that they have rights. When a zealous creditor figuratively points a loaded gun at their temples, it is virtually guaranteed that Mr. Good Guy creditor will be threatened with a "harassment" or "tortuous interference of contract" lawsuit. Utilization of these techniques mandates that you maintain a legal foundation coupled with the staying power to eventually overcome resistance. The practitioner must maintain momentum, convincing not only the debtor but also his attorney that you will not relent. Almost 99% of the time, debtors will acquiesce, waving the white flag of retreat if you remain firm and do not succumb to their threats. A small percentage, however, *will* attempt to intimidate you and/or file a lawsuit. If you have properly prepared a legally correct and convincing prosecution, your chances of success are excellent.

RISK VERSUS REWARD

Mastery of applicable legal principles governing your lawsuit is mandatory. Showcasing a threatened lawsuit replete with errors will not only diminish your posture but will also make you look foolish. The practitioner who exercises these advanced techniques should always consult with legal counsel. Make certain your "ducks are in a row," "cross every 't'," and "dot every 'i'." Once you have perfected this technique, you will be able to duplicate your success cookie cutter style, reiterating it over and over.

APPLICATION OF LEGAL PRINCIPLES

Most lawsuits are for goods sold and delivered. The legal term is *quantum meruit*, meaning merchandise delivered or services provided and not paid for. Before we showcase specific legal remedies, it is important to understand the chronology of a customer default in relationship to its multi-mix genre. Exhibit 7.1 illustrates the progressive cycle from credit inception to default, through the litigation process to final judgment.

Other genres ensue if you win your lawsuit and your judgment debtor/defendant appeals. In this scenario, your debtor is labeled appellant/defendant and you, the creditor, are plaintiff/respondent. The terms in Exhibit 7.1 apply during different stages of the

| Exhibit 7.1 | PROGRESSIVE CYCLE FROM CREDIT INCEPTION TO DEFAULT AND JUDGMENT |

Genre	Definition
Customers/Clients	The "honeymoon" stage of the credit relationship. Customers/clients have profited from instant gratification; they want immediate benefit from your merchandise/services and commit to pay you; the value of legal tender is secondary to need.
Debtors	Instant gratification subsides. Your customers have profited from your products or services and payment is no longer important. Customers transition to debtor status the moment they are in default. If your terms are "net 30," on day 31 your customers transition to debtor, which is applicable throughout their default. The value of retaining legal tender in relation to possession is more important than payment for your goods or services.
Defendants	If you sue your debtors, their legal status changes to "defendant."
Judgment Debtors	Once the legal system acknowledges the debt in relation to liability and renders judgment, your debtors' posture transitions to judgment debtors.

credit/default/lawsuit chronology of the relationship. There is one legal term, however, which applies throughout the default status—a term that is not only legally correct but also has a humorous ring: *Tortfeasor.*

Tortfeasor is made up from two words: "tort," a civil wrong, and "feasor," a person who commits a tort. Thus the breach of the credit sale is the tort, while your debtor who defaulted is the feasor. Keep these genres in mind as you navigate the complexities of credit and collection management.

POSITIONING YOUR NONPAYING CUSTOMER IN A VEXING LEGAL PREDICAMENT

Although most debt/default litigation is cut-and-dried, there are exceptions. For example, many regulated industries have their own rules—legal criterion that will work to the creditor's advantage. Consider the trucking industry, which was formally regulated by the Interstate Commerce Commission. Today, its policies are governed by the Department of Transportation (DOT).

Trucking companies enjoy added flexibility pursuant to Title 49 of the U.S. Code permitting shippers to recover from consignees and/or brokers in the event of shipper default. For example, assume a shipper defaults to the carrier relevant to merchandise delivered to a consignee. Where applicable, the carrier may collect freight charges from the consignee although the receiver of merchandise has no contract with the trucker and is innocent of the shipper's default. Incredible as it may seem, there may even be multiple liability if an intermediary (i.e., a broker) was paid by the shipper, who in turn pocketed the money.

In other words, the hapless consignee (recipient of the goods) may be legally compelled to pay the carrier, although the originating shipper paid the broker (intermediary). From a collections standpoint, this is one of the most difficult of all recovery efforts because the creditor (trucking company) is attempting to convince a third party (consignee) to pay a debt for which it has not contracted with, or worse, where a broker pocketed the money having been paid by the shipper. Unfair as it may seem, trying to convince an innocent third party to pay a debt it has not incurred is "mission impossible."

LONG-ARM STATUTE LITIGATION WITH APPLICABLE CASE LAW

ABC Truck Lines, an interstate carrier, retained a collection consultant to effectuate recovery of its delinquent receivables. Virtually every freight bill was "mission impossible," most having been consummated by fly-by-night brokers who are typically paid by shippers. Exhibit 7.2 illustrates an Introductory Statement to be incorporated into a complaint by showcasing case law, which can be utilized.

Unlike typical collection agencies, which initiate an ineffective campaign of letters and phone calls, the Long-Arm Statute Complaint, replete with Title 49 Case Law, is initiated against all responsible parties (i.e., shipper, consignee, and where appropriate, the broker). The results are predictable, bearing pressure on third parties. This technique is especially

---

EXHIBIT 7.2   TITLE 49 INTRODUCTORY STATEMENT

PRELIMINARY STATEMENT

Plaintiff is a common carrier governed by the rules and regulations of the former Interstate Commerce Commission (now Dept. of Transportation), particularly United States Code Title 49, Provisions 204 SEC. 10743 and 10744 which govern Bills of Lading.

Title 49 USC Section 3(2) note 13 states in relevant part that "a consignee cannot accept delivery of an interstate shipment of goods without incurring liability for the carriers lawful charges, known or unknown, prepaid or otherwise, nor relevant to the consignees actual relationship to the shipper"—see Western Atlantic Railroad Co. vs. Underwood DC. GA 1922-281 E891.

As further upheld in AFD Inc. vs. Barry Oil, 1945 58 NYS 2d 41 NYS 234 123 Misc C 907:

"A consignee becomes liable to carrier for charges when he accepts the interstate shipment, regardless of the contract between shipper and consignee".

In the case at bar, Interstate Transportation of Freight was originated as evidenced by the annexed Bills of Lading contract for which consignee accepted goods. Plaintiff sues shipper and consignee for unpaid freight charges, together with interest and reasonable attorney's fees as governed by statute.

Defendants filed various claims per the movement of freight in Interstate Commerce; Said claims were deemed frivolous and denied. In retaliation, defendants willfully offset invoices due ABC TRUCK LINES and in flagrant violation of Title 49 US code which specifically forbids offset.

Plaintiff sues defendants for unpaid freight bills, including punitive damages and attorney's fees as governed by statute.

effective in situations where the consignee maintains an ongoing relationship with the shipper. Under these conditions the defaulting shipper is wedged into an embarrassing legal predicament. The result is a path of least resistance and an accelerated recovery. The primary benefit, however, is that the creditor secures its monies from third parties who did not directly contract with the creditor. In many instances, the shipper and/or broker went out of business, leaving the consignee liable to the trucking company.

CALIFORNIA LONG-ARM STATUTE LITIGATION "OPEN BOOK" STATUS

Many states provide jurisdiction over out-of-state defendants. For California clients, the "open book," "stated amount" complaint is augmented with a summons. The strategy positions the nonpaying customer in his creditor's venue, wherein they are forced to retain counsel out of state. The leveraged settlement is initiated via a triune conference call between the debtor, his attorney, and the collection office. The strategy works 50+% of the time because the defendant's counsel maintains influence over his defaulting customer. Because the debtor's home state attorney cannot legally represent his client in California, coupled with the added expense of out-of-state representation, the situation usually results in favorable disposition.

This technique will work within the creditor's venue because most states maintain a Long-Arm Statute. From a collections standpoint, the technique is potent because it centralizes the creditor's litigation within its forum state, while forcing the nonpaying customer to retain counsel outside its jurisdiction.

Because the success rate of this technique is about 50%, the question of what happens to the other 50% is important. The remaining 50% of debtors who do not respond will result in a default judgment status. At this juncture, it must be domesticated within the debtor's jurisdiction—a secondary legal process. One benefit, however, is that during the secondary process creditors hit the ground running with a legal judgment. Although most states will honor an out-of-state decree, some will not. Oddly, the variables are diversified; some states are peculiar in whether they grant full faith and credit to a foreign judgment. For example, New York will not honor a foreign judgment rendered on default (i.e., the debtor/defendant does not defend). If the judgment is on the merits (i.e., as a result of a trial), New York may honor it.

This process opens a can of worms because jurisdictional defenses can be imposed. Generally, in order for a creditor to succeed in suing an out-of-state debtor, the criteria of "minimum contacts" and/or "continuity and regularity of contacts" must be met. This varies from state to state. Refer to Chapter 10 for more information. Creditors should seek the advice of counsel in both its forum state and that of the debtor's jurisdiction. Overall, however, the 50+% success rate of this strategy makes economic sense. Illustrated in Exhibit 7.3 is a sample complaint referencing long-arm jurisdiction for New York, which will give the practitioner an overview of this technique. Again, make certain to consult with an attorney before proceeding.

EXHIBIT 7.3   SAMPLE COMPLAINT REFERENCING
LONG—ARM JURISDICTION

SUPREME COURT OF THE STATE OF NEW YORK
COUNTY OF WESTCHESTER

GOOD FAITH CREDITOR.,

Plaintiff, COMPLAINT

-against-

WILLIAM PASTDUE, INDEX NO.

Defendants.

COMPLAINT

Plaintiff complaining of the Defendants, alleges as follows:

1. Plaintiff, was and still is a domiciliary of The State Of New York and is in the business of distributing heating and air conditioning components;
2. Upon information and belief, defendant, WILLIAM PASTDUE conducts business which is within The State of Wyoming and subject to the jurisdiction of this Court;
3. Defendants are liable for goods sold and not paid for in the amount of $17,000.00, together with contract liability interest and collection fees;
4. New York courts are liberal in extending the "Long Arm Statute" against foreign corporations, even when there is no subject matter jurisdiction provided:
   A. The action seeks damages for breach of contract if it arose in New York, or a litigant does business in New York, or
   B. Any wrongful act by a defendant out of state, but affects a plaintiff residing in New York.

Jurisdiction is applicable and arises pursuant to the aforementioned criterion. In Kulko vs. Superior court, 463, U.S. 84, the Court determined that any of these events (per Paragraph 4 (a)(b), coupled with the supportable conclusion that the defendant could "reasonably have anticipated being haled before a New York Court supports the exercise of jurisdiction". The trial of this action supports the exercise of jurisdiction, and New York is an appropriate forum;

5. Annexed hereto as Exhibit "A" is vendor GOOD FAITH CREDITOR'S receivable.
6. Defendant is indebted to plaintiff for various open invoices which remain unpaid and total $17,000.00 P & I, plus punitive damages and attorney's fees;
7. Plaintiff has duly demanded payment from defendant;
8. Plaintiff is entitled to judgment against Defendant for $17,000.00, together with attorney's fees of a total to be determined by this court;
9. Annexed hereto as Exhibit "B" are invoices in support of various unpaid invoices, all of which remain unpaid;

FEAR-FACTORED RECOVERIES

Early in his career, the author represented a leading manufacturer of office products. During the course of routine collection activity, a proficient debtor who owed the client $423.67 not only refused to satisfy his debt, but worse, willfully evaded his creditor. The client authorized suit, which was filed in small claims court. Eventually, a judgment was secured for $423.67, together with $91.16 interest and disbursements, a total of $514.83. Despite a reasonable effort to effectuate execution of the $514.83 judgment, it was not satisfied via an attempted levy on the debtor's bank account (judgment debtor changed his corporate name). Because there was a personal guarantee, the next step was to perform an asset search of the judgment debtor's personal assets. At this juncture, costs exceeded economic benefit; however, the client underwrote the investigation, a decision that at the time seemed foolish. The asset search revealed that the debtor's investment and banking relationships were in his wife's name—a happenstance that would have rendered the $514.83 judgment unenforceable. The collector terminated pursuit, advising the client that recovery costs far exceeded recovery potential. The client, however, had other ideas.

During a face-to-face interview with the client, the chief financial officer motioned me into his office, wherein he opened a file cabinet drawer marked "attitude adjustments." Within this drawer were several folders and VHS cassettes appropriately labeled with the name, account number, and amount recovered from what I later learned were hard-core deadbeats. The CFO proceeded to lecture me on the merits of extreme debt recovery and particularly how to capitalize on them:

> Mike, you're a good collector and I don't hold it against you that this $514.83 receivable (judgment) wasn't collected. You're correct that we're putting good money after bad, and on the surface it appears it's just not worth spending several thousands of dollars to collect such a negligible sum. There is, however, an economic benefit by subjecting this wisenheimer [actually he used more graphic words] to a lesson—one he will never forget, and one which we'll capitalize on for years to come.

At this point the CFO retrieved one of his "attitude adjustment" files, inserted the accompanying video into a VCR, and pressed the play button. The tape was a visual record of a sheriff's levy relevant to the execution of a judgment debtor's personal effects that occurred within sight of onlookers, curiosity seekers, and his family. The CFO continued:

> Notice how our hired photographer captured the drama and humiliation as the sheriff sold this judgment debtor's personal effects, even his children's toys [bicycles, etc. were auctioned while his kids were crying profusely]. Our visual presentation is a convincing documentary of what a nonpaying customer can expect. Why did we go through such extremes? Because a visual record is preserved for all time—and used to put the fear of God in the next guy who tries to rip us off. Any time we encounter a similar situation, we simply duplicate the file and copy the video. Then we present it to the nonpaying customer along with a verbal threat: "This is a preview of what you're going to go through."

The CFO went on to boast that his write-offs were less than one-tenth of 1%, practically nothing as compared to an industry that historically encounters 2% to 3% write-offs. After viewing the embarrassing sheriff's levy, I was provided with select copies of his "attitude adjustment" files and instructed to present it to the resistant judgment debtor with a copy of the video. He was then threatened that he too would suffer a similar fate. The judgment debtor was agitated with both what he had read and viewed. Relenting, this hardened judgment debtor voluntarily satisfied the $514.83. The CFO anticipated the favorable outcome: Pay up or your worst legal nightmare will become a reality.

A Lesson Learned: Deriving Profit from Hard-Core Recoveries

My exposure with this progressive office products company taught me a valuable lesson, one that I have reiterated hundreds of times over the years. Although the economics of spending several thousands of dollars to recover a receivable for a lesser sum may seem to be a waste of money, the fact is that a progressive creditor can utilize the dirty laundry from one full-circle recovery to motivate a nonpaying customer. Over the years I have duplicated the success of this strategy thousands of times by presenting credit criminals with both incriminating documents and a visual record of dire consequences. The result has almost always been expedient recovery. Why reinvent the wheel when several difficult recoveries can ride on the coattails of a previous success?

External Factors: A Reputation

The benefits of capitalizing on slam-dunk tactics do not end with one recovery. The positive economics extend into the psyche of a nonpaying customer's mentality. When a company maintains a wimpy posture, its industry reputation encourages abuse. *Case in point:* A manufacturer of sporting goods maintains a liberal credit policy with extremely lenient payment terms. Its philosophy: "Goodwill." Unfortunately for this company, its reputation is widely known (e.g., allowing a $30,000-plus defaulting customer to pay $50 per week!), resulting in detrimental word-of-mouth publication. To replenish its huge bad debt, this publicly owned company regularly issues stock to compensate for its losses (in effect transitioning write-offs to its shareholders). Having gotten away with this scam for several years, the Securities and Exchange Commission (SEC) prosecuted its principals while the company's shares plummeted to near worthless value. Today, this credit-liberal company is on the verge of bankruptcy. If customers discover that their creditors are lenient, then this policy becomes industry knowledge; however, if a creditor has a reputation for aggressive debt collection, then this stimulates compliance with terms. The word-of-mouth factor—over time—plants seeds that result in either a negative or positive accounts receivable.

The CFO who resorted to extreme measures against his nonpaying customers may be labeled as barbaric. Whatever your opinion, the facts are that this office products company maintained the healthiest profit margin among its competitors and had an industry reputation as a well-managed company. It amazes me to what extent companies will go to maintain "customer service" and "goodwill," even when they are being royally ripped off. Incredibly, this mentality is the same as giving away your company's hard-earned money. Yet, despite negatively impacting the bottom line, many companies foolhardily write off accounts rather than exert pressure, practicing charity rather than common sense. The real economic loss, however, extends far beyond the actual debt; there are the hidden costs to create the sale, administrative and collection costs, not to mention gaining a reputation for leniency. A sound policy is one that practices good customer service but also draws the line when the company becomes a victim of credit abuse. The more aggressive a company is in policing its receivables—even if it means exercising legal rights to the max—the more it will solidify an industry reputation for being tough. Practicing customer service is a virtue, a good philosophy, but remember, you are running a business, not a charity.

Destruction of an Employer's Property Results in Creditor Ammunition

A metal fabrication plant owed Lehigh Safety Shoes $5,860—a debt derived for providing steel tip safety shoes. Lehigh sells its safety shoes to blue-collar factory workers for whom their employer is responsible to pay the debt. As a security measure, Lehigh secures from each employee a guarantee to pay one-half the cost. The end result is that the employer deducts 50% of the cost for the safety shoes from the laborers' paycheck. When a company defaults, it casts its employees in a vulnerable position. During one difficult recovery, we recommended Lehigh sue the defaulting company's employees for their 50% share of the liability. Although there were a large number of employees, we initially sued only a half-dozen, which was intended to exert pressure on the employer. This tactic not only satisfied this particular debt but also capitalized on the result for future situations wherein the employer defaulted. From an initial economic standpoint, Lehigh expanded about $4,000—a disproportionate sum in relation to the $5,860 due—but the tactic has and continues to pay dividends far beyond expectations.

Disgruntled Employees Destroy Hundreds of Thousands of Dollars in Equipment

During six employee small claims actions, the labor force mustered momentum in retaliation against their employer for its deliberate failure to reimburse them for their safety shoes. As the intransigent employer refused to pay the debt, the steel workers united (resenting that each was sued and their credit damaged) and sabotaged their workplace; expensive dies were ruined, machinery was destroyed, and components were stolen. The uproar was so financially devastating that the already cash-starved employer filed bankruptcy. Although Lehigh never recovered its $5,860, nor the approximate $4,000 in legal fees (it did recover a few small payments from the steel workers), it nevertheless was the catalyst for what was to become a success recipe for many future recoveries. This well-documented and publicized crisis paid dividends far in excess of the original write-off and legal fees. The destruction of the steel fabrication plant, together with having sued innocent—but jointly liable employees—yielded Lehigh with powerful ammunition, which it utilizes as a persuasive tactic to intimidate nonrelated corporate deadbeats. Overall, the losses sustained from this one expense deterred enough bad debt write-offs to pay for itself many times over.

Today, Lehigh's investment for having underwritten employee-driven small claims lawsuits continues to be utilized with chronically delinquent customers who default. Where appropriate, the CEO's lesson is implemented (i.e., capitalizing on the success of ABC to intimidate and recover monies from XYZ). By showcasing to the nonpaying customer a preview—a coming attraction of dire consequences—the end result is that most debtors will pay rather than risk retribution. Once the incriminating documentation is provided to chronically delinquent customers, it is usually conveyed to their attorneys who advise their clients that they should satisfy the outstanding debt rather than succumb to retaliatory measures by the labor force. Lehigh's approximate $9,000 write-off/legal fees have been repaid many times.

BANKRUPTCY REMEDIES

Bankruptcy is a subject that requires its own treatise. This section provides a bare bones overview of possible creditor remedies. Creditors should always consult with counsel, preferably an attorney who maintains experience in this area. Bankruptcy assumes many forms categorized by chapters. A chapter 11 filing is a reorganization that compromises or extends the debt, whereas chapter 7 is a liquidation of assets. Chapter 13 is liberal and generally provides creditors with the best possibility for maximum recovery.

Contrary to common belief, a bankruptcy is not necessarily a fatal blow to a creditor. A chapter 11 filing provides a two-step democratic process relevant to the debtor's disclosure statement. Creditors are permitted latitude to challenge the debtor's financial representation. Creditors cast votes according to their designated class. If more than one-half in number and two-thirds in claim amount accept the plan, it becomes a new, binding contract. Timing and creditor vigilance are prerequisites if the proposed plan of reorganization is to be implemented.

Chapter 13 plans are not as complex as those of chapter 11. The provisions for administering this plan are found in 11 U.S.C. section 1322 and include identifying classes of claims, priority claims, waiving defaults, and committing disposable income to fund distribution. Chapter 13 plans are administered for no less than 3 years nor more than 5 years. Unlike a chapter 11 reorganization, a chapter 13 bankruptcy *does not* require a disclosure statement, nor are ballots cast by creditors. Two of the most frequently litigated aspects challenging confirmation are "good faith" and "feasibility."

Once a customer files for bankruptcy protection, an automatic stay ensues pursuit to 11 U.S.C. section 362. Only under specific situations can a creditor petition the court for relief from a stay, so it may continue with another legal proceeding. For example, foreclosure on a mortgage, an eviction of a tenant, payment of child support, or alimony will not be discharged by bankruptcy. A creditor in this situation is only temporarily delayed from prosecuting a case until a relief from the automatic stay is obtained.

CREDITOR REMEDIES FOR CHALLENGING FRAUDULENT CONVEYANCES AND ADVERSARY PROCEEDINGS

11 U.S.C. section 548 provides remedies to creditors who are prejudiced by a debtor's intended sale of assets with intent to defraud. 11 U.S.C. section 341 permits creditors and/or a trustee to examine debtors. A Rule 2002 examination is a more formal deposition of the debtor, wherein subpoenas to produce financial records and relevant documents are available. If a trustee serves on a particular bankruptcy and he determines the debtor has concealed or

liquidated assets, or has misrepresented any facet of true financial status with intent to defraud creditors, a section 707(B) motion to dismiss may be appropriate. Creditors also have adversarial remedies governed by 11 U.S.C. sections 523 and 727. Creditor complaints must be exercised within 60 days of the date of a creditor's meeting; however, there are exceptions. Debtors cannot discharge debts arising from "fraud, defalcation, embezzlement or larceny." *It is the creditor's burden to develop information and/or evidence to challenge the bankruptcy and to prosecute an adversary proceeding.* Where creditors' claims are economically justified, a Rule 2002 examination of the debtor is the best resource. Creditors should use due diligence to assemble and subpoena incriminating documents favorable to their cause. Adversarial bankruptcy proceedings are complex, and legal representation is recommended. Creditors can gain invaluable experience by serving on a creditors' committee.

UNCONVENTIONAL BANKRUPTCY RECOVERIES

Over the years, challenges have been made on all forms of bankruptcy, particularly the dreaded chapter 7 that accounts for more than 70% of filings. In many insolvencies, monies have been recovered that would otherwise have been written off, but not all recoveries followed protocol. Some have been accomplished by scorched-earth tactics, which were so potent as to position dishonest debtors in checkmate.

One client, a distributor of truck parts, was owed $53,241.16 by a Winnebago dealership. For years this customer maintained an exemplary relation with the client, but the customer became tardy and eventually defaulted. No sooner had collection activity begun than the Winnebago dealership filed a chapter 7, no-asset bankruptcy. The attorney who represented the defaulting dealership would not voluntarily provide a schedule of the debtor's assets and liabilities—a happenstance for which he was not legally obligated. (Most attorneys representing their clients will voluntarily provide this information.)

A search firm provided photocopies of the schedules filed by the debtor. Here is a synopsis of relevant information filed by the debtor:

Assets		Liabilities	
Cash on hand including checking accounts	$ 167,421	Notes due	$2,647,673
		Rent arrears	$ 63,400
Estimated fixtures and equipment	$ 216,000	FICA & sales tax	$ 37,940
Floor planned vehicles estimated	$ 721,000	Federal tax liabilities	$ 109,600
Accounts receivable	$ 119,002	Shareholder loan	$ 847,970
Misc.	$ 43,000		
Total Assets	$1,266,423	Total Liabilities	$3,706,583

Note: The above figures are excerpts from schedules filed by the debtor, with cents omitted. The overall financial condition as represented by the debtor was suspicious. An investigator was dispatched to inventory the debtor's place of business. Here is what was uncovered:

New Vehicles	Used Vehicles
16 Pop-up trailers	8 Pop-up tent trailers
11 Large motor homes	4 Large motor homes
9 Medium motor homes	7 Medium motor homes
23 Small motor homes	16 Small motor homes

Miscellaneous recreational and diversified vehicles 27

Because most of these vehicles were void of license plates, tracing the legal owner had to be accomplished by securing each vehicle's identification number (VIN). An investigator copied down each VIN. The next step was to perform a motor vehicle search to determine each vehicle's owner and lien status. Rather than perform this task manually, a Texas law firm was hired, which specializes in debt collection and maintains online software to provide a printout (they were not retained to collect the debt). They charged $675.

The DMV printout revealed that a large number of vehicles were owned outright by the dealership—a figure inconsistent with the schedules filed by the debtor. The next problem was to ascertain the vehicles' worth. This was accomplished by providing a copy to another recreational vehicle dealer, who was paid $500 to estimate the approximate market value, together with providing a sworn affidavit. The valuation of the vehicles was closer to $2.5 million—a sum that far exceeded the debtor's representations and approximately $1 million in equity that was not disclosed. Comparing apples to oranges, it was clear that not only had the debtor intentionally misrepresented his assets, but worse, he grossly understated their value. The chapter 7 bankruptcy was ripe for dismissal on the grounds of fraud.

Armed with incriminating evidence, an adversary petition was drafted relevant to sections 523 and 727 of the Bankruptcy Code charging the debtor with fraud. The document *was not filed.* Instead, it was faxed to the debtor, augmented with a verbal threat that unless the client was paid, the collector would blow the whistle, petition the court to dismiss the bankruptcy, and move for sanctions; negotiations ensued. Although this debtor had willfully filed false documents, he was not an intentional deadbeat. It unraveled that he and his second wife assumed ownership of the dealership from his elderly parents and were trying to revive the business from a financial mess resulting from his father, whose drinking problem substantially depleted their assets and cast them into debt; he wanted to settle.

At this juncture negotiations were made directly with the debtor, without the knowledge of his attorney. The debtor, who candidly revealed his finances, was unable to borrow the money needed to settle. Attention was then focused on barter (i.e., trading off the debt for a motor home).

At first the client was reluctant, insisting that an adversary proceeding be filed; however, this legal maneuver would be expensive and time consuming. Instead, a novel solution was offered. The client maintained an army of commissioned sales reps. It was proposed that the client take a motor home in trade and maintain it for incentive use. That is, sponsor a contest for the sales reps, awarding the best producer use of the motor home for a designated time frame. To support this proposal, the cooperation of the sales manager was elicited, and together with the president, it was emphasized that the public relations value of providing sales reps with an incentive had far greater value than the debt; the creditor agreed.

The client took possession of a used, medium-sized Winnebago motor home, which had about 28,000 miles on it. Its market value was between $37,000 and $40,000, less than the client's $53,241.16 debt. To sweeten the settlement, the dealership provided a three-year/100,000-mile extended warranty worth about $2,000. The deal was consummated, and the client took possession of the motor home. It did not take long for the creditor to profit. Other than routine maintenance and insurance, the motor home is utilized by the creditor's highest-producing sales reps, who in turn generate the most business.

Two years after the creative disposition of what otherwise would have been zero recovery, the client purchased a second motor home from the same dealer (at a respectable discount) to service its expanding incentive-driven sales force. The client credits the creative disposition of its $53,241.16 claim with having achieved a result in far greater proportion than the debt. The creditor not only consummated the deal quickly, but it also saved considerable legal fees, not to mention the incalculable goodwill and public relations value.

Within our archives are volumes of similar success stories. The ingredients to achieve spectacular results are always as a result of thinking outside the box. Never view a receivable with tunnel intelligence, but rather explore the possibilities—get creative. Accounts receivable success is a definitive recipe of intuition, applied creativity, and the fortitude to chart new waters. Every job, every endeavor is a self-portrait of its architect. Autograph your work with excellence.

CHAPTER **8**

Skip Tracing and Asset Searches

Acollection manager must be alert and informed. Nowhere is this more critical than
in the area of skip tracing and asset searches. What are the prerequisites to be a good skip
tracer? Learn basic sources of debtor information—public, private, and personal. This
chapter explains how to develop information to support your claim from conventional
skip-tracing sources you may have overlooked (e.g., the county tax assessor's office, voter
registration lists, the post office, the department of motor vehicles, court records, utility
companies, licensing agencies, the secretary of state, the department of revenue services,
the Securities and Exchange Commission, trade associations and unions, the military, and
credit bureaus). You will learn how virtuoso skip tracers develop information and zero in
on debtors. You will also discover how to deal with different categories of skips, including
the criminally minded debtor who thrives on beating you out of your money.

We will analyze the economics of pursuit, scrutinize relevant court proceedings, and put
your options into perspective. Do you know why it is vital to search public records before
you invest large sums to sue a debtor? If you bypass these remedies, you could be throwing
good money after bad. You will be introduced to myriad little-known sources of information. In addition, you will learn how to use the telephone company to locate debtors, how
to get an unlisted number, and how to use a reverse telephone directory.

This chapter will show you how to find out where your debtor banks and explain how
to get information from banks, collection agencies, other creditors, and landlords. Sample
forms are provided to request information from banks and landlords. You will also see how
many collectors seek the right information in the wrong manner.

Finally, you will discover how to make money as a professional skip tracer.

How to Locate Debtors and Their Assets

Skip tracing and asset searches are necessary evils, intrinsic elements of the collection
process. A professional collector must be a keen investigator who knows how to develop
information to support a creditor's claim. Skip tracing and asset searches are interrelated.
The term "skip tracing" refers to attempts to locate an individual or a responsible princi-

pal. Asset searches are undertaken to develop information that could be crucial in the execution of a judgment or in structuring collection strategy.

The demand for public records retrieval has soared because of the electronic information craze. For creditors, the opportunities are virtually limitless. This is even more relevant in skip tracing, debt collection, and post-judgment pursuits. This phenomenon has spawned a new breed of information retrieval providers. Surprisingly, 62% of public record retrievers have been in business less than 10 years, as a result of the recent awareness among creditors. For the collector, credit professional, bookkeeper, or anyone charged with debt recovery, an exciting universe of unparalleled opportunity awaits.

Many types of records are translated into electronic form, the list of which is virtually endless. For the bill collector, a basic search will aid in most collection situations. In this chapter, you will learn how record retrieval will help you accomplish three objectives:

1.   Find your target.

2.   Gauge recovery potential.

3.   Locate debtor's assets.

All three are interwoven in the debt collector's arsenal, an intrinsic part of the receivable recovery process.

Virtually any person, including evasive debtors, can be located. There is always a "paper trail," albeit it assumes many forms. Thanks to computers and database management companies, you can quickly and cost-effectively access various records that will likely pinpoint the location of your subject, gauge collectibility, and sometimes provide a glimpse of attachable assets.

Numerous types of records are accessible: driving records, vehicle registrations, credit files, post office changes-of-address, magazine subscriptions, bad checks, judgments, tax liens, bankruptcy, real property, deeds, voter registrations, corporate filings, professional licenses, and telephone listings, to name a few (see Exhibit 8.1 for a sample search report). National profiles are at the forefront of uncovering debtor information. They provide recent address(es), Social Security number, possible aka's (also known as), date of birth, and other relevant data. This information is critical to the creditor for locating skips and gauging collectibility. Keep in mind, however, that a profile report is not all-inclusive. Although it does not divulge all legal proceedings, including judgments, pending litigation, and/or bankruptcies, it does, however, provide creditors with important information.

These records usually originate in the county courthouse or clerk's office, where voluminous files can be expeditiously searched. By referencing each county and checking its department index, the collector is ideally positioned to discover critical information. Many of these searches are available via a computer and modem. Once you gain access within a system, the possibilities are virtually limitless.

Businesses specializing in records research buy records from each pertinent source and input them into a computer database. Then, the information is searchable by various methods (e.g., by referencing last and/or first name; Social Security number; date of birth,

EXHIBIT 8.1   INVESTIGATIVE REPORT

```
LOCATE:   SUZANNE L. JONES
D.O.B.:   04/12/67
_____


SUZANNE L JONES              DOB: 04/12/67
SS#: 140-69-1229 Was issued in New Jersey between 1975 and 1976

Possible AKAs
-------------
   MURPHY, SUZANNE L              SS#: 140-69-1229


Known Addresses For Subject
---------------------------
   APR-97/APR-97 - 596 N 10TH ST  SCOTTSDALE AZ 85220  (602) 502-1234
   JAN-97/JAN-97 - 3196 JOHNSON AVE  HACKENSACK NJ 07610
   NOV-95          69 E ANYPLACE DR  SCOTTSDALE AZ 85254


Possible Liens, Judgments and Bankruptcies
-------------------------------------------
   ** No Liens, Judgments or Bankruptcies found during search **


Relatives (* - denotes address match with Subject)
--------------------------------------------------
   JONES, GREGORY J             DOB: 9/2/69
      SS#:194-44-1234 Was issued in New York between 1972 and 1974

      APR-96/APR-96 - *596 N 10TH ST SCOTTSDALE AZ 85220   (602) 502-1234
      DEC-95/DEC-95 - *3196 JOHNSON AVE HACKENSACK NJ 07610
      JUN-95/OCT-95 - 5255 PASSAIC AVE WEST CALDWELL NJ 07009

   MURPHY, MIKE J SR            DOB: 8/21/42
      SS#:227-36-3456  Was issued in Maine between 1955 and 1956

      MAY-91/JUN-97 - *69 E. ANYPLACE DR  SCOTTSDALE  AZ  85254  (914) 762-1234

                    *** End Of Report ***
```

DISCLAIMER: This report is provided with the understanding that the terms of The Fair Credit Reporting Act and all Federal, State and Local laws will be strictly observed. Although this information is obtained from reliable resources, the accuracy of the information is not guaranteed. The information provided within this report is intended for investigative purposes only.

Reprinted with permission from Investigations Unlimited, Inc.

a surname, and age range; address and/or a telephone number. Retrieval of information is easy; you can research right from your office without ever traveling to the source. Sometimes you can research a smorgasbord of records at one time. Thanks to the marvels of automation, the process is economical and convenient. There are, however, some drawbacks.

The disadvantages of searching by computers are the following:

- Locating geographic location is spotty and/or information is incomplete.
- The information is sometimes not current (updates may occur weekly, monthly, or quarterly).

EXHIBIT 8.1   INVESTIGATIVE REPORT (CONT'D.)

```
596 N 10TH ST, SCOTTSDALE  AZ 85220
----------------------------------------
          Arizona Assessment Record - County of: MARICOPA
          Owner Name: JONES GREGORY & SUZANNE L
       Parcel Number: 212-11-301
     Short Legal Desc: JASPER RANCH PARCEL B MCR 344/05 LOT 15
       Property Type: RESIDENTIAL
            Recorded: 4/24/1996
           Document#: 96-341187           Book/Page: 5/42
       Situs Address: 596 N 10TH ST
                      SCOTTSDALE, AZ 85220
          Assessment Year: 1996                    Tax Year: 1996
       Assessed Land Value: $2,700       Market Land Value:
     Assessed Improvements:              Market Improvements:
       Total Assessed Value: $2,700      Total Market Value:

          Most Recent Sale: $205,437        Prior Sale Price: $189,232


                    *** End Of Report ***
```

DISCLAIMER: This report is provided with the understanding that the terms of The Fair Credit Reporting Act and all Federal, State and Local laws will be strictly observed. Although this information is obtained from reliable resources, the accuracy of the information is not guaranteed. The information provided within this report is intended for investigative purposes only.

Note: Knowing whether your debtor owns real property, particularly if equity exists, provides an advantage. Property reports reveal descriptions, taxes, prior or recent sales, and sometimes mortgagors.

Important: Astute debtors may resort to deeding their properties to a limited partnership. Under these legal structures, a trust is usually a beneficiary. Unearthing this data is cumbersome, since the partnership will have its own Tax ID number. There might even be bogus liens. A comprehensive property search can unravel the mystery and expose an attachable asset.

- There may be limitations on how records are searched. (You may need a date of birth (DOB) or a Social Security number (SSN) in order to access relevant information.)
- The start-up and per-inquiry fee may be too costly for low-volume searching. (By using a reseller, you can bypass the costs of a computer and start-up fees accessed by the record owners.)

The advantages of computer research are the following:

- It is fast and cost-effective.
- It offers expanded coverage. You can search, by county or state, all discoverable records.
- There is flexibility to use different inputs to locate relevant records and/or cross-referencing.
- A computer is not required. (You can contract with a reseller by fax, phone, or e-mail and have that party perform the search for you.)

EXHIBIT 8.1   INVESTIGATIVE REPORT (CONT'D.)

```
TODAYS NATIONAL BANK
234 MAIN STREET
BANK, AZ    12345


ACCOUNT TYPE:   CHECKING
ACCOUNT NUMBER:   2345678
ACCOUNT BALANCE:   $4,236.24
ACCOUNT NAME:   SUZANNE L. JONES


ACCOUNT TYPE:   SAVINGS
ACCOUNT NUMBER:   694932
ACCOUNT BALANCE:   $9,867.00
ACCOUNT NAME:   SUZANNE L. JONES




                    *** End Of Report ***
```

DISCLAIMER: This report is provided with the understanding that the terms of The Fair Credit Reporting Act and all Federal, State and Local laws will be strictly observed. Although this information is obtained from reliable resources, the accuracy of the information is not guaranteed. The information provided within this report is intended for investigative purposes only.

Note: Bank account information is crucial for creditors. Social Security and/or Tax ID numbers are electronically scanned.

Most records are in the category of "public records." Other records, such as credit files, are covered by the Fair Credit Reporting Act, which deals with the legitimacy of obtaining a credit report on an individual. The law is specific in that credit reports may be obtained with a signed release from the subject of the report in connection with a credit transaction involving a consumer. A consumer report may also be obtained for review, the collection of an account, or post-judgment procedures.

Let us examine how information is retrieved from an online computer data bank or information reseller. Exhibit 8.1 is an example of an information report that is obtainable for a fee of $30 to $60. Although this report is elementary, it does provide creditors with the basics. Comprehensive searches can reveal substantially more data. Some specialized searches can be expensive, especially if they have to be expedited manually or are all-inclusive. Bottom line? Information retrieval is to a creditor what gasoline is to an automobile: It is the fuel that propels receivables on the road of recovery.

There is a definite distinction between "vertical" and "horizontal" debtor pursuit. Here is the difference:

- *Vertical debtor pursuit* is a noninvestigatory process that involves direct debtor contact—telephone and/or written communication. Most collection problems are resolved this way.

EXHIBIT 8.1   INVESTIGATIVE REPORT (CONT'D.)

```
Possible Vehicles Located
-------------------------

   Tag#: MHJ421       State: AZ     Exp: 04/98
   Date Registered: 06/06/97   Title: H9KB1232640208
   Title Date: 09/22/95   VIN: 124FG3478912A6
   Veh Yr: 1995   Type: FORD    Model: 150

   CO-OWNER: SUZANNE L. JONES
             596 N 10TH ST
             SCOTTSDALE  AZ 85220


                 *** End Of Report ***
```

DISCLAIMER: This report is provided with the understanding that the terms of The Fair Credit Reporting Act and all Federal, State and Local laws will be strictly observed. Although this information is obtained from reliable resources, the accuracy of the information is not guaranteed. The information provided within this report is intended for investigative purposes only.

Note: Motor vehicle searches often uncover attachable assets. Sophisticated debtors can thwart creditors by registering vehicles in nearby states. Tapping this source may uncover exotic or collectors' cars, commercial vehicles, and/or other attachable assets

- *Horizontal debtor pursuit* involves more sophisticated investigatory techniques. This process draws information from many sources. The information is then used to develop leverage to influence your debtor in direct communication (vertical pursuit). The information gained by horizontal pursuit can be used to:
  - Entice the debtor to pay.
  - Influence third parties that can, in turn, influence the debtor.

Reminder: Various state and federal laws prohibit creditors and/or collectors from revealing information about debts to third parties. The laws apply primarily to consumer debts, but some state statutes and the Federal Trade Commission Act extend prohibitions to commercial debt collectors as well. Generally, you have a right to exchange credit data, payment profiles, litigation experience, and similar information with third parties. You even have a legal right to question a potential garnisher or to inquire of other creditors about the possibility of forcing a debtor into involuntary bankruptcy. But be careful not to make any false or defamatory statement about your debtor. Although you do have a right to develop information to support your claim, improper contacts can create legal consequences. Consult with a reputable collection attorney before contacting third parties.

For all practical purposes, skips fit into one of only two categories:

1. *Unintentional or accidental skip.* These are debtors who do not intentionally circumvent their obligations. They simply move to new addresses and neglect to notify their creditors. These debtors are easily located.

2. *Intentional or deliberate skips.* These debtors are more sophisticated. They may be "credit criminals" who "with malice aforethought" conceal their whereabouts. There are two levels of intentional skip.

   - *Novice deadbeats.* These skips cover most of their tracks, usually by not leaving forwarding addresses and not revealing their whereabouts to neighbors. In most cases, attempts to thwart creditors are haphazard, and with a little digging, you can easily find these deadbeats.

   - *Hard-core skips.* These debtors are true professionals. Chances are that they have been through the mill and know the game. In addition to the obvious evasive actions (e.g., failing to leave a forwarding address), these debtors take great care to conceal their whereabouts and may even go so far as to make themselves judgment-proof. These debtors are devious and cunning. They may change their driver's licenses, reregister their vehicles, and use "front addresses" for such essentials as transferring school and medical records and sometimes to maintain prestigious credit cards (e.g., American Express or Diner's Club). These debtors characteristically shaft *everyone*. They have no sense of ethics and thrive on beating their victims. Unfortunately, most skip tracers lack the skills and resources to locate and collect on this kind of mastermind debtor. A virtuoso skip tracer could probably locate and confront the criminal-minded debtor, but collecting what is owed is another story. However, these debtors *can be dealt with*. Their actions of intentional concealment and subterfuge can be used as a powerful advantage.

How to be a Good Skip Tracer

Good skip tracers are perceptive, creative, intelligent, and cunning. Skip tracers should have endurance, be inquisitive, and be masters of the art of persuasion. It is essential that they develop a "sixth sense"—keen insight and strong intuition. Skip tracers are, after all, detectives. They must gather and carefully put together puzzle pieces to locate debtors and assets. Most collectors are not good skip tracers, but most skip tracers are very good collectors.

Able Conversationalists

In the "negative selling" and "boomerang" collection techniques, the debtor is encouraged to do most of the talking. The information the debtor provides is then used to formulate strategy. Skip tracing also demands an ability to listen. It is easier to talk than it is to listen. Yet the ability to listen and stimulate conversation are absolute prerequisites. You must learn to recognize potential information sources and tune in to opportunities. The knowledge you gain from contacts will be the catalyst that enables you to locate debtors and motivate them to pay.

Professional Credit Abusers

Professional deadbeats will go to extraordinary lengths to conceal their whereabouts. People who use the protection of a "corporate veil" to escape liability tend to be ruthless, insensitive, hard-core individuals. These white-collar criminals are expert manipulators. They know how to falsify information to procure credit. Interestingly, people of this type usually do *not* have criminal records because most of their crimes are considered victimless.

White-collar crime: The fact is that credit crime just is not punishable in this country. Professional debtors know this and usually escape prosecution.

TO TRACE OR NOT TO TRACE

Before you decide to locate a skip, you should consider the economics of pursuit. Will the end justify the means? If you locate the debtor, what are your chances of recovery? Is it a corporate debt or a consumer debt? If it is a business debt, have you verified the business entity so that you can determine liability? There are three primary types of business entity:

1. Corporation (Generally, no individual liability, but there are exceptions—a principal of a corporation can be named a defendant in relevant legal proceedings.)
2. Partnership (limited liability)
3. Sole proprietorship (individual liability)

It might be a waste of time to locate the principals of a defunct corporation if you cannot legally hold them liable for corporate obligations. Many creditors insist on personal guarantees from principals, corporate officers, shareholders, or even family members if dealing with closely held corporations. Personal guarantees offer additional security if a corporation goes out of business. Armed with a personal guarantee, you *can* legally pursue the individual who signed that instrument. (See Exhibit 8.2 for a sample personal guarantee form.)

If a debtor is a partnership or sole proprietorship, there is individual liability, and a search for the principals might be appropriate.

Subterfuge and Impersonation

Many skip tracers resort to subterfuge and impersonation to gather information, but federal regulations prohibit use of the telephone to "frighten," "abuse," "torment," or "harass" another person for any "unlawful" purpose. Ironically, subterfuge may sometimes be necessary to stay within the law. There are numerous contradictions in these regulations, and by adhering to one law, you might inadvertently be breaking another. Use good judgment, and *always consult with an attorney* before engaging in any form of investigation.

EXHIBIT 8.2 **PERSONAL GUARANTEE FORM**

GUARANTEE

The undersigned does hereby guarantee prompt and full performance and payment of the obligations of _____ Corporation, a Corporation in which the undersigned guarantor is a Principal, Officer, and/or Stockholder, and in the event of a default authorizes the creditor to proceed against the undersigned for the full amount due including reasonable attorney's fees, and the undersigned does hereby waive presentment, demand, protest, notice of protest, notice of dishonor, and any and all other notices or demand of whatever character to which the undersigned might otherwise be entitled. If more than one guarantor, the obligation of each shall be joint and several.

WITNESS the hand and seal of the undersigned, this _____ day of _____,20_____.

_____

Are You an Investigator?

The fact of the matter is that any form of skip tracing or asset search is an investigatory function. Many states have ironclad laws that require "investigators" to be licensed. If you tell a third party that you are an investigator, you could open a Pandora's box. By telling a third party that you are conducting an investigation, you become an investigator, and if you are not *licensed,* there could be civil or criminal consequences. Use substitute words instead. For example, you might tell a third party that you are "developing information." Most attorneys confirm that you have a right to develop information for your files, but you do not have a legal right to investigate. Ironically, a creditor in contemplation of a credit decision would never be challenged if it undertook a credit investigation, but a bill collector attempting to collect a debt might run afoul of laws banning private investigations by unlicensed parties.

Credit Reporting: The Fair Credit Reporting Act strictly regulates consumer reporting agencies (anyone who charges a fee to assemble consumer information for third parties). These agencies can furnish consumer reports only in the following conditions:

- By court order
- If so instructed by the consumer
- To a person who has a legitimate business need for the information

Investigative consumer reports relating to consumers' "character, general reputation, personal characteristics, or mode of living" gathered by personal interviews with "neighbors, friends, or acquaintances" are subject to further restrictions. Unless these reports are to be used only for employment purposes for which consumers have not specifically applied, the credit reporting agency must inform the consumers *in writing* that such reports are in the works and of the consumers' right to request further disclosures regarding the nature and scope of the investigative reports.

Consult an attorney for details regarding federal and state regulation of credit reporting agencies.

Maintain Accurate Records

It is important to maintain accurate records. No activity is more conducive to complaints and litigation than third-party contacts. *Do not* rely on memory. Take notes when talking to debtors or third parties and retain these notes in your files. Notes should include the following information:

- The dates and times you spoke with the contacts
- The names of the people to whom you spoke
- Descriptions of each conversation

Make these records an intrinsic part of each debtor's file.

BASIC SKIP-TRACING SOURCES

Sources of information are virtually limitless. The voluminous sources can be likened to branches on a tree (see Exhibit 8.3). Like a branch, each primary source has many smaller shoots or appendages from which you can develop information. Some of these primary sources and the offshoots that are most commonly fruitful include the following:

PUBLIC RECORDS

- County tax assessor
- Voter registration records
- U.S. Postal Service—Freedom of Information Act
- Department of Motor Vehicles
- Court records
- Municipal water district
- Local schools

PRIVATE RECORDS

- Telephone company
- Telephone directories
- Criss cross directories
- Banks and financial institutions
- Landlord or mortgage holder
- Gas and electric companies

EXHIBIT 8.3 SKIP-TRACING SOURCES

EXHIBIT 8.3 SKIP-TRACING SOURCES

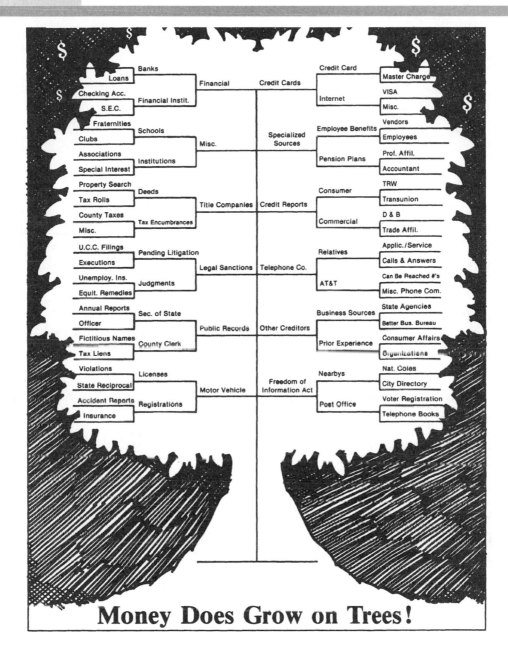

Money Does Grow on Trees!

- Collection agencies
- Credit bureaus
- Local merchants
- Trade associations and unions
- Fraternal organizations—memberships

PERSONAL CONTACTS

- Relatives
- Friends and acquaintances
- Neighbors
- Employers and former employers
- Work and business associates
- Leaders of membership groups

Court Procedures

Our judicial system does not guarantee success to the party whose cause is "just." The system does provide for discovery, but the real drama takes place outside the courtroom because a successful conclusion depends on the cooperation of your adversary. The subpoena is the most common device to gather information in court proceedings. There are two types of subpoena:

1. *Subpoena Duces Tecum* (to take the deposition of a witness) commands a witness to appear for examination, often with records concerning the debtor's assets and financial resources. Note that in some jurisdictions the creditor might have to pay the witness a fee to appear.

2. *Information subpoena* (interrogatory) requires the recipient to fill out an attached question form and return it to the creditor's attorney.

To gather information about the judgment debtor, the creditor's attorney might subpoena any of the following sources:

- The judgment debtor
- The debtor's spouse
- The debtor's bank(s)
- Work and business associates
- Utilities (which provide useful credit information about the debtor)
- Employers and former employers
- Friends and relatives
- Neighbors
- Leaders of membership groups

Other court procedures that can be used by a creditor's attorney to uncover information about the debtor and the debtor's assets include the following:

- *Discovery.* A creditor can also make a motion of discovery, by which the creditor asks the court to order the debtor or a party to disclose facts that are necessary to the creditor's cause of action.

- *Notice to Produce.* This is a notice in writing that requires the debtor to produce specified papers or documents before trial.

- *Interrogatories.* These are written questions to which the debtor must respond in writing. The problem with interrogatories is that both sides tend not to provide substantive answers.

Discovery Within Our Legal System

The most expensive, time-consuming, and drawn-out means to uncover debtor information is via the lawsuit. Legal discovery requires depositions, interrogatories, bills of particulars, subpoenas, and other forms of examination. One disadvantage is that the system operates extrajudicially. That is, the discovery process is *supposed* to function between the litigants without court intervention. More often than not, this does not pan out because recalcitrant witnesses, who may have personal relationships with your debtor, tend to hold back crucial information.

The only remedy is for the creditor's attorney to go back to court and file a motion to compel disclosure. If refused, the attorney must make another motion to hold an uncooperative witness in "contempt." Even if the judge grants this motion, it is unlikely that the witness will be subjected to any penalty. Courts are reluctant to impose prison terms for violations of civil contempt orders. In most cases, the witness gets off with a slap on the wrist.

Even if you successfully extricate needed information, what guarantee do you have that the information will result in payment? This is especially uncertain if you are looking for hidden assets. The assets in question could easily be sold or otherwise hidden or disposed of long before you can execute a judgment. You might have further recourse if you have been the victim of fraud, but fraud is difficult and costly to prove.

This whole scenario of discovery costs big bucks. Your attorney and the debtor's attorney will be the only ones to profit. In short, if you can develop information through a few phone calls, without going to court and without your debtor's knowledge, you are much better off.

There are ways to expand the discovery process at minimal expense. Refer to Chapter 10.

PUBLIC RECORDS: DOCUMENT RETRIEVAL

Public records are a virtually limitless resource and are open for inspection. They are a valuable resource, not only to locate debtors but also to determine collection potential. Generally, the most important documents you will retrieve concern:

- Pending litigation
- Judgments
- State and federal tax liens

The importance of retrieving pertinent documents cannot be overemphasized. When you secure this information, it can prevent your having to pay unnecessary legal expenditures and can help you gauge collection potential. You should not depend on a collection agency or even an attorney to develop this information because most will not. Reputable search firms can retrieve information from public filings at minimal cost. Infosearch, Equifax, and Julius Blumberg are established search firms. Check your Yellow Pages under *Research Services* or *Lawyers Service Bureaus,* or ask an attorney for search firms in your area.

The experience of one judgment debtor in a civil action illustrates how important it is to search public records before investing large sums to sue debtors. In this case, the attorney successfully secured a judgment in the amount of $5,958, *but the judgment was uncollectible* because other uncollectible judgments totaling almost $2 million were already outstanding. If other creditors cannot collect, how can you expect to be successful? In this particular case the judgment debtor also had an unsatisfied federal tax lien against him.

All of this vital information did not surface until well into the litigation. The bottom line is that the client squandered $770 to get a judgment that ended up being just a worthless piece of paper. If the creditor had had this information beforehand, the debt could have been written off and out-of-pocket legal expenses would not have been wasted. From another perspective, any time you sue a debtor, you expend good money after bad; litigation is often a crap shoot.

PERSONAL CONTACTS

Other good sources of information are your debtor's personal contacts, including business associates, friends, relatives, neighbors, landlords, and so on. If the debtor rents or has rented space, the landlord's name and address can be useful. To find out the name of the owner of property rented by your debtor, consult one of three sources:

1. The office of the county tax assessor or local tax collector
2. The customer service department of a title guaranty company
3. A *Cole* or *Criss Cross* cross-referenced directory, available at most libraries (See also "Using the Telephone Company to Locate Debtors" section.)
4. Various Web sites

A landlord is likely to have valuable information, including a forwarding address and other references. Again, some landlords may require a request to be in writing. (See Exhibits 8.4 and 8.5 for examples of an Applicant's Referral Form (Landlord's Form) and a Landlord-Tenant Association form.)

PLOYS TO GET INFORMATION FROM DEBTORS

Some collectors have given the collection industry a bad name by using ploys, deception, and impersonations to get information from evasive debtors. The following list describes

EXHIBIT 8.4   APPLICANT'S REFERRAL FORM (LANDLORD'S FORM)

We have been given your name as a reference by a person we are considering for a position. Can you please fill out the following form and return it to us in the prepaid envelope? All information will be held in confidence, and we thank you for your assistance.

Name of Applicant _____

Name of Referral _____

Relationship to Applicant_____

How long have you known this tenant? _____

If this tenant has rented from you less than three years, what was this tenant's previous

address? _____

_____

Who is this tenant's current employer?

    Name of Employer_____

    Address _____

How does this tenant usually pay you?

    Check_____   Money Order_____   Cash_____   Credit Card_____

    Name of Bank or Credit Card _____

    Account Number _____

---

four such gimmicks perpetrated to extract information. These methods are illegal for third-party consumer collectors and are questionable for commercial collectors and creditors. They are presented here to make you aware of some of the tricks being used in the collection field.

- *Contest Winner.* Here the collector lets the debtor think that he has won a prize or contest, baiting the debtor to get information.

- *Research and Opinion Poll.* People are responsive to surveys, and they like to cooperate. If debtors think they are part of a research project, they may be willing to cooperate.

- *Employment Agency.* It is always gratifying when a management recruiting firm calls a prospective candidate for a new position. It boosts our ego to know that someone is interested in our abilities and might be willing to pay more for having the benefit of our services. If the debtor thinks an employment agency or a management recruiting firm is interested in him, the debtor can be encouraged to talk and reveal important information.

EXHIBIT 8.5   LANDLORD-TENANT ASSOCIATION FORM

Account XJ2034

Dear Landlord:

You are requested to provide the following information on one of your tenants:

(Name of Tenant)

Is the above person a current tenant?   Yes_____ No_____

How long? _____

What is the monthly rent? _____

From which bank does this tenant pay you? _____

    Account Number _____

If the tenant is employed, what is his/her place of employment?

    Company Name _____

    Address or Location _____

If the tenant is self-employed, please indicate:

    _____

Thank you for your cooperation.

- *The Jury Duty Ruse.* In this deceitful strategy, the collector posing as the court clerk states that the debtor has been selected for jury duty. The unsuspecting debtor reveals pertinent information about employment, finances, assets, and so on.

USING THE TELEPHONE COMPANY TO LOCATE DEBTORS

We generally think of the telephone company as a limited source of information. If a telephone is disconnected, we assume that the debtor is a proficient deadbeat and, therefore, the obligation is uncollectible. Interestingly, *just by calling directory assistance,* you can develop information. If the debtor is not listed, ask the operator for other listings in that county with the same last name as your debtor. (Obviously, if a debtor's name is Smith or Jones, this will not work.) Often debtors have relatives in the area with the same last name, and their numbers may be listed. Call them after you have exhausted the preliminaries.

Advanced Telephone Company Information Sources

Assume that you have a telephone number with no name or address. You can verify the subscriber name and address from one of several sources:

1. *Reverse telephone directories, which contain numerical listings of phone numbers and addresses.* This works only for listed numbers. Unlisted numbers are not recorded.

2. *Telephone company calls and answers (C & A) office.* All telephone companies maintain such an office. This office can tell you the name, county, and, in some cases, even the address of a subscriber. It is a useful tool for verifying telephone numbers, and all it takes is one call.

3. *Header reports.* The top portion of a credit report—the nonfinancial portion—reveals Social Security number, date of birth, previous and last known address(es), telephone numbers (even cell phone numbers), and place of employment. Refer to the section on credit reports in Chapter 12.

Now the bad news: Unfortunately, many overzealous collectors have abused the privilege of access to subscriber information. Phone companies have become aware of such subterfuge and have imposed security codes limiting access to the system. This information is now available only for internal security purposes, and phone companies require positive identification. Security codes are changed frequently to prevent outsiders from accessing the system. Some collectors with inside contacts manage to get these security codes. It is helpful to know somebody in the phone company. One of the most valuable sources of information is a local area telephone access list, also called a LATA list, which is trade terminology for retrieving copies of someone's phone bills. Access to this information can produce extraordinary results because, armed with this information, a shrewd collector has access to any person with whom your debtor communicates. Repeat numbers reveal established relationships. One tip to know is that some investigative research firms have access to this information. *Warning:* Access to this information is illegal and an invasion of privacy.

Advanced Skip-Tracing Technique

Assume that your debtor is a professional deadbeat who is astute and has covered his tracks. Nonetheless, there are two types of bills on which even hard-core debtors will dutifully make payments:

1. Phone bills
2. Prestigious credit cards

Consider those debtors who have beaten everyone out of money. They usually continue to pay their phone bills because the phone company will not tolerate lengthy indebtedness. A debtor who is late in paying the phone bill is typically shut off in 90 to 120 days. You can use this information to your advantage. If a debtor's business is telephone oriented, it is probable that the debtor will apply for a new telephone number at a new location. If the debtor's payment history is good, he will not have to post a security deposit to commence service. You will note that telephone companies routinely exchange information concerning their subscribers. Again, it is nice to know someone who works for the telephone company.

How to Get an Unlisted or CBR Number

At the time debtors file applications for phone service, they must include telephone numbers where they "can be reached" (CBR). Often these are the numbers of other business ventures or even their home numbers. If they are residential numbers, they might be unlisted. A collector who calls a telephone company to verify credit information about a subscriber could also ask the phone company business office for the "can be reached" number on the subscriber's application. All the collector has to do is tell the phone company representative that he is having trouble reaching the subscriber (debtor) at telephone number _____. Does the phone company have a CBR number? The telephone company representative reviewing the application for pertinent credit information may give the CBR number to the collector even if it is a home listing or an unlisted number. You might want to tell the telephone company representative that Bill Pastdue listed the phone company as a reference and that you are making a credit inquiry.

Another source of extracting this data is an electronic information retrieval firm or a header report.

Note: Credit reports often reveal telephone numbers, even if they are unlisted.

Cross-Reference Directories/Online Services

One of the most valuable skip-tracing, asset-search tools available is the cross-reference (reverse) telephone directory. Directories cover most metropolitan areas. They list information according to street address, phone listings, and geographic location rather than by name. Suppose that your debtor, William Pastdue, formerly resided at:

27 Spring Street
Allentown, Pennsylvania

If the phone was disconnected, mail was returned, or the post office did not have a forwarding address, you could look up "nearbys" (homes and businesses near the debtor's former address) in the reverse directory. You could find out who lives at 21, 23, 25, 29, and 31 Spring Street (addresses on the same side of the street) and also get the names and phone numbers of neighbors across the street at 20, 22, 24, 26, 28, 30. Armed with this information, you can then call these "nearbys." Often they have had some communication with your debtor. If so, they might tell you where the debtor is and/or provide other valuable information. There are many techniques to get "nearbys" to reveal the information you want. Use your imagination!

Cross-reference, or reverse, telephone directories can be leased, or you can subscribe to a service from most cross-directory manufacturers. They all have this information on computer, which is available through a single telephone call. To find out what cross-directory to use, look in the Yellow Pages under "Publishers—Directory & Guide," or inquire of local libraries, fire departments, or real estate offices. One of these sources should tell you which publishers cover their areas, or Cole Publications (901 West Bond Street, Lincoln, Nebraska 68521) will field inquiries regarding availability of cross-reference directories and refer callers to the appropriate company. Cole Publications also sells software so its users can access their database online.

Cross directories are still published, but most services are accessed online. Some provide disk updates based on geographic locations. Any firm that sells skip tracing can provide creditors with a menu of vendor services.

But remember: The federal Fair Debt Collection Practices Act prohibits professional debt collectors, attorneys included, from revealing to third parties that the subjects of their inquiries owe money or anything about their indebtedness. Generally, the law will not apply to creditors directly or even to third parties if a debtor is already in litigation. If you have a judgment against a debtor, you have a right to make inquiries, but note that federal restrictions may be extended by state law, so make sure you check with an attorney well-versed in state collections law.

Obviously, regardless of the existence or nonexistence of explicit state regulations, a creditor may not use or threaten violence or use any criminal means to collect a debt or punish a debtor for nonpayment.

COUNTY TAX ASSESSOR'S OFFICE

The tax assessor is an excellent source to verify property owned by a debtor. Information from this office can be cross-referenced by street and owner's name to give you the block and lot number. You can then determine whether there are any liens or encumbrances on the property, or whether there are improvements that would increase the property value.

Statewide alphabetical listings of property owners, a source used by most title companies, are often overlooked by collectors and even by attorneys. This list covers the entire state and is referenced alphabetically by owner's name. To find out whether your debtor has any property in a state, call a local title company. Determine whether the title company has a state list of property owners and what it charges to search a property. A debtor often owns property in different parts of the state in which he resides or does business. Information from the state lists is useful to locate both debtors and their assets.

VOTER REGISTRATION LISTS

If your debtor is a registered voter, voter registration lists will provide his name, address, telephone number, and date of birth. They will also tell you the debtor's political party affiliation, if any, and date of registration. If your debtor is not a registered voter, you may find the names and phone numbers of relatives with the same last name as the debtor. Voter registration lists are usually available at city hall. If not, contact local offices of one of the political parties or the League of Women Voters to find out where the lists are kept.

POST OFFICE

The easiest, least expensive, and *best* way to locate debtors is via the Freedom of Information Act. If a debtor has moved, any information provided to the post office on the debtor's change-of-address form is available to you under the Act. In most cases, you can get the information over the phone. In some cases, you may be required to document a legal proceeding or indicate an index number.

Note: In some situations, it is advisable to speak with the postal courier regarding your nonresponsive customer. Generally, the person who delivers the mail knows something about your subject, information that can be valuable. Simply inquire with your debtor's post office and ascertain the name and best time to speak to the mail carrier.

SKIP TRACING AND COMMUNICATION

Establishing communication with your nonpaying customer is an essential prerequisite. The following are two resources that can increase your chances of success.

FREEDOM OF INFORMATION ACT

At one time the U.S. Post Office was required to voluntarily reveal information relevant to its files, including change of address, box holder's street address, and so on; however, today the information seeker must either have filed a lawsuit or is contemplating suit to compel the U.S. Post Office to release information.

The request for change of address of a boxholder or addressee can be obtained by using the form in Exhibit 8.6. Information seekers should provide a self-addressed, stamped envelope.

DEPARTMENT OF MOTOR VEHICLES

The Department of Motor Vehicles is another good source of tracking information. Not only can you determine your debtor's current address, but you can also verify an asset and even get a physical description of the debtor. Many states provide information about operators' insurance coverage, which can be a gold mine in terms of tracking debtors and their assets. Let us look at some conventional ways of tracking information. Then we will explore some lesser-known methods that can provide better information for locating debtors and/or their assets.

EXHIBIT 8.6   REQUEST FOR CHANGE OF ADDRESS OR BOXHOLDER FORM

Postmaster   Date:_____

_____
City, State, Zip Code

Request for Change of Address or Boxholder
Information Needed for Service of Legal Process

Please furnish the new address or the name and street address (if a boxholder) for the following:

NAME: _____

ADDRESS:_____
Note: The name and last known address are required for change of address information.
The name, if known, and post office box address are required for boxholder information.

The following information is provided in accordance with 39 CFR 265.6(D)(6)(11). There is no fee for providing boxholder information. The fee for providing change of address information is waived in accordance with 39 CFR 265.6(d)(1) and (2) and corresponding Administrative Support Manual 352.44a and b.

1. Capacity of requester (e.g., process server, attorney, party representing himself):_____

2. The names of all known parties to the litigation:_____

3. The court in which the case has been or will be heard:_____

4. The docket or other identifying number if one has been issued:_____

5. The capacity in which the individual is to be served *(e.g. defendant or witness)*:_____

WARNING

THE SUBMISSION OF FALSE INFORMATION EITHER (1) TO OBTAIN AND USE CHANGE OF ADDRESS INFORMATION OR BOXHOLDER INFORMATION FOR ANY PURPOSE OTHER THAN THE SERVICE OF LEGAL PROCESS IN CONNECTION WITH ACTUAL OR PROSPECTIVE LITIGATION OR (2) TO AVOID PAYMENT OF THE FEE FOR CHANGE OF ADDRESS INFORMATION COULD RESULT IN CRIMINAL PENALTIES INCLUDING A FINE UP TO $10,000 OR IMPRISONMENT OF NOT MORE THAN 5 YEARS, OR BOTH (TITLE 18 U.S.C. SECTION 1001).

I certify that the above information is true and that the address information is needed and will be used solely for service of legal process in connection with actual or prospective litigation.

_____   _____
Signature   *Address*

_____   _____
Printed Name   *City, State, Zip Code*

FOR POST OFFICE USE ONLY
                                                            Postmark
☐ No change of address order on file.   NEW ADDRESS or BOXHOLDER NAME
☐ Not known at address given.   and STREET ADDRESS
☐ Moved, left no forwarding address.   _____
☐ No such address.   _____
                                         _____

Information from the Department of Motor Vehicles (DMV) can be broken down into two primary categories:

1. Vehicle registrations
2. Driver's licenses

Driver's licenses are generally cross-referenced by name, date of birth, and street address. Registered vehicles are referenced by plate numbers and owners' names. Disadvantages?

Conventional searches are time-consuming and expensive. Also, the law generally limits disclosures to basic information. The most comprehensive information, which is exchanged through reciprocal agreements between the states, is usually not available through conventional sources. To tap motor vehicle records, you can file an information request directly with the state DMV, usually at a cost of $2 to $3 per request, or you can use a search firm, or information broker, which will do the research on a fee basis. Intelligent-e-Commerce, Inc. (c/o infosearch.com, P.O. Box 12382, La Jolla, CA 92039, (858) 587-8259) is one company that provides search and retrieval services for law firms and financial institutions. The company also has offices in most state capital cities.

Note: National profiles also contain motor vehicle/driver ID information.

Conventional DMV Searches

To initiate a conventional motor vehicle records search, you file a "request for information" and pay a fee, usually $2 or $3. For example, if you wanted information from the state of California, you would get a Registration Record Request from the DMV. The form requires the person making the request to provide information about himself, to give the specific reason for the request, and to explain what the information will be used for. To enable the DMV to search its records, you must also provide the vehicle owner's date of birth, the plate or identification number of the vehicle, or the owner's first and last names. In some states DMV information is cross-referenced by street addresses or even Social Security numbers.

Submit the filled-out request form to the appropriate DMV office. In a few weeks, you will get a printout with information on the vehicle or other registered owners.

B 3P SMITH JOHN

A681

C211

DATE: 07/19/02 TIME: 09:50

MATCHED ON ⋆L/N⋆F/N⋆ Z

NAME: SMITH JOHN ADD: 166 CITY: SUNNYVALE VR# 1HAL1 FC:L YR: 95 MK: BMW

NAME: SMITH JOHN ADD: 166 CITY: SUNNYVALE VR# 469RNE FC:A YR: 96 MK: FORD

ANI END

Once you have a plate number, the same procedure will get you more detailed information, including the owner's address and ownership status of the vehicle. This will tell you whether the debtor is the legal owner, as well as the registered owner, and whether there are any liens or loans against the vehicle. Such information is important because a vehicle can hardly be considered an asset if your debtor is not the legal owner. You should check to make sure your debtor has enough equity in the vehicle, after outstanding encumbrances are satisfied, to make the vehicle an asset worth levying against.

The Internet has provided a wealth of instant access information. Check with a service provider.

Alternative, Sometimes Questionable, Tactics

Scenario 1: Assume that your car is parked in a busy shopping center. While you are doing your grocery shopping, somebody sideswipes your automobile. The person who hit your car drives off, but fortunately a witness to the accident took down the license plate number and left a note on your windshield. What do you do? Typically, you would report the matter to the police. Of course, the police can access motor vehicle information instantly and locate the vehicle that caused the damage, whereupon you could swear out a warrant for the arrest of the hit-and-run driver.

Scenario 2: Now suppose that the most beautiful, gorgeous, sensuous person you have ever laid eyes on pulls up alongside you on a major thoroughfare. There is a certain magic in the air as your eyes meet for an instant. You are just about to speak when the light turns green. The person of your dreams floors the accelerator and leaves you in the dust. What if you wanted to meet that gorgeous person? What would you do? Certainly the police department would not be a viable source because no crime was committed. You are left with two alternatives. You can proceed via the conventional route by contacting the motor vehicle department, getting a registration record request, filling out the form, paying your fee, and waiting for a response (or accessing information online). This process will cost you a few dollars and could take several weeks, but eventually you will find the registered owner of the vehicle.

Carry this scenario one step further. Suppose the information was needed not because a crime had been committed or to communicate with the man or woman of your dreams, but to locate a debtor. Your interest is not romance, but money. I have known collectors who, using various degrees of creativity, could trace a motor vehicle operator's address within a matter of seconds. One technique is to simply call the DMV. Identify yourself as a legitimate business and tell the clerk that there is an unknown car on your premises and that you want to get in touch with the owner because the vehicle is blocking your driveway. If you sound convincing enough, the clerk might plug the plate number into the computer and give you the information, or the clerk might refer you to the local police department. It all depends on how convincing you are. This innocuous approach may be a little deceptive, but it will work most of the time, and you do have a perfectly legitimate right to know your debtor's address.

Some collectors will stretch this technique into territory that definitely violates the law by representing themselves to the motor vehicle department as government officials, stating that they have suspicious cars on the premises and wish to contact the legal owners. This, of course, is somewhat risky. Impersonation of government officials carries strong consequences. Incidentally, the DMV is not the only source of motor vehicle registration and licensing information. Police departments, the FBI, sheriff's departments, and other agencies also access DMV information because they are all connected by one computer network.

Driver's License Identification

You can also use the DMV to determine whether an individual is a licensed driver in that particular state and to get that individual's current address. The procedure for tracking individuals is similar to the aforementioned procedure for tracking plate numbers; that is, you can request information by filling out forms and paying a fee, or you can be creative and try to get the DMV to release information on the strength of a telephone call. But, again, some information-gathering methods are illegal. For example, some innovative collectors calling the DMV of a particular state represent themselves as officials of another state's DMV and say they are "just checking" the driving record of a particular individual. Sometimes a DMV will divulge information to an insurance company over the telephone, particularly if an automobile has been involved in an accident. An unscrupulous tracer might call, say, the Nevada Department of Motor Vehicles and represent himself as a representative of one of the big insurance companies. The collector would explain that he is trying to locate Mr. Accident-Prone Deadbeat because the company is a defendant in a serious lawsuit over an accident involving that person. The collector would then ask the clerk for the individual's last known address. Note that all states operate differently. Most reference driver's licenses by date of birth and the last seven digits of a person's last name.

Assume you successfully secure a debtor's last known address from the DMV only to learn that the debtor has fled and the address is no longer valid. In that case, contact the debtor's insurance carrier for information because it is possible that the debtor notified the insurance company of his change of address. Of course, to use this technique, you must make absolutely certain to ask the motor vehicle department for the name and address of the debtor's insurance company and the policy number.

Con of the Century

What follows is a true story of one of the most outrageous cons in the annals of accounts receivable recovery. Mark Hall, a virtuoso skip tracer, had exhausted all conventional sources in his efforts to locate a particular debtor. He learned that the debtor had moved out of state, but he did not know to which state the debtor had moved. Finally, Hall turned to the DMV. The debtor's prior address was in New York, and Hall knew that New York (like many other states) exchanged normally inaccessible information on a limited basis. Hall called the New York DMV, and the conversation went something like this:

Hall: "This is the Bergen County Coroner's Office. We just had a terrible accident on Route 46. The deceased is a white Caucasian male, 46 years old, five foot eleven inches, 170 pounds. He had in his possession an American Red Cross card indicating that his name was William Pastdue, last known address, 711 Deadbeat Street, Anytown, New York. There's a notation on the driver's license that upon his death the deceased wishes to make an anatomical gift of organs or parts for transplantation.

"The state police dispatched an officer to the last known address, but Mr. Pastdue no longer lives there. It is imperative that we remove the organs from the deceased for transplantation within the next hour and notify the next of kin. Can you run Mr. Pastdue's name through your computer and see whether you can come up with a current address? Maybe another state contacted your office to request Mr. Pastdue's driving record."

DMV clerk: "Spell the individual's last name and give me a date of birth if you have it."

Hall: "The deceased had only a New York state driver's license and wasn't carrying any other identification with a date of birth."

DMV clerk: "Well, it's going to be difficult with this limited information, but I'll see what I can do." (The clerk enters the name of the "deceased" into the computer.) Some minutes later . . .

DMV clerk: "We checked the information you provided and found that the deceased applied for a driver's license in the state of Michigan. He is no longer on file as an operator with a valid driver's license in the state of New York."

This is all Hall needed to know. He proceeded to call the Michigan DMV and fed a clerk there the same or a similar ruse. The clerk revealed the debtor's address. Of course, this whole process is highly illegal, but most times a motor vehicle department will not question a call from a coroner's office, especially if there seems to be an urgent need to notify next of kin or remove organs or body parts.

Caution: The preceding illustration is not intended to encourage readers to embark upon such an illicit campaign to develop information. It is included here for information purposes only, to show that almost any information in government files can be accessed by almost anyone. The reason this con works so well is because it puts the computer operator on the hot seat and does not give him or her time to question the caller's legitimacy.

Nonresident Violators Compact

According to the *I.D. Checking Guide* published by the Drivers License Guide Company (Redwood City, California), most states have joined in the Non-Resident Violators Compact (NRVC) to exchange information about motorists who have committed moving violations and failed to answer summonses.

This network of motor vehicle jurisdictions can be a valuable source of information in tracking debtors, especially if a debtor has failed to answer a summons regarding a moving traffic violation, even if that violation has been satisfied. This information is logged into the computer, since, for example, Kentucky would like to know about moving violations committed by a Rhode Island driver should that person ever apply for a driver's license in Kentucky. The computer network that makes up the NRVC could provide useful information to collectors, including debtors' whereabouts. I know of several instances where collectors, upon finding out that certain debtors were guilty of moving violations and that warrants were outstanding, confronted the debtors with that information to bring the debtors to the table. In one instance, there were four warrants out against a debtor from New Jersey who failed to answer summonses for moving violations. The DMV did not have a valid address, but the collector did find the address. The collector confronted the debtor, giving the warrant numbers, the dates of the violations, and the information about possible penalties, and told the debtor that if he did not pay up, the collector's next call was going to the sheriff. A harsh remedy, yes, but collectors have been known to resort to extortion-like remedies.

COURT RECORDS

In many instances, your debtor may have been involved in litigation. Whether the debtor was the defendant or the plaintiff in legal proceedings, court records are available for public inspection. They can be a fertile source of information and even serve as leverage to collect a debt. It is important for you to know the status of previous or pending legal proceedings.

Court records reveal the name of your debtor's attorney. You can then enlist that attorney's help in locating the debtor. The debtor's attorney has had previous experience with the debtor and may have information that would be valuable to you.

Real-life application: One collector learned that a debtor who had intentionally absconded was involved in divorce proceedings. The debtor concealed his whereabouts, not because of the debts he owed, but because his ex-wife had a substantial judgment against him. The potential damage and monetary loss from the judgment in favor of his ex-wife were more detrimental than all the debts owed to other creditors. The collector, armed with this information, communicated directly with the debtor. The collector told the debtor that he could buy the collector's silence if he paid the debt. In that case, the debtor was glad to pay the $6,500 he owed. That was a small price to pay as compared with what his ex-wife would do to him.

Be alert for similar opportunities. They will come up—if you do your homework. A debtor's vulnerability represents leverage.

Review Legal Records

Legal records of proceedings in federal, state, and county courts are available from the courts or via a search firm. Most court documents are preserved on microfiche that are easy to find and use. Just look under the alphabetical listings of both defendants and plaintiffs by year (or by month for most recent cases). A search through the alphabetical listings will determine whether the debtor has been involved in litigation. Armed with that information, you can further research court records to learn the specifics of each case.

Mercantile information brokers and credit-reporting agencies provide a centralized source for public records on bankruptcy and tax liens that can be used to supplement a creditor's own research. (*Statewide Information Systems* is one such source serving credit reporting agencies. Consult your local phone directory under "Public Record Search Firms.")

Research resources: Call your state judicial department and find out how to get a *Judicial Department Directory.* This resource will help narrow your inquiries to state or municipal courts in your debtor's area where proceedings most likely would be brought by or against the debtor. A *United States Court Directory* is available from the Superintendent of Documents, U.S. Government Printing Office, Washington, DC 20402.

Opposing Litigation

If you find that your debtor is involved in litigation, you might consider joining forces with the creditors involved in the suit(s). Sometimes by concerted action, you create opportunities that might not otherwise be available. For example, creditors acting together may be able to achieve the following:

- Force the debtor into involuntary bankruptcy.
- Initiate equitable remedies, including injunctions or show-cause orders.
- Develop criteria for summary judgment or attachment.

Of course, you will have to consult with your attorney to initiate any such actions.

Involuntary petitions: Action to force a debtor into involuntary bankruptcy generally requires a minimum of three petitioners whose unsecured claims meet statutory requirements. A single creditor may be allowed to force a debtor into bankruptcy if it was a victim of fraud, trick, artifice, or scam, or if the creditor would otherwise be without adequate remedy under state or federal law.

UTILITY COMPANIES

Water companies and other utilities are also excellent sources of information. If you have not been able to locate a debtor's current mailing address through conventional sources, there is a good chance you can get it from a utility company. In some cases, debtors who are about to make a move pay their electric bills, believing that a reference from the electric company will induce utilities at their new location to waive deposit requirements—as the phone company will often do if accounts with previous service providers are current.

To learn your debtor's current mailing address, call the customer service department at the local utility and be creative. If the debtor has moved to another state, there is a good chance that the debtor used the utility as a reference. If the utility was asked to provide account data in a reference check, it might have records that will show the new address.

Statistics show that debtors are more likely to pay their phone and credit card bills than their utility bills, but utilities can also be useful. Also, where legally permissible, obtain a consumer credit report on your debtor. The payment history is not only a valuable source of information, but also a skip-tracing/asset search tool.

IS YOUR DEBTOR A LICENSED BUSINESS?

The odds are good that you will be able to find commercial debtors because businesses generally must be licensed by the state, city, and/or county in which they operate. These licensing agencies are a viable information source. In addition, commissioning a national profile report on your debtor will usually indicate some but not all licensing.

State Licensing Agencies

Licensing requirements for businesses vary widely from state to state. In some states wholesalers, retailers, and manufacturers may be required to have licenses issued by the state department of revenue services or the state tax commission. Service companies, including plumbers, electricians, contractors, and others, may be required to register with or obtain licenses from the consumer protection department or other state agencies. In other states, such licenses are issued only on a local level—every county and city may maintain a licensing authority that licenses certain types of businesses. At any rate, it is generally worthwhile to track down the state or local department or agency that licenses your debtor's industry because it will usually have valuable information, including your debtor's most recent address.

County Clerk's Office

In many states, businesses that are operating as sole proprietorships must file certificates in the county where they do business. The names and addresses of these businesses and their owners are on file with the office of the county clerk. Even if your debtor is doing business under a fictitious name, you might be able to find it by searching the owners' names.

SECRETARY OF STATE

The secretary of state is another source of information. This state office maintains information regarding corporations and the responsible principals of those corporations. The secretary of state will usually possess the most recent annual reports, authorizations to do business, and other pertinent documents. Often you can discover the number of shares issued, the number of stockholders, and the addresses of responsible principals. The secretary of state will even act as an agent to serve writs, summonses, and legal processes on the corporation.

Normally, if you were to retain a search firm to retrieve this information, you would pay a fee; however, a law firm can call the office of the secretary of state to verify a trade name at no charge because it is not possible to incorporate a business if the business name is already taken. To get this free information, call the office of the secretary of state. Say that you are with the firm of McLaughlin, Kelly & O'Reilly (or whatever). This implies that you are a law or accounting firm, but do not *state* that you are. Tell the clerk that you need information to verify formation of a "new" corporation. The clerk will enter the corporate name into the computer and relay all the information. Of course, you do not really want to know whether the name is already taken. Your objective is to access the system. Once the clerk has the corporate file at hand, you can ask for such information as:

- How long has the corporation been in business?
- Who are the responsible principals, and what are their addresses?
- Is there any litigation or are there any judgments pending against the entity?
- When was the last time it filed an annual report?
- Who is the principal stockholder?

Remember, this office will reveal this information free only because attorneys need to know before incorporation papers are filed to avoid a name duplication. Use a name that *sounds* like a law firm, but do not represent yourself as a law firm (unless, of course, you are a law firm). The office of the secretary of state may get the impression that you are a law firm, but that is no crime. (Check the blue pages of the local telephone directory for the phone number of the secretary of state or refer to their Web site.)

Many offices of secretaries of state have become automated. It is now possible to order every conceivable report simply by responding to numerical queues and/or voice prompts. Many states also have Web sites. Payment is via credit card.

REVENUE SERVICES

Businesses may be required to report sales tax revenues or have other tax liabilities to the state. They might also owe local property taxes. Often if you cannot get the debtor's current address from the collecting agencies (local tax collector, or state tax commission or department of revenue services), you can find the name of the accountant who files the tax returns. The accountant might divulge the whereabouts of your debtor. Also find out whether your debtor is making required tax payments. If not, ascertain how far the debtor is in arrears. If your debtor has not met state or local tax obligations, there is a good chance you will not be paid either.

SECURITIES AND EXCHANGE COMMISSION

If your debtor's business offers stock or other securities for sale to the general public, the securities must be registered with the SEC. This information then becomes a matter of public record and is open for inspection.

Smaller publicly held corporations might be registered under a "Regulation A" filing. Check with the SEC or a stockbroker to verify whether your debtor has in fact "gone public."

Other Items to be Checked

Other areas that the collector should investigate are as follows:

- *Assumed name record and corporate charters.* In looking up the names, addresses, and dates on file with the state or county, you or the specialist you have employed may find additional local and/or out-of-town business interests.

- *Miscellaneous personal records (MPR).* Many counties retain copies of professional certification records, notary bonds, and military discharge forms.

In many cases, the county courthouse is the repository of all records pertaining to property, local taxes, lawsuits, and professional certification.

Also, in most cases, you will find the assumed name and MPR records in the county courthouse.

Trade Associations and Unions

If your debtor is affiliated with a labor union, call the local office and ask the union to help you locate the debtor. Many different occupations are unionized, including airline pilots, clothing and textile workers, printers, transit workers, truck drivers, government employees, teachers, postal workers, bakers, painters, carpenters, longshoremen, department store employees, hospital workers, hotel and restaurant employees and bartenders, machinists, laundry workers, plumbers, printers, retail clerks, and transport workers. If you know your debtor's occupation, and you know that occupation is unionized, take a chance and call the local union. Check the Yellow Pages of your phone book under "Labor Organizations."

Similarly, commercial debtors may belong to industry groups or trade associations. Such groups could provide valuable information about the debtor or its assets. Your local library will have the *Encyclopedia of Associations;* to find local business groups, simply check the Yellow Pages under "Associations."

The Military

For consumer debt obligations, if your debtor is in the military, you can locate the appropriate branch as follows:

- *Army.* Write to Commander, U.S. Army Enlisted Records & Evaluation Center, Attn: Locator, Ft. Benjamin Harrison, IN 46249-5301.

- *Marines.* Write to Commandant of the Marine Corps, Headquarters, USMC, Code MMSB-10, Quantico, VA 22134-5030; or call Marines Locator Service at (703) 784-3942.

- *Navy.* Write to Navy Worldwide Locator, Navy Personnel Command, PERS 312F, 5720 Integrity Drive, Millington, TN 38055-3120; or call (877) 414-5359. The fee for researching an address is $3.50 per address made payable by check or money order to the U.S. Treasurer.

- *Air Force.* Write (include the person's Social Security number) to HQ AFMPC/ RMIQL, 550C Street, West, Suite 50, Randolph AFB, TX 78150-4752; or call (210) 652-5774 or (210) 652-5775.

Credit Bureaus

There are many consumer credit bureaus and mercantile agencies throughout the United States.

A debtor's credit report will include most major credit accounts, a profile of the debtor's payment history, public record information (e.g., judgments, tax liens, bankruptcy), and personal information, including employment verification, income, home ownership, and so on. Armed with this knowledge, you can develop a targeted collection technique.

How to Use Credit Reports

The credit profile is often overlooked as a valuable source to develop information or to locate assets and/or skips. Dun & Bradstreet used to pretty much corner the market in the commercial sector; however, TRW (Experian) is an industry leader. (See Exhibit 8.7.) Commercial reports generally provide basic information creditors need to make credit decisions. Because of space limitations, legal sanctions imposed against a commercial entity (i.e., a corporation, partnership, or even a sole proprietorship) may not always show up on a commercial report. For this reason, it is always advisable to initiate a public records search, more particularly a search for pending litigation, outstanding judgments, and tax liens that may not be reported in the commercial report. Conversely, consumer credit reports can take you directly to attachable assets, help you locate hard-core skips, and provide a storehouse of other valuable information.

Assume that you are trying to collect a consumer debt. The debtor has skipped town, and you have been unable to secure a forwarding address. Because the debtor did not have his mail forwarded, there would not be much point in requesting information from the debtor's local post office pursuant to the Freedom of Information Act. Postal regulations now require a pending or contemplated civil case to release information. Assume you have also done a motor vehicle search only to come up with the same address you already have on file. You have struck out both times at bat. Do you give up? Let us see where the credit report can be a viable tool. But first, let us analyze the sources of available information. Whereas Dun & Bradstreet is the first name in commercial credit information, TRW is number one in the consumer area. TransUnion and Equifax run a close second. Beyond those three giants, there is a string of smaller credit reporting agencies. Generally, a debtor can be found in the memory banks of one or more of these agencies.

How to Access Your Debtor's Credit Profile

Information from most credit reporting agencies is accessed by:

- *Social Security number.* Most credit records are accessed through the debtor's Social Security number, so it is always a good idea to secure the number on your credit application and employer tax identification number. (See Exhibit 8.8.)

- *Date of birth.* If you do not have the debtor's date of birth, you can usually get it from the state department of motor vehicles. (See "Department of Motor Vehicles" in this chapter.)

- *Residence.* Credit bureau information also can be accessed by the debtor's last known address.

EXHIBIT 8.7   SAMPLE EXPERIAN CREDIT REPORT

Consumer credit report sample

THIS IS YOUR CONSUMER
IDENTIFICATION NUMBER. PLEASE
REFER TO THIS NUMBER WHEN   **ID# 1234567890**
YOU CALL OR WRITE US.

JONATHON QUINCY CONSUMER
12345 WEST MAINE STREET
BURBANK, CA 90210

HOW TO READ THIS REPORT:

EXPERIAN IS THE INDEPENDENT COMPANY FORMED FROM TRW'S INFORMATION SERVICES BUSINESSES.

AN EXPLANATORY ENCLOSURE ACCOMPANIES THIS REPORT. IT DESCRIBES YOUR CREDIT RIGHTS AND OTHER HELPFUL INFORMATION. IF THE ENCLOSURE IS MISSING, OR YOU HAVE QUESTIONS ABOUT THIS REPORT, PLEASE CONTACT THE OFFICE LISTED ON THE LAST PAGE.

AS PART OF OUR FRAUD-PREVENTION PROGRAM, ACCOUNT NUMBERS MAY NOT FULLY DISPLAY ON THIS REPORT.

YOUR CREDIT HISTORY:

THIS INFORMATION COMES FROM PUBLIC RECORDS OR FROM ORGANIZATIONS THAT HAVE GRANTED CREDIT TO YOU. AN ASTERISK BY AN ACCOUNT INDICATES THAT THIS ITEM MAY REQUIRE FURTHER REVIEW BY A PROSPECTIVE CREDITOR WHEN CHECKING YOUR CREDIT HISTORY. IF YOU BELIEVE ANY OF THE INFORMATION IS INCORRECT, PLEASE LET US KNOW. FOR YOUR CONVENIENCE, INSTRUCTIONS FOR REINVESTIGATION ARE INCLUDED ON THE LAST PAGE OF THIS REPORT.

EXPERIAN INCLUDES THE FOLLOWING STATEMENT IN ALL REPORTS OF YOUR CREDIT HISTORY.

MY IDENTIFICATION HAS BEEN USED WITHOUT MY PERMISSION ON APPLICATIONS TO OBTAIN CREDIT. VERBAL CONFIRMATION FROM ME AT 805-969-9601 OR 123-456-7890 IS REQUESTED PRIOR TO CREDIT APPROVAL.

EXHIBIT 8.7   SAMPLE EXPERIAN CREDIT REPORT (CONT'D.)

ACCOUNT	DESCRIPTION
1 *US BKPT CT MD 101 W LOMBART ST. BALTIMORE MD 21002 DOCKET # 08511002	VOLUNTARY BANKRUPTCY CHAPTER 13 DISCHARGED ON 05/23/02. PETITION ON 06/01/00. RECORDED ASSETS: $100,000, LIABILITIES: $8,000. YOU ARE SOLELY RESPONSIBLE FOR THIS PUBLIC RECORD ITEM.
2 * HOPKINS COUNTY COURT MADISON CNTY CT HOUSE MADISONVILLE KY 42111 DOCKET # 2005355267 BK PG SEQ # 1386520381	SMALL CLAIMS JUDGMENT SATISFIED ON 02/23/02. ORIGINAL FILING DATE 06/08/01. AMOUNT: $4,100. PLAINTIFF: WILSON AND MCPHERSON. YOU HAVE JOINT RESPONSIBILITY FOR THIS PUBLIC RECORD ITEM.
3 * LEE CO CIVIL COURT P O BOX 408 FT MYERS FL 33403 CERTIFICATE # 211412123 BK PG SEQ #	COUNTY TAX LIEN ON 05/19/01. AMOUNT: $2,000. YOU ARE SOLELY RESPONSIBLE FOR THIS PUBLIC RECORD ITEM.
4 * WELLS FARGO BANK P O BOX 2096 CONCORD CA 94520 BANKING ACCT # 200543445667XXXX	THIS CREDIT CARD ACCOUNT WAS OPENED 02/05/91 AND HAS REVOLVING REPAYMENT TERMS. YOU HAVE CONTRACTUAL RESPONSIBILITY FOR THIS ACCOUNT AND ARE PRIMARILY RESPONSIBLE FOR ITS PAYMENT. CREDIT LIMIT: $5,000.

AS OF 02/22/94, THIS CLOSED ACCOUNT WAS CURRENT AND ALL PAYMENTS WERE
MADE ON TIME. BALANCE: $0 ON 04/30/94. MONTHS REVIEWED = 59.
*** ACCOUNT CLOSED-CONSUMER'S REQUEST-REPORTED BY SUBSCRIBER.

5 * CHEMICAL BANK 300 JERICO QUADRANG JERICO NY 11753 BANKING ACCT # 456920095206XXXX	THIS CREDIT CARD ACCOUNT WAS OPENED 05/04/79 AND HAS REVOLVING REPAYMENT TERMS. YOU HAVE CONTRACTUAL RESPONSIBILITY FOR THIS ACCOUNT AND ARE PRIMARILY RESPONSIBLE FOR ITS PAYMENT. CREDIT LIMIT: $3,500, HIGH BALANCE: $2,512.

AS OF 01/15/03, THIS OPEN ACCOUNT IS 120 DAYS 2+ TIMES PAST DUE. BALANCE: $1,695
ON 12/15/95. SCHEDULED MONTHLY PAYMENT IS $73. MONTHS REVIEWED = 99.

PAYMENT   44332211CCCCC CCC-CCCCCCCC 999999999999   999999999666
HISTORY: 5443221111CC   CCCCCCCCCCCC CCCCCCCCCCCC

NUMBER OF TIMES LATE: 30 DAYS = 6, 60 DAYS = 4, 90+ DAYS = 11, DEROG = 21.

EXHIBIT 8.7   SAMPLE EXPERIAN CREDIT REPORT (CONT'D.)

YOUR CREDIT HISTORY WAS REVIEWED BY:

THE FOLLOWING INQUIRIES ARE REPORTED TO THOSE WHO ASK TO REVIEW YOUR CREDIT HISTORY.

	INQUIRY	DESCRIPTION
6	CELLULAR ONE 651 GATEWAY PL. SAN FRANCISCO CA 94082 UTILITIES	07/14/02 INQUIRY MADE FOR CREDIT EXTENSION, REVIEW OR OTHER PERMISSIBLE PURPOSE.
7	METROPOLITAN NATL BK 406 8TH STREET OAKLAND CA 94206 FINANCE	09/29/01 INQUIRY MADE FOR REAL ESTATE LOAN FOR 30 YEARS REPAYMENT TERMS. THE AMOUNT IS $200,000. THIS INQUIRY WAS MADE ON BEHALF OF ABC MORTGAGE.

THE FOLLOWING INQUIRIES ARE **NOT** REPORTED TO THOSE WHO ASK TO REVIEW YOUR CREDIT HISTORY. THEY ARE INCLUDED SO YOU HAVE A COMPLETE LIST OF INQUIRIES.

	INQUIRY	DESCRIPTION
8	EXPERIAN P O BOX 2103 ALLEN TX 75013 UNDEFINED FIRM TYPE #9877333456789023	01/11/03 INQUIRY MADE FOR CONSUMER DISCLOSURE OF YOUR CREDIT HISTORY.

PLEASE HELP US HELP YOU:

AT EXPERIAN WE KNOW HOW IMPORTANT YOUR GOOD CREDIT IS TO YOU. IT'S EQUALLY IMPORTANT TO US THAT OUR INFORMATION BE ACCURATE AND UP TO DATE. LISTED BELOW IS THE INFORMATION YOU GAVE US WHEN YOU ASKED FOR THIS REPORT. IF THIS INFORMATION IS NOT CORRECT, OR YOU DID NOT SUPPLY US WITH YOUR FULL NAME, ADDRESS FOR THE PAST FIVE YEARS, SOCIAL SECURITY NUMBER AND YEAR OF BIRTH, THIS REPORT MAY NOT BE COMPLETE. IF THIS INFORMATION IS INCOMPLETE OR NOT ACCURATE, PLEASE LET US KNOW.

YOUR NAME:	JONATHON QUINCY CONSUMER	SOCIAL SECURITY #:	123456789
ADDRESS:	12345 WEST MAINE STREET BURBANK, CA 90210	YEAR OF BIRTH:	1951
OTHER ADDRESSES:	55 OLD CREEK ROAD LITTLETON, NH 03303	SPOUSE:	SUSAN

IDENTIFICATION INFORMATION:

THE FOLLOWING ADDITIONAL INFORMATION HAS BEEN PROVIDED TO US BY

EXHIBIT 8.7   SAMPLE EXPERIAN CREDIT REPORT (CONT'D.)

ORGANIZATIONS THAT REPORT INFORMATION TO US.

Social Security #:	123656789	REPORTED 3 TIMES
	123456789	REPORTED 6 TIMES
Addresses:	1314 SOPHIA LANE SANTA ANA CA 92708	GEOGRAPHICAL CODE=123-4632-7

THIS SINGLE-FAMILY DWELLING ADDRESS WAS FIRST REPORTED 11-93 AND LAST REPORTED 12-95 BY UPDATE. LAST REPORTED BY CHEMICAL BANK. ADDRESS REPORTED 11 TIMES.

Employers: AJAX HARDWARE
              LOS ANGELES CA 90019

FIRST REPORTED 6-94 AND LAST REPORTED 6-95 BY INQUIRY. LAST REPORTED BY METROPOLITAN NATL BK.

Other:	Year of Birth:	1961
	Name:	CONSUMER, JONATHAN CONSUMER, JON Q
	Spouse:	PATRICIA

FROM 02/01/01 THE NUMBER OF INQUIRIES WITH THIS SOCIAL SECURITY # =5

FACS+ TRANSPORTATION SERVICE ON FACS+ FILE/LUX TRANS/10655 N BIRCH ST/BURBANK CA 91502

SOCIAL SECURITY NUMBER YOU GAVE WAS ISSUED: 1950-1953

* * * END OF THE REPORT * * *

Information for collection: It is common knowledge that credit reports are useful to determine a debtor's creditworthiness before a transaction is consummated; however, credit reports are often overlooked as a source of information in the recovery stages. Do you have a right to access the debtor's consumer credit report? Yes. The Federal Fair Credit Reporting Act specifically provides that a consumer report may be furnished to a party that intends to use the information in connection with collection of an account, provided that the debt is consumer originated.

Normally, a credit report will show most common credit transactions, including Visa, MasterCard, oil company credit cards, department store accounts, loans, and the like. The reports will show when the accounts were opened, credit balances, and mortgage payment profiles. Usually, creditors will also list their phone numbers, sometimes even unlisted ones.

Cautionary note: Many small vendors and some major, prestigious credit cards do not report into the credit–reporting database. Credit reports will not show any information on these creditors that do not report into the system. Countless times, hard–core debtors who do not pay most of their obligations take pains to maintain satisfactory credit relationships

EXHIBIT 8.8   SOCIAL SECURITY NUMBERS BY STATE

The following list indicates in which states a Social Security number was assigned. By looking at the first three digits of the number, you will have another clue that may lead to the location information.

001–003	New Hampshire		425–428	Mississippi
004–007	Maine		429–432	Arkansas
008–009	Vermont		433–439	Louisiana
010–034	Massachusetts		440–448	Oklahoma
035–039	Rhode Island		449–467	Texas
040–049	Connecticut		468–477	Minnesota
050–134	New York		478–485	Iowa
135–158	New Jersey		486–500	Missouri
159–211	Pennsylvania		501–502	North Dakota
212–220	Maryland		503–504	South Dakota
221–222	Delaware		505–508	Nebraska
223–231	Virginia		509–515	Kansas
232–236	West Virginia		516–517	Montana
237–246	North Carolina		518–519	Idaho
247–251	South Carolina		520	Wyoming
252–260	Georgia		521–524	Colorado
261–267	Florida		525	New Mexico
268–302	Ohio		526–527	Arizona
303–317	Indiana		528–529	Utah
318–361	Illinois		530	Nevada
362–386	Michigan		531–539	Washington
387–399	Wisconsin		540–544	Oregon
400–407	Kentucky		545–573	California
408–415	Tennessee		577–579	Dist. of Columbia
416–424	Alabama		700	Railroad Employee

with certain creditors, making regular payments on loans or credit cards, or perhaps even keeping current with discretionary creditors.

Address/Asset Location

Assume that your debtor maintains an oil company credit card, a department store charge card, and revolving credit with MasterCard or Visa. Simply call these credit grantors. Tell them that you are a creditor, and exchange information on the account. Almost every credit grantor who inputs into the system will share such basic knowledge as when the account was opened, average balance, and payment trends. But beyond that information, which is already listed on the credit report, you can ask the creditor for a forwarding address, telephone number, and place of employment.

Tip: In some instances, creditors will not divulge information per their customer's accounts. Shrewd collectors circumnavigate these situations by impersonating the customer's identity. The application of creativity will almost always yield relevant data.

Elements of defamation: If the debtor is a skip and has not paid his creditors, you might convey vital information in an exchange. Is this legal? Again, as a collector or creditor, you certainly have a legal right to exchange information on the account, but do not be tempted to make potentially libelous (written) or slanderous (spoken) statements about the debtor. A false statement of fact, negligently made to a third person, which causes damage to the debtor, could make you or your company liable for defamation: In libel law a court will *presume* at least some damages from false statements of fact to third parties. That is not to say you should not talk to other collectors or creditors, but be careful what you say, and limit your words to factual statements about the debtor.

There have been many instances when hard-core debtors, shielded by unlisted telephone numbers and transient places of employment, have been located solely through information provided by credit reports. Valuable information, including unlisted telephone numbers and vital employment data, can be secured from this minimal investment. The credit report is the consumer collector's most valuable tool to locate and track information. This is especially true when a debt has escalated to the litigation phase and an income execution must be levied upon the employer, which will act as garnishee.

For example, suppose you have a money judgment, but you cannot locate the debtor, who has changed his residence and place of employment. If the debtor values select creditors (such as MasterCard, Visa, etc.), the debtor might very well provide that creditor with his new address and place of employment, including his unlisted telephone number. This information is *gold* to you because many states permit a judgment creditor to execute a judgment against the debtor's wages.

Income executions: Garnishment laws vary from state to state. But in most cases, *federal* law controls, and it generally maximizes the amount of wage garnishment to 25% of disposable earnings per week, or the amount by which weekly earnings exceed 30 times the hourly wage. Wage garnishments are controlled by state law only where state statutes are substantially similar to federal law, or are even more favorable to the *debtor,* than federal law. Some states do not permit wage garnishment. Comprehensive strategies on judgment recovery are presented in Chapter 10.

Never underestimate the value of a credit report. If you extend credit to more than 100 customers within a calendar year, it is highly recommended that you subscribe to either TRW, TransUnion, Equifax, or a credit bureau in your locale. The small investment is more than offset by the potential rewards. Even if the information in a credit profile does not lead directly to settlement of a debt, at least you have secured vital information, including the debtor's current address, that will enable your attorney to effect proper legal service of process, should you proceed via the litigation route.

A credit profile further provides a viable negotiation tool. When communicating with debtors, you can impress upon them your knowledge of their credit histories and make innuendos regarding the potential ramifications of the unpaid accounts on their credit records (i.e., rejection). Sometimes that is enough to intimidate and motivate debtors, especially if they do have other creditors they are paying and wish to preserve their creditworthiness. The credit report is one of the best tools at your disposal—use it!

To Draw a Credit Profile

To extract credit information reports, you must either be a member of an interchange group or subscribe to a credit-reporting service. Either way, you must be a credit-granting entity and use the reports in credit decisions. As a rule, the minimum number of reports you can order in a year is 100. If you need only an occasional report, you will have to depend on another source. Information retrieval provides this service on an à la carte basis.

Here is how: Contact the credit-reporting agency and say you are interested in subscribing to the service. The agency will give you an information package. Ask for a directory of subscribers. You will not be subscribing to the service, so keep the directory. Examine the membership list carefully. Look for smaller businesses (e.g., service companies, property managers, retail store owners). Stay away from banks and major credit card companies. Call the small subscriber and try to make a deal whereby they agree to draw credit reports for you. In return, you will pay a fee for each report. Generally, subscribers to credit-reporting services pay about $3 for each report. Maybe you can get your contact to draw reports for $10 or $20. You get your reports, and they make a profit. Another good source are real estate brokers. Realtors often secure reports for landlords or to prequalify a home buyer.

Important: Note that any creditor or debt collector who "regularly" accesses consumer reports is considered a credit-reporting agency, subject to the procedural requirements of the Fair Credit Reporting Act (FCRA). Commercial transactions are not subject to the federal law. Note also that the Act imposes criminal and civil liability on those who obtain credit information under false pretenses and that you could be liable if you furnish a consumer credit report to someone who will use the information for a purpose not permitted under FCRA.

State laws: Check with your attorney general, per state laws.

Consumer credit bureau files are accessed via a debtor's Social Security number and/or last known address. Credit reports can be a potent collection weapon to collect delinquent accounts. (See Exhibit 8.9 for a sample credit bureau report.)

Unlawful practice: Assume your debtor has an account at a major department store, a secured loan, a Visa card, or MasterCard. Some debt collectors will use the debtor's credit report to lull the debtor's suspicions and glean valuable information. Here is how:

Collector: "Ms. Customer, this is Bill Smith from the credit department at _____'s. I am calling in reference to your account, number XYZ-23417-Y. Ms. Customer, it is the policy of _____'s to verbally update customers concerning their account status on an annual basis. We'd like to thank you for using our credit card and to assure you that we appreciate the opportunity to serve you. We value your business . . .

(The unsuspecting debtor thinks the voice on the phone is that of a credit representative from the prestigious store. Because the collector had pertinent information about the debtor's account (i.e., status and account number), the debtor also accepts the collector's further statements as valid.)

Collector: "Ms. Customer, it is necessary for us to update our files, so that we may continue your charge privileges. To expedite this process and ensure that there is no

EXHIBIT 8.9   SAMPLE CREDIT BUREAU REPORT

NAME AND ADDRESS OF CREDIT BUREAU MAKING REPORT

☐ SINGLE REFERENCE   ☒ IN FILE REPORT   ☐ TRADE REPORT
☐ FULL REPORT   ☐ EMPLOY & TRADE REPORT   ☐ PREVIOUS RESIDENCE REPORT
☐ OTHER _____

CREDIT BUREAU OF ANYTOWN
1131 MAIN ST.
ANYTOWN, ANYSTATE 12345

FOR   FIRST NATIONAL BANK
       ANYTOWN, ANYSTATE 12345

Date Received	4/11/01
Date Mailed	4/11/01
In File Since	APRIL 1999
Inquired As:	JOINT ACCOUNT

CONFIDENTIAL **crediscope® REPORT**

Member
Associated Credit Bureaus, Inc.

REPORT ON:	LAST NAME	FIRST NAME	INITIAL	SOCIAL SECURITY NUMBER	SPOUSE'S NAME
	CONSUMER	ROBERT	G.	123-45-6789	BETTY R.

ADDRESS:	CITY	STATE:	ZIP CODE	SINCE:	SPOUSE'S SOCIAL SECURITY NO.
1234 ANY ST. ANYTOWN	ANYTOWN	ANYSTATE	12333	1973	123-45-6789

COMPLETE TO HERE FOR TRADE REPORT AND SKIP TO CREDIT HISTORY

PRESENT EMPLOYER:	POSITION HELD:	SINCE:	DATE EMPLOY VERIFIED	EST. MONTHLY INCOME
XYZ CORPORATION	ASST. DEPT. MGR.	10/01	12/01	$2500

COMPLETE TO HERE FOR EMPLOYMENT AND TRADE REPORT AND SKIP TO CREDIT HISTORY

DATE OF BIRTH	NUMBER OF DEPENDENTS INCLUDING SELF:			OTHER: (EXPLAIN)
5/25/50	4	☒ OWNS OR BUYING HOME	☐ RENTS HOME	☐

FORMER ADDRESS:	CITY:	STATE:	FROM:	TO:
4321 FIRST AVE.	ANYTOWN	ANYSTATE	1970	1973

FORMER EMPLOYER:	POSITION HELD:	FROM:	TO:	EST. MONTHLY INCOME
ABC & ASSOCIATES	SALES PERSON	2/99	9/01	$1285

SPOUSE'S EMPLOYER:	POSITION HELD:	SINCE:	DATE EMPLOY VERIFIED	EST. MONTHLY INCOME
BIG CITY DEPT. STORE	CASHIER	4/01	12/01	$1300

CREDIT HISTORY *(Complete this section for all reports)*

WHOSE	KIND OF BUSINESS AND ID CODE	DATE REPORTED AND METHOD OF REPORTING	DATE OPENED	DATE OF LAST PAYMENT	HIGHEST CREDIT OR LAST CONTRACT	BALANCE OWING	PAST DUE AMOUNT	NO. OF PAYMENTS	NO. MONTHS HISTORY REVIEWED	30-59 DAYS ONLY	60-89 DAYS ONLY	90 DAYS AND OVER	TYPE & TERMS (MANNER OF PAYMENT)	REMARKS
2	CONSUMER'S BANK B 12-345	2/6/01 AUTOMTD.	12/01	1/02	1200	1100	-0-	-0-	2	-0-	-0-	-0-	INSTALLMENT $100/MO.	
3	BIG CITY DEPT. STORE D 54-321	2/10/01 MANUAL	4/96	1/01	300	100	-0-	-0-	12	-0-	-0-	-0-	REVOLVING $25/MO.	
1	SUPER CREDIT CARD N 01-234	12/12/00 AUTOMATD.	7/96	11/00	200	100	100	1	12	1	-0-	-0-	OPEN 30-DAY	

PUBLIC RECORD: SMALL CLAIMS CT. CASE #SC1001 PLAINTIFF: ANYWHERE APPLIANCES
AMOUNT $225 PAID 4/4/97
ADDITIONAL INFORMATION: REF. SMALL CLAIMS CT. CASE #SC1001--5/30/97 SUBJECT SAYS CLAIM PAID
UNDER PROTEST. APPLIANCE DID NOT OPERATE PROPERLY.

interruption of your credit privileges, we are asking that you provide this information over the telephone. Can you tell me, Ms. Debtor:

- Let me verify your Social Security number. It's XYZ–1234–ABCD. Is this correct?

- Are you still working? If so, what is your employer's address?

- What is your annual income?

- Do you have any other sources of income and, if so, what are they?

- Have you applied for any other credit cards or lines of credit since you opened your account with us?

- What is the name and address of your bank? What are your account numbers?

- Do you own any real property? If so, where and who is the mortgage holder?

- Is your husband employed? If so, where and how much does he earn?

- Ms. Customer, do you have any investments, own any stocks, etc.?

The unscrupulous collector continues to ask pertinent questions. Once the collector has gained the debtor's confidence, the debtor will spill her heart out, unaware that she is being manipulated by a debt collector using illegal tactics to plumb the debtor's personal and financial records.

Professionals who use this technique are cunning and convincing. They know how to gain debtors' confidence by encouraging them to talk. This technique motivates debtors to cough up all the information the collectors need to collect their debts. If debtors come up shaky or suspicious, the shady collectors remind them that it is the prestigious department store's policy to review information by telephone so as to save their valued customers any inconvenience.

Again, such deception is illegal under numerous federal and state statutes. It is submitted here for cautionary purposes.

Using Credit Cards to Locate Debtors and Assets

A wealth of information can be obtained by merely securing a credit profile on your debtor. Information contained on a credit report very often will lead you directly to the debtor and provide pertinent information concerning the nature and location of his assets. Credit reports can be an effective source to effectuate information subpoenas. Refer to Chapter 10 for more information. If you do not already subscribe to a credit information service, you are impairing your effectiveness as a skip tracer. There are numerous nation-wide and local credit-reporting agencies. TRW, Trans Union, and Equifax are three of the largest that report *consumer* information. Dun & Bradstreet and TRW are the largest providers of *commercial* credit data. Check the Yellow Pages of your phone book under "Credit Reporting Agencies" to locate credit bureaus serving your area. Sometimes it pays to draw reports from more than one agency because there may be gaps in a particular agency's data that can be filled in by drawing a credit profile from another source. Another strategy is to obtain a triune report combining all three major credit report sources (i.e., TRW, Trans Union, and Equifax).

As long as a debtor has an ongoing credit history, you can secure a credit profile. If the information you need is not included in the credit profile itself, you can get additional information by simply contacting the merchants or suppliers named on the report. If, for example, your debtor holds a credit card from a department store or oil company, a phone call to the credit grantor will usually provide the information you need (e.g., current address, phone number, place of employment). All creditors make note of a debtor's bank account and of payments received. This information can be crucial in minimizing your efforts to attach the debtor's assets should it prove necessary to proceed into litigation.

You should be aware of several points concerning the various credit cards. Most important, not all credit card companies report to a credit-reporting database. Thus your debtor might very well have one of these cards, but you will not be able to access the payment history. In situations like this, should the balance owed warrant it, it might be to your advantage to contact the credit card company directly to determine whether your debtor is a cardholder and, if so, the status of the person's account.

Normally, these credit card issuers will not divulge information about their subscribers, but anybody with a little creativity and ingenuity can illegally access another person's credit file. Some dishonest collectors use a clever approach to extract information. For example, criminal collectors might call the credit card companies and say that they are the debtors and that they have inadvertently lost their cards and want to report them "missing." If the debtors are cardholders, and the customer service representatives think they are talking to the cardholders, the reps might divulge the information. Another way dishonest collectors extract information is by using the last known address of the debtors. Once they have verified that the debtors do in fact hold certain credit cards, they call the card issuers to give them their new addresses or to complain that they have not been receiving their statements. As you can see, there are many ways for an unscrupulous individual to get around reporting restrictions and access confidential credit data. But it is illegal to impersonate a debtor to access information, and it is not the purpose of this book to encourage you to engage in any illegal act. To stay within the law, it is suggested that you contact the creditor directly for the legitimate purpose of exchanging credit information.

Very useful tool: Anyone who engages in skip tracing or asset searches should possess a current copy of the *I.D. Checking Guide,* published by Driver's License Guide Company (Redwood City, California). This directory contains information about driver's licenses (including how to detect fraudulent licenses), identification cards, credit cards, and automobile registration plates. The guide also contains telephone numbers and security contacts regarding lost or stolen credit cards. The *I.D. Checking Guide* is not a comprehensive how-to manual because it was not intended for skip tracers and asset locators, but used properly the guide can help you develop more information, which will make your job easier and expand the results of your efforts.

INFORMATION FROM COLLECTION AGENCIES

Normally, collection agencies do not divulge information from their debtor files; however, because collection agencies cross-reference debtors alphabetically, you can at least find out if there are multiple claims against your debtor. Call a collection agency in the debtor's locale and represent yourself as a creditor. Tell the agency that your debtor's account is delinquent. But before you turn the account over, ask the agency if it has had experience with the debtor. If the answer is yes, ask what that experience has been. Then you can either turn the account over to the agency (remember the value of prior experience with a debtor) or you can pursue it yourself with a better idea of the account's collectability. To contact an agency in the debtor's locale, simply go to your local library and look under "Collection Agencies" in the phone directory for the debtor's city, or use online Yellow Pages.

INFORMATION FROM OTHER CREDITORS

If you have a credit application from your debtor that lists references, or if you know other creditors who do business with your debtor, you might try the following approach.

Call the references or other creditors. Introduce yourself as a creditor who is trying to locate Mr. Pastdue. Tell them their names were provided as references by Mr. Pastdue and ask about their experience with the debtor. They might be willing to share the information. If it turns out that they are still doing business with your debtor, that is a healthy sign that increases your chance of collection. If, however, the creditors are also victims of unpaid debts, you should exchange information for mutual benefit.

CROSS-REFERENCING BANKS IN A DEBTOR'S LOCALE

The easiest way to find out where a debtor banks is through the debtor. An innovative collector can coax a debtor to reveal this important information. If this does not work, verify the debtor's address. Assume that the debtor does business with a bank or savings institution close to his home or business address, and refer to the Yellow Pages in the debtor's locale. Another source is *Polk's World Bank Directory,* which lists all banks and branches alphabetically. Call the banks within this area. The chances are good that you will hit upon the debtor's bank. Obviously, this would not work in major cities, but in rural areas it is a viable technique. An electronic search firm is another source to locate bank accounts. To access the system, you need either a Social Security number (if the debt was incurred by an individual) or a federal tax ID number (if the debtor is a corporation). Both access numbers are obtainable by a search firm.

Banks are protective of their customers and resist giving account data, but they can be manipulated to reveal important information about their customers. Here are several techniques used by professionals:

- Call the bank and tell a bank officer that you are considering a credit application from John Smith. Then read off the debtor's telephone number, afterward exclaiming to the bank officer, "Oh, I just did something really stupid. I took the phone number instead of the account number. I'm sorry. I wonder if you could help me? I'd appreciate it very much if you would give me the account number, so that I can correct our records."

    This is yet another application of the "negative selling" technique. If you are convincing, you can usually prompt the bank to give you the correct account number and the address where your debtor's statements are sent.

- Give the bank officer all the correct information, with the wrong account number, so that the bank officer can correct it.

- State that you are trying to verify an account number on a check that has bounced. Tell the bank that you cannot read the account number because the check is torn, or because your bank punched a hole in it, or because you have a bad photocopy. Sound distressed, as though you have a legitimate problem. If the bank employee believes you, he will cooperate.

- Send the bank a verification form (see Exhibit 8.10). Many banks will insist that credit inquiries be made in writing. If this is the case, and you cannot prompt a bank to give you information orally, then use a bank verification form, being sure to enclose a postpaid, self-addressed envelope. This is a routine procedure, and it will usually elicit a prompt reply from commercial banks. Savings and loan associations are somewhat more restrictive.

EXHIBIT 8.10   BANK VERIFICATION FORM

Can you please provide us with the following information on the account listed below? Information is for verification purposes.

Name: _____

Address: _____

City, State, Zip: _____

Checking Account Number: _____

Savings Account Number: _____

Thank you.

You need to know a debtor's bank balance, or you received a check returned for "insufficient funds." Banks cannot legally reveal customers' account balances, but they can tell you how "short" their customers are to clear checks, if a check drawn on the debtor account for a specific amount will clear.

Example: Call the debtor's bank and say you are in receipt of a check from William Pastdue for a substantial amount of money. Ask the bank if the check will "clear," because you want to get the check certified. Most likely, the debtor will not have these funds, but that does not matter; your objective is to find out the debtor's balance. Or in the alternative, call the bank and pose as the person. Armed with the tax ID number, it is easy to secure the desired information.

Strategy: Tell the bank that you will have your representative at the bank in person to make up that portion of the check that will not clear, that amount to be deposited will be in cash and/or by wire transfer to the debtor's account. If the bank will tell you how much you must deposit to give the debtor sufficient funds to clear the check, you can figure out the debtor's balance. For example, if you tell the bank that you are in possession of a check for $10,000 and ask the bank to certify the check, the bank will check the account record. If the account has only $6,000, the bank will tell you No. Then tell the bank that you will pay the difference between the debtor's balance and the face amount of the check. Then it only remains for the bank to tell you how much your representative should deposit in the debtor's account. If the bank tells you $4,000, then you know that the difference between that amount and the amount of the fictional check ($10,000) is the debtor's account balance ($6,000). This is a great tool you can use for a variety of applications.

OPPORTUNITIES FOR SKIP TRACERS/ASSET LOCATERS

Skip tracing can be profitable *if it is done correctly.* Collection agencies are reluctant to pursue hard-core skips or search for hidden assets because such cases are not profitable. Routine collections might be completed with a few phone calls, but to locate a debtor and/or assets, a collector might have to invest many hours with no guarantee of success. Search procedures can be expensive and time-consuming. Compounding the problem is the fact that collectors earn most of their money on a commission basis, so there is really no incentive for them to divert attention from accounts with direct debtor contact (vertical pursuit) to accounts that may require sophisticated investigation (horizontal pursuit). (See the section on "How to Locate Debtors and Their Assets" in this chapter for more about *horizontal* and *vertical* pursuit.) Even if a collection agency were to charge a 50% commission to locate and collect a skip, the account would still, in most cases, be marginally profitable. There simply is no incentive for a commission collector to focus his income-producing time on the myriad details necessary to locate a debtor and/or assets. As a result, most collection agencies do a haphazard job in locating debtors.

Problems with skips and/or asset location usually come about because creditors, for reasons of economy, resist turning their accounts over to collection agencies. Unfortunately, many creditors do not recognize that time is money. If an account is turned over for collection at an early date, not only does the creditor enhance the collector's chances of success, but the creditor is also in a better position to negotiate rates.

By the time many creditors finally turn to professional collectors, the accounts in question are dead or on the verge of bankruptcy. Creditors, which originally resisted paying any fee at all, are now willing to pay a high percentage to anyone who can successfully collect their accounts. If you are proficient in this area, then you are indeed a fortunate individual. Many credit grantors are willing to pay for quality service. Here are just some areas where excellent employment opportunities exist for collectors who have the ability and knowledge to locate debtors and/or assets:

- Collection agencies and law firms
- Repossession agents
- Banks and finance companies
- Private investigators
- Leasing companies
- Other creditors and commercial entities

A professional skip tracer is not just someone who knows how to secure a forwarding address. A professional is someone who knows how to use his creative intellect to the utmost to track down intentional skips and concealed assets. A professional easily commands a six-figure income. If you are interested in pursuing this profession, there are abundant opportunities.

Many professionals are women: Historically, skip tracing and asset location has been an industry dominated by men, but times are changing. Today many excellent professional skip tracers are women. Women may have an advantage over men because debtors are often more inclined to let down their guard with a woman than with a man. A woman with a friendly voice can be very convincing.

Law firms are among the best sources of referral business. Major litigation, deadlocked in discovery, can yield a small fortune to the enterprising professional who breaks the deadlock by uncovering the information sought in discovery proceedings. An attorney cannot split fees with a collection agency, but the attorney's client can pay you a fee based on results. I have had many cases in which a private or corporate attorney paid me a fixed fee with the balance contingent on results. The fixed fee offsets my expenses, and the contingency is the incentive.

Be wary of the enticing deal that offers you a hefty percentage. You would be wise not to sell skip-tracing/asset location services on a straight contingency basis. Remember, a percentage of nothing is still nothing. You are a professional. Your time is valuable, and the service you provide is unique. You deserve to get paid. If a creditor tries to lure you with a pie-in-the-sky contingency fee, remind the creditor that you are results oriented and that you will give 110% in your efforts to locate a debtor and/or assets. If the creditor does not want to pay the fee, it is not going to get the results. Consider this analogy: A business had an accountant who charged $250 per hour. At the end of the year the business got a $50,000 tax rebate. Feeling that it paid too much for accounting services, the next year the business hired some schnook, but at the end of the year the business had to pay $30,000 in taxes. In collections, as in all services, the adage holds true: You get what you pay for.

For every 250 collectors (commercial or consumer), there is only one good skip tracer. Only 1 in 2,000 collectors is a virtuoso skip tracer. I know most of the virtuosos in this business, and very few of them are good enough to be called professionals. If a collector is earning an executive-size income, he is at the head of the class.

There is demand for individuals with the skills necessary to locate debtors and/or assets. Even if you do not engage in private practice, a mastery of these skills will make you more valuable to your employer, improve your chances of success, and increase your income. Moreover, these skills will aid you in many areas of your personal and business life.

CHAPTER 9

Legal Recovery

In this chapter you will learn how to avoid unnecessary legal expenses and improve collection potential over your competitors. Today's dishonest debtor is a sophisticated customer, keenly aware of his rights and of the limits of litigation. This chapter examines techniques involving consumer and commercial collection attorneys. These are techniques to be applied to hard-core debtors by experienced collectors. You can sometimes manipulate your debtor's attorney to act as your liaison to successful collection. Learn about the unwritten law of attorney-to-attorney respect and how to use this principle to create collection opportunities.

This chapter provides a complete system for forwarding legal claims to attorneys. The local influence factor can be critical to the successful collection of a past-due account. Find out how to use corresponding attorneys to bring this factor to bear, and how to use law lists to find commercial and consumer collection attorneys in your debtor's locale. You will even learn why it is generally possible to use an attorney's influence free for 15 days.

Every professional collector needs a working knowledge of basic principles of state and federal laws. In this chapter legal experts reveal "universal" principles of law that will help you formulate strategies to maneuver debtors toward payment. You will learn about the summary judgment (aka accelerated judgment) collection technique that can compel a debtor to come to terms without your having to go through complex discovery processes or trial.

Find out how to strengthen your bargaining position and create leverage by painting in the debtor's mind graphic illustrations of court proceedings and making him dread the spectre of looming legal expenses. You will discover possible remedies—including attachment, restraining orders, and injunctions—should you have reason to believe that your debtor will dispose of funds or property before you can complete legal action. This chapter also explains how a debtor that is generally not paying its debts as they become due can be forced into involuntary bankruptcy. This tactic sometimes presents a viable collection opportunity. Most important, you will learn how to use legal knowledge to bring your debtor to the bargaining table.

How to Protect Yourself from a Scam Operation

Commercial fraud robs American business of billions of dollars per year. Every company at one time or another has been ripped off by unscrupulous operators who procure credit under false pretenses. Credit fraud ranges all the way from small mail-order scams to multimillion-dollar commercial transactions. Every credit grantor is vulnerable.

Every company that extends credit has bad debts. Granting credit is risky business, but it is essential to build sales volume. It would probably be impossible for you to screen every credit application or conduct a thorough investigation before each transaction, but there are steps you can take to minimize risk. Before we examine available remedies, let us analyze the reasons credit crime is a big problem in the United States.

- The mere retention of counsel and civil pursuit can be counterproductive. While such action might induce some debtors to pay (probably those who would have paid anyway), it might lead those who are judgment-proof (alas, all too many debtors are!) to dig in their heels and adopt a "take it or leave it" attitude. Furthermore, our overburdened legal system is time- and cost-intensive. Often, the cost (as well as the risk) is not justified.

- The great debtor "cop-out" is filing for protection under Bankruptcy Laws. There are several forms of bankruptcy, but they all protect the debtor and not the creditor. Simply put, the bankruptcy laws make it easy for a debtor to walk away from an obligation, leaving creditors with little or no recourse.

- The corporate veil protects officers and shareholders from personal liability for corporate debts. Extraordinary evidence that the principals have acted in a fraudulent or negligent manner is required to pierce the corporate veil and expose individual liability.

- The passing of bad checks: Most states have laws that establish procedures by which creditors can prosecute people who issue bad checks. But again, the creditor must be prepared to go through extraordinary efforts and great expense to bring about results that may or may not be satisfactory.

- An aggressive sales force and liberal credit policies will almost certainly result in a high percentage of uncollectible debts.

- Too much reliance on credit bureau reports is another factor that facilitates credit fraud. The mere scrutiny of a credit report is not sufficient basis for intelligent credit decisions. Credit reports should be regarded as a source of *basic* information (a mirror image). Many credit-reporting agencies do not investigate the information in their reports. Even a respected credit reporter like Dun & Bradstreet should not be relied on exclusively in credit decisions. An unscrupulous operator, intending to defraud, can easily fabricate and falsify credit information.

- Restrictions on collection agencies (i.e., the Fair Debt Collections Practices Act and other federal, state, and local laws) severely curtail third-party debt collectors and, in some cases, creditors.

Safeguarding Your Interests

The first and most important rule is never to extend credit if there is any likelihood that you will be defrauded. How do you find out whether a transaction is risky? Unfortunately, there is no simple method. The naked fact is that *if a potential customer wants to beat you, he will*. Never be lulled into a false sense of security by credit reports and trade references. Use them with discretion. When in doubt, always insist on money up front or, at least, on a substantial deposit to minimize your risk. Some credit grantors ask for a deposit equivalent to their cost of providing goods or services, to offset the risk of loss.

The next rule is never to rely on a collection agency to resolve a fraudulent account. You will be wasting your time. Collection agencies are powerless. They lack the resources to deal with this kind of collection problem. Do not have too much faith in your attorney either. The legal system does provide some remedies, but if you decide to go that route, be prepared to spend a fortune.

Take the Customer to Court?

Litigation is a time-consuming and expensive process. Even reputable attorneys will tell you that if a debt can be resolved any other way, try to do so before filing a claim with the courts. (Exhibit 9.1 provides a sample Legal Representation Letter.)

Consider this: If a dispute can be adjudicated in small claims court (the maximum amount that can be awarded in such courts differs from state to state), consider that route. One rea-

---

EXHIBIT 9.1   SAMPLE LEGAL REPRESENTATION LETTER

```
    RE:

Gentlemen:

        Please be advised that I am the attorney for
                            I have been retained
in connection with its claim against you in the sum of $
which includes accrued interest.

        If it is your desire to avoid additional expense, it
is imperative that you forward bank check, certified check, or
money order in the sum of $        payable to John Doe,
as attorney.

        If there is any reason why you should not or cannot
make this payment, it is imperative that you contact the under-
signed on or before                    If I have not heard
from you or received payment by this date, I have been instructed
to proceed with suit. You may then be required to pay all court
costs and accrued interest in addition to the above amount.

        Thank you for your attention in this matter.
```

son is that your case will likely be heard much sooner in this forum than in a county or state court. In addition, most small claims courts permit pro se representation. Refer to Chapter 6, Suing in Small Claims Court.

What Evidence Do You Need?

Most lawsuits to settle debts are based on written contracts, personal guarantees, promissory notes, or open accounts. If the transaction behind the suit is based on a written contract or promissory note, then that document is your evidence. If you are trying to collect an open-account debt, your proof would be copies of the statement of account, all invoices, credit memos, and so forth. Your attorney can always do a better job if he or she has all available information concerning the debt and the debtor. You will save time and money if you research your debtor before turning the account over for legal action.

If a debtor does not respond to pretrial proceedings, the court will usually award a judgment to liquidate your claims against the debtor. If the debtor does not dispute the facts of your claim, but says that legally it owes you nothing (or less than what you are asking for), the judge will then issue a ruling based on the law.

If the debtor does dispute the facts as you have presented them in your claim, the debtor files its response with the plaintiff's attorney. (In most states, a copy also goes to the court.) If it is a general denial (we do not owe the plaintiff anything), you, the creditor, then have to file an affidavit with the court certifying that the facts in your claim are true and correct. The court will ask the defendant to respond specifically to the facts as you have presented them. The defendant may also include evidence, such as copies of shipping invoices for returned merchandise, and so on, with its affidavit.

After service of the summons and complaint, the next step is discovery. The cost and time factors of discovery are cumbersome. These conventional methods include the following:

- *Interrogatories.* These are written questions submitted by either the plaintiff or the defendant to the other party, who then must either respond to the questions or file an objection to the questions with the court. Generally, respondents provide "icicles in wintertime" responses.

- *Bill of Particulars.* This is a detailed itemization of the creditor's (plaintiff's) demand or of the debtor's (defendant's) response to the creditor's demand. Bill of particulars are intended to amplify the complaint.

- *Subpoenas.* These court orders require people to appear and give testimony at a particular time and place. These witnesses may also be required to bring records or documents that may be relevant to the issue at trial (*subpoena duces tecum*). Information subpoenas are another discovery device.

- *Testimony.* This is evidence given orally in a court of law or before a magistrate.

- *Depositions.* These are oral testimonies that have been reduced to writing and authenticated, and that are intended to be used in court.

All of these discovery sources operate extrajudicially, meaning that they are supposed to function between the litigants without court intervention. More times than not, that does not happen. Securing information as evidence is most important to prove your case, but an evasive debtor may not voluntarily surrender information. In that event, your attorney will have to go back to court and file a separate motion requesting the judge order the debtor to provide the information sought. Often, this tactic fails to produce results, and the attorney must go back to court again, this time to argue a motion for contempt—another separate (and expensive) proceeding. Even if your attorney is successful and the debtor is cited for contempt, it is unlikely that anything earth-shattering will occur to forward your cause. The debtor may be fined a few hundred dollars, as violators of contempt orders seldom go to jail. Even if you get the information you seek (the location of concealed assets, funds, property, hidden bank accounts, merchandise, etc.), the very instrument of discovery puts your adversary on notice of your intentions and gives the debtor an opportunity to foil your efforts by devising alternative strategies to place assets out of your reach. The burden is always on you to prove that the debtor owes you money and has the assets to satisfy a judgment. Unfortunately, this process costs money—and all along your debtor has been making profit from your product. It is not fair, but justice is not cheap.

Who is the right lawyer for the job? Most attorneys specialize. Always retain a lawyer who specializes in collection law. Your attorney may, with your permission, try to help you and the debtor settle the dispute out of court. Once again, settlement is always better than litigation.

Most Commercial Litigation Is Nonproductive

After the discovery process, the court will schedule the case for trial. From the ensuing proceedings, you might secure a money judgment, but that does not mean you are going to get paid. The court will not collect for you. Once a money judgment is rendered, the clerk of the court will issue, at your request, a *writ of execution*. It is your responsibility to forward this writ, together with a check to pay the nominal fee, to the *appropriate* constable or sheriff for collection—if the debtor's principal business address (if your money judgment is against the business) or place of residence (if your judgment is against the individual) is in the same state as you.

If your debtor is located in another state, you will have to "convert" your money judgment under terms of that state's Uniform Enforcement of Foreign Judgment Act. (Most states have passed such acts.) The simplest way to do this is to be represented by a local attorney in the debtor's state.

Important consideration: The courts do not guarantee payment after awarding you a money judgment and issuing a writ of execution. The debtor can go into bankruptcy court and file for protection against you—and all its creditors. Your money judgment and writ may prove as uncollectible as the original debt.

206   CHAPTER 9 LEGAL RECOVERY

Do Not Throw Good Money After Bad

Contrary to popular belief, most claims that proceed through litigation and result in judgments are uncollectible. There are many reasons why creditors, after having endured the litigation route, end up with paper victory, a worthless judgment. Most attorneys require noncontingent suit fees. Legal fees average between 5% and 10% of the claim, including court costs and disbursements, up front. Thus most of the financial risk in litigation is absorbed by the creditor, not by your attorney.

To minimize the risk of expensive litigation, you should conduct a due diligence debtor evaluation. You might want to hire a search firm to conduct a public records search. Your objective is to find any detrimental public filings or unknown liabilities before filing suit. As was shown in Chapter 8 on skip tracing, there is a tremendous volume of information available from public records. But, generally, in prelegal evaluations, you can narrow your search to cover these areas:

- Pending litigation
- Judgments
- Tax liens (state and federal)
- Unsatisfied employment withholding tax obligations

Never rely solely on credit reports. Space limitations may force credit bureaus to leave out important information. Often valuable information is simply not recorded. There are many reputable search firms like Infosearch that have offices in most major cities. Check the Yellow Pages under "Attorney Services" to locate a service company, or dial 800-USA-INFO to get the Infosearch, Inc., office in your region. A Uniform Commercial Code (UCC) search, depending on where it is, how fast it is required, how many document copies there are, the volume you are doing with the search firm, and other variables, could cost anywhere from $35 to $100. Obviously, the cost multiplies as you seek additional information. A few full-service agencies also provide investigation services. A collection agency will usually provide these services for less than $200. This is a small price to pay if it determines the collectability of a claim early in the collection cycle.

Many unsuspecting creditors have paid large up-front attorney fees only to end up with worthless judgments. They could have been avoided had the credit grantor taken the initiative and screened potentially legal accounts before taking the plunge into litigation. Never assume that your attorney will exercise this precaution; most will not. Preventive medicine and early diagnosis can thwart costly mistakes. Electronic search firms such as Investigations Unlimited are another resource.

Bad-Check Summary

Contrary to general belief, the passing of bad checks does not necessarily mean criminal culpability. The reason for nonpayment by the drawee bank (e.g., "payment stopped," "account closed," "insufficient funds"), the state in which the check was drawn, and numerous other factors determine whether a drawer is subject to criminal and/or civil prosecution. In some states, passers of bad checks are subject to criminal prosecution only in C.O.D. transactions or if checks were returned "Account Closed." Most states require that Not Sufficient Funds (NSF) checks be deposited twice before any legal action can be commenced. Some states require a payee to protest the bad check.

Criminal liability does not usually exist in most credit transactions because it is generally accepted that creditors enter into these arrangements knowing that there is an element of risk. Even if there was criminal intent on the part of the person who passed a bad check, such intent to defraud must be *proved* in court. Overworked district attorneys, a huge backlog of criminal cases, and the enormous costs of such proceedings are all factors that discourage criminal prosecution on bad checks. You should always seek the advice of competent legal counsel with respect to any bad check. (See Exhibit 9.2 for a sample Legal Bad-Check Letter.)

To collect on NSF checks: Bad-check statutes differ from state to state, but most are the same in principle. When you receive an NSF check, inform the maker of the returned check of the amount owed, including a service charge—the amount of which depends on state statute. Tell the maker that he must exchange cash for the NSF check by such and such a date or you will turn the maker's name, amount of check, bank name, and the number of the maker's driver's license over to a check verification service so that in the future the debtor will find it hard to write checks in the district covered by that organization. There is no charge for this procedure. If you do not get cash by the deadline you set, turn the information over to the check verification service as promised. You then have two choices for further action:

1. Turn the check over to a check collection agency, which will charge a contingency fee.

2. Write a certified collection letter, allowing 10 working days to make good on the check and service charge. The time limit is set by bad-check statute and varies from state to state, but written notice is generally a prerequisite to legal proceedings. The certified letter must be mailed *return receipt requested*. If there is no response after 10 days, you can take the original check and the signed receipt to the district attorney's office for collection. There is no charge for this procedure.

Out-of-state checks should be returned to the bank on which they were drawn *for collection purposes only.* This procedure ensures that should the check writer make a deposit, the first payment the bank makes from those funds will go to you to cover the NSF check. Banks charge collection fees for this service.

Fees for returned checks: If you decide to charge customers fees when their checks are returned NSF, make sure you abide by statutory limits. Every state has different rules governing returned check charges.

EXHIBIT 9.2   SAMPLE LEGAL BAD-CHECK LETTER

DEMAND FOR PAYMENT OF DISHONORED CHECK

(WARNING, YOU MAY BE SUED 30 DAYS AFTER THE DATE OF THIS NOTICE
IF YOU DO NOT MAKE PAYMENT)

     Your check in the amount of
dated   , payable to the order of
has been dishonored by the bank upon which it was drawn because:

     1) Insufficient funds on deposit with the bank;
     2) You had no account with that bank

     If you do not make payment you may be sued under
§11-104 of the General Obligations Law to recover payment. If
a Judgment is rendered against you in court it may include not
only the original face amount of the check, but also an additional
liquidated damages as follows:

     If you had insufficient funds on deposit with the bank
upon which the check was drawn, an additional sum which may be
equivalent to twice the face amount of the check or $400.00,
whichever is less.

     If you had no account with the bank upon which the check
was drawn, an additional sum which may be equivalent to twice the
face amount of the check or $750.00, whichever is less.

     Please promptly arrange to make payment by bank check,
certified check or money order, payable to _____

_____

     If you dispute any of the facts listed above, contact
the undersigned immediately.

TURN YOUR DEBTOR OVER TO THE IRS

Commercial fraud robs American businesses of billions of dollars. It is easy for credit criminals to obtain credit under false pretenses, convert the goods obtained into cash, and skip town with the proceeds. Furthermore, if you are trying to collect from a corporation, the corporate veil shields principals and shareholders from personal liability except under extraordinary circumstances. One of the best safeguards in transactions with corporations is a personal guaranty. (See Exhibit 8.2.) Then if the corporation goes out of business, you can at least pursue the individual who signed the guaranty, but even so, you are still subjected to certain risks. Today's dishonest debtor is sophisticated, keenly aware of his rights, and knowledgeable about the limitations of litigation.

Powerful Last Resort

If you have taken all conventional steps and determined that a debtor is judgment-proof, you still have a unique, little-known option: Turn your debtor in to the IRS for tax evasion, and stake a claim for the reward under Section 7623 of the Internal Revenue Code (see Exhibit 9.3). If your debtor has been engaging in misappropriation of funds, transference of assets, or fraudulent transfers, the chances are that the debtor is also evading federal taxes. But before you become too enthusiastic, you should know that you must submit a *prima facie* case to the IRS.

This strategy is at the extreme end of the collection spectrum, but it provides a powerful, devastating remedy. It can, however, be risky on several fronts. This is to commercial collections what chemotherapy is to the treatment of cancer. It is a potent remedy that requires mastery of highly specialized, advanced collection techniques. The innocuous Form 211 (application for reward), available from any IRS office, is easy to fill out. The hard part is to build a *prima facie* case of tax evasion that will induce the IRS to investigate, audit, and punish your debtor. The result if you are successful? Federal law mandates that an informant be paid a percentage of the gross tax deficiencies recovered by the IRS. (See Exhibit 9.4 for a schematic of the procedure the IRS will employ to evaluate a claim, the resulting tax collateral, and the reward, if any.)

Threat May Be Enough

Essentially, the strategy is to let the debtor know that you have evidence that the IRS could use in a commercial fraud investigation to determine tax evasion. While this ploy does occasionally trigger an IRS audit and result in a reward for the creditor that is as large as or larger than the original debt, this is an infrequent outcome.

What you are really trying to accomplish is to reopen negotiations and create substantial collection leverage. That is not to say the threat of an IRS audit need not be rooted in fact. It *must* be rooted in fact—that is, "probable cause" must be established. Work this strategy in conjunction with a knowledgeable attorney, and use the debtor's attorney (and accountant) to pressure the debtor.

RECOMMENDATIONS

- Conduct a thorough investigation of the debtor's business dealings and establish illegal improprieties.
- Conduct a thorough investigation of the debtor's cash-flow management practices and establish the criteria for tax evasion.
- Avoid a direct connection between an IRS audit and resolution of the debt. Words to be avoided are connectors such as "unless," "if you don't," and so forth.
- Explain that you want to involve the debtor's attorney, preferably a criminal law attorney.

EXHIBIT 9.3 IRS DEBTOR INTERVENTION

Receivable Management, Investigations and Document Retrieval . . . Everywhere

I.R.S. DEBTOR INTERVENTION - AUDIT - REWARD
(211 – APPLICATION FOR REWARD BASED ON ORIGINAL INFORMATION)

For the first time, under a little-known and seldom-used provision under Federal Law (Section 7623 IRS Code), a creditor can compel direct IRS debtor intervention. Under extraordinary circumstances where Coleman & Coleman, Inc. has investigated and confirmed that your debtor may be involved in any of the following deceptive business practices encompassing possible tax fraud:

- Illegal transference and/or a conveyance or concealment of assets.
- Illegitimate liquidations, bulk sales, or general assignments, with intent to defraud.
- Multiple corporate entities to intentionally circumvent legal pursuit and frustrate the enforcement of a money judgment.

- Fraudulent capital involvement of the principals.
- Fraud, stock manipulation, altering of financial statements, etc. . . .
- Financial manipulation to procure credit via creation of a corporate shell to escape personal liability.

Where there is probable cause to support that your debtor may be in violation of Title 26 USCA Section 7201 (tax evasion) and where there appears an impenetrable corporate veil, illegal transference of assets, or where debtor is judgment proof by reason of tax fraud, a remedy is available wherein the creditor has the option to pursue the filing of an IRS application for reward based on original information. This approach is used on the stringent end of the collection spectrum where Coleman & Coleman, Inc. is authorized, has conducted an extensive in-depth investigation of your debtor and probable cause exists to substantiate a prima facie case that will support the IRS intervention.

Because of the relatively unknown nature of this means of debtor pursuit, the following questions may come to mind!

- **Is IRS intervention more productive than a lawsuit?**
  - Yes. Where financial manipulation exists, pursuing your debtor as a *tax evader*, in lieu of litigation, will provide an effective remedy against a judgment proof debtor, where appropriate.

- **What procedure does the IRS follow to evaluate/audit claims and to ascertain civil and/or criminal liability?**
  - IRS Code 4569.22(1)(A)(B) dictates that informant's correspondence, immediately upon recognition, is to be sealed in two envelopes and forwarded to Criminal Intelligence for review. Cases lacking criminal potential will be referred to the district examination director, and where substantial liability exists, civil prosecution will be forthcoming. (4569.34(1)–IRM 4211.11)

- **Q What is the criteria to support filing of an IRS 211?**
  - Because of potential devastating effects, Coleman & Coleman, Inc. exercises great discretion incorporating built in safeguards before IRS intervention is initiated. Subject to creditor approval, advice of counsel and where a prima facie case is evident, Coleman & Coleman, Inc. will file the necessary moving papers.

- **U What is required of the IRS upon the filing of a 211?**
  - Assuming they deem the claim worthwhile for pursuit, our experience with the IRS has shown that a number of factors must be considered. Typically, this is the criteria used in evaluation of your claim:
    1. The extent of the taxpayer's (debtor) financial dealings and the approximate tax deficiencies.
    2. The local IRS office's timetable and staff to pursue the matter.
    3. The intent of the alleged tax evader, whether criminal and/or civil liability.

- **E**
- **S Scope, quality and substance of the accompanying evidence in support of the 211 application.**

- **T What are the factors in determining allowability of claims?**
  - Rewards are paid *only* with respect to deficient taxes, fines, and penalties collected. No reward, however, is paid on *interest* collected.

- **I Are rewards paid where tax deficiencies from related taxpayers recovered?**
  - Yes! Section 4569.7(2) of the IRS Code clearly specifies that the informant (creditor) is entitled to an *additional* reward where the violation or pattern of tax evasion prompted the initial investigation/audit to discover discrepancies in returns of related taxpayers.

- **O**
- **N What rewards are obtainable under this system, if any?**
  - Under Federal Law, the district director will determine whether a reward will in fact be paid and its amount. The IRS in making this decision, will evaluate all factors and determine the relationship to the evidence developed by the resulting investigation. The reward will not exceed $50,000 or 15%, whichever is greater. Any reward will be paid as soon as possible after collection of deficient taxes recovered and the amount of said reward will always be at the discretion of the IRS.

- **S How do clients of Coleman & Coleman, Inc. benefit financially under this system?**
  - When Coleman & Coleman, Inc. has been engaged to pursue an investigation and developed a prima facie case to support the filing of an IRS 211, any resulting reward is shared equally with the creditor. In addition to any financial remuneration, the creditor achieves the psychological satisfaction of knowing that once IRS intervention commences, devastating consequences befall the debtor (tax evader). The results can be overwhelming.

- **How long before a reward can be realized?**
  - The time span can be months or even years depending on the IRS's own timetable and priorities.

- **Can partial rewards be paid in a case where criminal prosecution and a conviction is obtained, irrespective of civil liability?**
  - Yes! Where the prosecution/conviction was attributable to the informant's information, a reward may be paid as partial allowance prior to civil resolution of the tax liability. (IRS Code 4569.9(11)(2) Revised 1/16/79).

- **Is the IRS concerned with the indebtedness to the creditor?**
  - No. The IRS is solely concerned with the tax liability. Hypothetically, where the IRS may recover $200,000 in back taxes a maximum reward of $50,000 will be equally shared with our client. (Rewards may exceed indebtedness owed to creditor.)

- **Are rewards taxable?**
  - Yes. Upon receipt and disbursement to the client, the IRS views any resulting reward as taxable income.

EXHIBIT 9.4   IRS DEBTOR INTERVENTION STEPS*

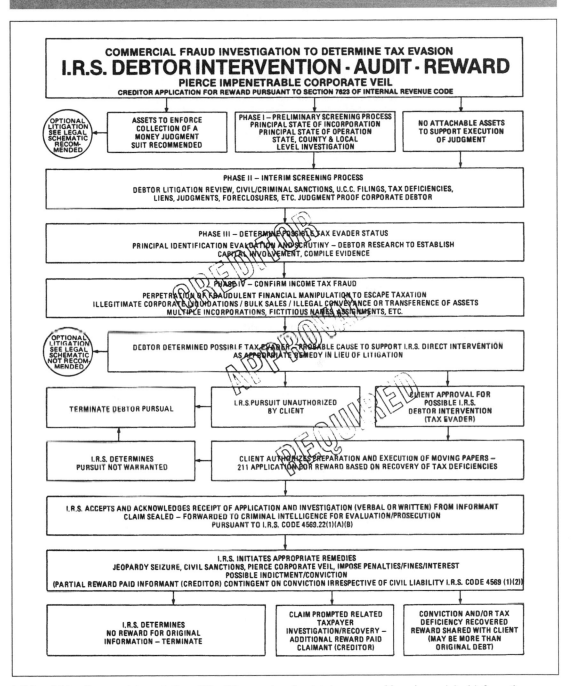

* This exhibit reflects an interpretation of the IRS procedure for claiming a reward based on original information. Individuals contemplating filing a claim Form 211 for reward should obtain the most recent IRS policy.

The main thing to understand is that there is a vast difference between threatening a debtor with a court case and threatening a debtor with an IRS audit. This is a litigious society, and bringing a matter to court is considered an acceptable means to resolve a civil conflict. That is not the case with an IRS audit. The latter will be interpreted as blackmail.

It is essential to have evidence that backs up your claim that the IRS would be interested in an investigation of the debtor's back taxes. The debtor's attorney can be your best source to influence the debtor to negotiate. If the debtor feels it has more to lose from an IRS audit/investigation than from paying your bill, it is likely to reconsider and settle its debt with you.

When you decide to go ahead with this strategy, you should follow the steps given in Exhibit 9.4.

- Use the term "evidence." This implies that an investigation has occurred.

- Ask the debtor if he is aware of the ramifications of Section 7623 of the Internal Revenue Code.

- State that you have "evidence" that will suffice to set the IRS in motion and that you will be filing a Form 211. (See Exhibit 9.5. This is the application form that makes you or your firm a stakeholder in an IRS audit.)

- Suggest that the debtor initiate a conference call with an attorney.

Although you do not want to be the one to state the possibility of a trade-off—the debtor settling up and you forgetting the 211 form—the debtor is likely to suggest this route. Accept it! This is exactly what you had hoped would happen all along.

Representing yourself as a potential IRS informant is no sure-fire approach. Use it only as a last resort, and above all, *use it with extreme caution.* You may want to write out a script before you call the debtor, but first, submit it to your attorney for review, just to make sure you are on solid ground.

To learn more about turning your debtor over to the IRS, visit any local IRS office, or purchase an IRS field manual directly from the U.S. Government Printing Office in Washington, D.C. You will find the procedure under section 7623 of the Internal Revenue Code. (See Exhibits 9.6 and 9.7 for sample letters to the IRS.)

CONFERENCE CALLS TO THE DEBTOR'S ATTORNEY

One of the most revolutionary, bold, and downright aggressive techniques is to encourage your debtor to give you his attorney's phone number and then take the initiative to arrange a conference call between you, the debtor, and the debtor's attorney. Why? Because chances are the debtor has not retained an attorney for this specific matter, and getting the attorney involved will automatically create an expense for the debtor. You should not attempt this technique until you have chalked up experience in the university of hard knocks. When you have paid your dues, here is how to implement the strategy:

EXHIBIT 9.5 APPLICATION FOR REWARD FOR ORIGINAL INFORMATION

**Rewards for Information
Provided by Individuals to the
Internal Revenue Service**

Section 7623 of the Internal Revenue Code and the regulation under it permit the Internal Revenue Service to pay a reward to anyone who provides information that leads to the detection and punishment of anyone violating the internal revenue laws.

Who May File a Claim for Reward

Under the above section, you may file a claim for reward unless:
1.   You were employed by the Department of the Treasury at the time you received or provided the information; or
2.   You are a present or former federal employee who received the information in the course of your official duties.
An executor, administrator, or other legal representative may file a claim form reward on behalf of a decedent if the decedent was eligible to file such a claim before his or her death. The representative must attach to the claim evidence of authority to file it.

Providing Information For A Reward

If you have information you believe would be valuable to the Internal Revenue Service, you may give it in person or in writing to a representative of the Criminal Investigation Division located at a local IRS District office. You may also give the information over the telephone, to a representative of the Customer Service located at an IRS Service Center. The toll-free number is 1-800-829-0433.

Useful information about persons who do not comply with the tax laws includes, but is not limited to, the following:
1. Tax years of violations.
2. Aliases.
3. Addresses.
4. Social Security Number and/or employer Identification Number.
5. Financial data (bank accounts, assets) and its location
6. Documentation to substantiate allegation (for example, books and records) and its location
7. Date of birth.

Filing A Claim For Reward

To file a claim for reward, you should
1. Notify the office or person to whom you reported the information that you are claiming a reward.

　　　　Department of the Treasury
　　　　Internal Revenue Service
　　　　Publication 733 (Rev. 06.97)

　　　Cat. No. 46729M

2.   File a claim for reward by completing Form 211, Application for Reward for Original Information, signing it with our true name, and mailing it to the Informants' Claims Examiner at the Internal Revenue Service Center for you area. The addresses are listed on the back of Form 211. If you provided the information in person, include in your claim the name and title of the person to whom you reported the information and the date you reported it.

If you used an identity other than your true name when you originally reported the information, attach to the claim proof that you are the person who gave the information. (IRS does not disclose the identity of its informants to unauthorized persons.)

Amount and Payment of Reward

The District Director will determine whether a reward will be paid and its amount. In making this decision, the information you provided will be evaluated in relation to the facts developed by the resulting investigation. Claims for reward will be paid in proportion to the value of information you furnished voluntarily and on your own initiative with respect to taxes, fines and penalties, (but not interest) collected. The amount of reward will be determined as follows:
1.   For specific and responsible information that caused the investigation and resulted in the recovery or was a direct factor in the recovery, the reward shall be 15 percent of the amounts recovered, with the total reward not exceeding $2 million.
2.   For information that caused the investigation and was of value in the determination of tax liabilities although not specific, the reward shall be 10 percent of the amounts recovered, with the total reward not exceeding $2 million.
3.   For information that caused the investigation, but had no direct relationship to the determination of tax liabilities, the reward shall be 1 percent of the amount recovered, with the total reward not exceeding $2 million.
4.   No reward will be paid if the recovery was so small as to call for payment of less than $100.00 under the above formulas.
5.   An informant who has received direct payment(s) for information provided to the Service is not precluded from filing a claim for reward for the same information. However to prevent duplicate payments, the amount of the reward payment will be reduced by the amount of the direct payment(s).
6.   Federal disclosure laws prohibit the IRS from providing information regarding specific actions taken by the Service with respect to the information provided.
7.   If an investigation is initiated as a result of the information provided, it can take two or more years before there is a final disposition of the investigation.

U.S. GPO: 1997-417 890A6T1

EXHIBIT 9.5   APPLICATION FOR REWARD FOR ORIGINAL
INFORMATION (CONT'D)

Form 211 (Rev. June 1997) Department of the Treasury Internal Revenue Service	**Application for Reward for Original Information**	OMB Clearance No. 1545-0409
		Claim Number

This application is voluntary and the information requested enables us to determine and pay rewards. We use the information to record a claimant's reward as taxable income and to identify any tax outstanding (including taxes on a joint return filed with a spouse) against which the reward would first be applied. We need taxpayer identification numbers, i.e., social security number (SSN) or employer identification number (EIN), as applicable, in order to process it. Failure to provide the information requested may result in suspension of processing this application. Our authority for asking for the information on this form is 26 USC 6001, 6011, 6109, 7802, and 5 USC 310.

Name of claimant, if an individual, provide date of birth	Date of Birth Month Day Year	Claimant's Tax Identification Number, SSN or EIN:
Name of spouse (if applicable)	Date of Birth Month Day Year	Social Security Number:

Address of claimant, including zip code, and telephone number (telephone number is optional)

I am applying for a reward, in accordance with the law and regulations, for original information furnished, which led to the detection of a violation of the internal revenue laws of the United States and the collection of taxes, penalties, and fines. I was not an employee of the Department of the Treasury at the time I came into possession of the information nor at the time I divulged it.

Name of IRS employee to whom violation was reported	Title of IRS employee	Date violation reported (Month,day,year)

Method of reporting the information – check applicable box   [ ] Telephone   [ ] Mail   [ ] In person

Name of taxpayer who committed the violation and, if known, the taxpayer's SSN or EIN

Address of taxpayer, including zip code if known

Relative to information I furnished on the above named taxpayer, the Internal Revenue Service made the following payments to me or on my behalf:

Date of Payment   Amount   Name of Person/Entity to Whom Payment was made

Under penalties of perjury, I declare that I have examined this application and my accompanying statements, if any, and to the best of my knowledge and belief they are true, correct, and complete. I understand the amount of any award will represent what the District or Service Center Director considers appropriate in this particular case. I agree to repay the reward, or an appropriate percentage thereof, if the collection on which it is based is subsequently reduced.

Signature of Claimant	Date

The following is to be completed by the Internal Revenue Service

Authorization of Reward

District/Service Center/Assistant Commissioner (International)	Sum recovered $	Amount of Reward $

In consideration of the original information that was furnished by the claimant named above, which concerns a violation of the internal revenue laws and which led to the collection of taxes, penalties, and fines in the sum shown above, I approve payment of a reward in the amount stated.

Signature of the Service Center Director	Date

MAIL COMPLETED FORM TO THE APPROPRIATE ADDRESS SHOWN ON THE BACK

EXHIBIT 9.5   APPLICATION FOR REWARD FOR ORIGINAL INFORMATION (CONT'D)

Send the completed Form 211 to the Internal Revenue Service Center for your area shown below.

Name of Service Center	Address
Andover Service Center	Internal Revenue Service Attention: I.C.E. Andover, MA 05501-0002
Atlanta Service Center	Internal Revenue Service Attention: I.C.E. Atlanta, GA 39901-0002
Austin Service Center	Internal Revenue Service Attention: I.C.E. Austin, TX 73301-0002
Brookhaven Service Center	Internal Revenue Service Attention: I.C.E. Holtsville, NY 00501-0002
Fresno Service Center	Internal Revenue Service Attention: I.C.E. Fresno, CA 93888-0002
Kansas City Service Center	Internal Revenue Service Attention: I.C.E. Kansas City, MO 64999-0002
Memphis Service Center	Internal Revenue Service Attention: I.C.E. Memphis, TN 37501-0002
Ogden Service Center	Internal Revenue Service Attention: I.C.E. Ogden, UT 64201-0002
Philadelphia Service Center	Internal Revenue Service Attention: I.C.E. Philadelphia, PA 19255-0002

PAPERWORK REDUCTION ACT NOTICE: We ask for the information on this form to carry out the internal revenue laws of the United States. We need it to insure that taxpayers are complying with these laws and to allow us to figure and collect the right amount of tax. You are required to give us the information if you are applying for a reward.

You are not required to provide the information requested on a form that is subject to the Paperwork Reduction Act unless the form displays a valid OMB control number. Books or records relating to a form or its instructions must be retained as long as their contents may become material in the administration of any internal revenue law. Generally, tax returns and return information are confidential, as required by Code section 6103.

The time needed to complete this form will vary depending on individual circumstances. The estimated average time is 15 minutes. If you have comments concerning the accuracy of these time estimates or suggestions for making this form simpler, we would be happy to hear from you. You can write to the Tax Forms Committee, Western Area Distribution Center, Rancho Cordova, CA 95743-0001.

Do NOT send the completed Form 211 to the Tax Forms Committee. Instead, send it to the IRS Service Center for your area shown above.

Form 211 (Rev. 6-97)

Collector: "Mr. Debtor, I have worked with you in good faith, but it has become evident that you are unwilling to come to terms to resolve this matter in a professional, ethical manner. Mr. Debtor, you may not be aware of the severity of the situation or of the potential legal consequences, but even though we are on opposite sides of the fence, I do share your concerns and don't want to do anything to hinder your position." (This is a softening statement that prepares the debtor for what is to follow.)

EXHIBIT 9.6   COMMERCIAL FRAUD REPORT LETTER

CASE NO.: *A1158*   CLIENT: *E & M Metal Products*

TO: The Internal Revenue Service
    1111 Constitution Avenue
    Washington, D.C.   20224
    ATTN: Intelligence Division/Criminal Investigations

                              Criminal Violation U.S. Code
                                   Title 26/Section 7201
                         Possible Criminal Intent to Commit
                         Tax Evasion/Fraudulent Conversion/
                      Illegal Conveyance of Assets/Illegitimate
                                   Corporate Liquidation

            RE: Quality Sheet Metal, Inc./Quality Mechanical Services
                     575 Kennedy Road, Hollywood, CA 90028
                          Mr. Edward Black, President

        APPLICATION FOR REWARD BASED ON ORIGINAL INFORMATION PURSUANT TO
                           IRS CODE SECTION 7623
    KINDLY ACKNOWLEDGE RECEIPT OF THIS CLAIM/INVESTIGATION ON YOUR FORM #500-4-214

Dear Sir:

Pursuant to Section 7623 of the Internal Revenue code, the undersigned herein
files claim for reward based on original information that the above noted com-
panies/individuals are perpetrating numerous financial schemes, incorporating
illegal conveyance of assets, transference of funds, and via possible illegitimate corporate liquidation are netting Mr. Black and Mr. Yeaman thousands of
dollars in unreported taxable income.

Based on our investigation, and incriminating statements made by Mr. Michael
Yeaman while under interrogation, there is probable cause to justify direct
IRS intervention/audit since a prima facie case does exist for possible tax
evasion.

Evidently, QUALITY SHEET METAL, INC. orchestrated a brilliant financial scheme
by fraudulent and deceptive practices. This enabled Michael Yeaman to secure
large lines of credit by falsifying and intentionally misleading creditors into
extending credit into six figures. Mr. Yeaman has capitalized on an impenetrable corporate structure to incur these liabilities, liquidating same for cash,
and totally escaping individual liability while making himself judgment proof.
Via the creation of a new corporate entity and through clever corporate manipulation, QUALITY MECHANICAL SERVICES, INC. has rendered QUALITY SHEET METAL, INC.
immune to execution of judgment.

Since the names are intended to be similar for credibility purposes, Mr. Yeaman

---

"Mr. Debtor, would you have any objection if I were to contact your attorney?"
(Wait for answer.) "Thank you, Mr. Debtor. Why don't we arrange a conference call
between the three of us, so that we can discuss this like reasonable people?" (Wait for
answer.)

Debtor: "It won't do any good. I've already told you I'm not paying. As far as I'm concerned, we have reached an impasse. My attorney will tell you the same thing (and
so on)."

EXHIBIT 9.6   COMMERCIAL FRAUD REPORT LETTER (CONT'D)

-2-

has in fact pulled off the perfect white collar crime. He has failed to satisfy the indebtedness of the prior corporation, at the same time capitalizing on a similar name while funneling the assets/cash that have been diverted for his own personal use. Edward Black apparently has some role in this corporate swindle, and allegedly is related to Yeaman.

While it is known that a number of creditors have pursued Mr. Yeaman for defaulting on obligations, one could easily be misled by the manner in which he successfully thwarts creditor/legal pursuit. Rather than evading communication with his creditors, Mr. Yeaman has skillfully managed to convince his creditors that two companies, QUALITY SHEET METAL, INC. and QUALITY MECHANICAL SERVICES, INC. are totally separate entities. He further conveys a hardship story of business failure and severe financial difficulties. As part of his pitch to thwart pursuit, Yeaman conveys that Mr. Edward Black has created a new company to continue to serve the needs of the prior company and the new corporation is not responsible for the debts of QUALITY SHEET METAL, INC.

Yeaman's clever scheme has worked! He has successfully outmaneuvered his creditors, dumbfounded collection agencies, manipulated attorneys, outsmarted the judicial system, and escaped prosecution.

In a few isolated cases, where suspicion has arisen with respect to the crimes being perpetrated by Yeaman, he intimidated the creditor's designated third party by stating that the conversation "is being recorded" and will be "used against" the collection agency or attorney. Even to this degree Mr. Yeaman has again successfully halted any further pursuit.

Pursuant to IRS Rule 4569-24 [4], the information contained herein, including Form 211, shall be forwarded to the Chief Claims Examiner in the district of the alleged tax evader's locale, and evaluated on a criminal basis. IRS Rule 4569.9 dictates the claimant shall receive a partial reward, contingent on criminal prosecution/conviction therein. If the IRS determines that no criminal liability exists, then it is our understanding that this case shall then be investigated for possible civil liability and any collection of deficient taxes will result in a reward.

Accordingly, it is our understanding that contingent upon any tax deficiencies recovered, Coleman & Coleman and the creditor shall receive a reward for providing the IRS with this information.

If we can be of any further assistance in the prosecution of this case, please do not hesitate to contact our office.

Very truly yours,

A. Michael Coleman

A. Michael Coleman
COLEMAN & COLEMAN, INC.

AMC/css
Enclosure

EXHIBIT 9.7   APPLYING FOR A REWARD*

```
Internal Revenue Service
Attention:  Hyman Leventhal
Special Agent - Criminal Investigations
P. O. Box 50456
Chicago, Illinois 60609

                              Criminal Violation U. S. Code
                              Title 26 - Section 7201
                              Intent to Commit Tax Evasion

            RE:   Salvatore Beroca & Associates
                  D/B/A  Master Craft
                  Mediaserv
                  The South Land Company
```

As per our research and your decision to commence an involuntary audit
and jeopardy seizure we are herein confirming the highlights of our
investigation.

The undersigned herein applies to the Internal Revenue Service, pursuant
to Title 26 of the U. S. Code, for a reward predicated on original
information that the above noted individuals and/or business entities
are engaged, amongst other things, in perpetrating numerous blatant,
deceptive, financial schemes, the result of which has netted Mr.
Beroca & Associates unreported income. We have concluded our extensive
investigation, which constitutes probable cause that the above-noted
Associates are at the head of a sophisticated scam operation, the
intricacies of which are as follows:

> The Associates referenced, first incorporate as a "legitimate"
> business, utilizing a name similar to one of a long
> established and creditworthy entity. Cleverly, a numeral
> "1" follows the corporate name so as to legally represent
> themselves as a separate operation. Now the Associates,
> with intention to defraud, misrepresent themselves as
> that of the legitimate business. A "round robin" commercial
> checking account is established utilizing upwards of
> 3 banks. Ingenuously, they draw a substantial draft
> from bank "A" payable to bank "B" and between banks "C",
> "D" and so on. Thereby as impression is falsely created
> where an actual balance of $20,000.00 can be shown to be
> assets in excess of $100,000.00 depending on the timing

* This is a sample IRS cover letter. It is a suggested format. Consult with the IRS for its requirements.

Collector: "Mr. Debtor, I can understand where you're coming from." (Empathy) "In your position, I might even feel the same way. But obviously we are not going to bury this matter, even though we do recognize your rights, and I think it would be prudent to get your attorney involved before we create an expensive and unnecessary litigious situation. Mr. Debtor, I know that your attorney has your best interests at heart, and I'd like to elicit his opinion. Certainly you don't need this matter hanging over your head any longer . . ."

EXHIBIT 9.7   APPLYING FOR A REWARD (CONT'D)

PAGE 2

and statements of the banks. By careful manipulation and with little cash, the Associates have successfully created the illusion of extensive bank deposits thereby yielding them availability to high lines of credit. With credit in hand, the Associates now commence their colossal swindle. The stage has been set, the facade is clearly designed to defraud credit grantors. Usually the first few billings are paid, sometimes within the period necessary to avail themselves of a discount thereby apparently showing a good account status. Within due time and a fictitious credit history, the full impact of the 'sting' will now be realized.

Now utilizing intense, fraudulent applications the goods and/or merchandise obtained are sold below market value to stimulate quick cash flow. The principals of the corporation, protected by the corporate veil, now leave a hollow shell of a defunct entity. Litigation follows, resulting in unsatisfied judgments establishing the Associates immune from liability.

The successful perpetration of white-collar crimes is as follows:

MASTERCRAFT WHOLESALE DISTRIBUTORS

An elaborate hoax wherein impressive multi-color catalogs were printed, offering brand-name merchandise below wholesale, most items requiring large deposits up front while they are non-existent in fact.

RESULT

Numerous unsatisfied judgments have been levied against the defunct corporate entity. No creditor satisfaction has been realized.

MEDIASERV INCORPORATED

A cleverly concocted fraudulent approach to multiple level market distribution. Actually fulfilling their contractual obligation to provide advertising space, however, severely undercutting the actual number of distributed materials and grandiloquent claims of performance and intentionally misleading advertisers.

RESULT

Protracted lawsuits commence, ultimate involuntary bankruptcy leaves creditors with no recourse.

EXHIBIT 9.7   APPLYING FOR A REWARD (CONT'D)

PAGE 3

THE SOUTH LAND COMPANY, INC.

An orchestrated play of words. The South Land Company, a facade illicitly intended to impersonate the legitimate Southland Corporation "7 - Eleven" stores. Under this scheme, the principals have again employed their prior deceptive tactics, resulting in immunity from both civil and criminal liability. Shielded by an impierceable corporate veil and homesteading exceptions, Salvatore Beroca & Associates maintain a recalcitrant attitude and escape prosecution as the crimes were committed out of state.

RESULT

Again, not one of the judgments against the entity has ever been satisfied.

Coleman & Coleman, Inc., has successfully uncovered, through our investigative procedures overlapping involvement of the same principals, transference of assets to avoid levy and hidden private funds for the use of the principals, all of whom are involved in each corporation in a different capacity.

Accordingly, we have filed an application for original information. It is agreed that we are to receive a reward contingent of tax deficiency recovered for providing the I. R. S. with this information, subject to jeopardy seizure execution and/or criminal prosecution.

The Associates (principals of the corporation) have successfully outwitted their creditors and brilliantly out-maneuvered attorneys, judges and even the sheriff. They have in essence committed the perfect crimes.

Our records are available at your request.

Sincerely,

A. Michael Coleman

A. Michael Coleman
COLEMAN & COLEMAN, INC.

AMC:kc
cc: R. V. Torre
        Investigative Research Department

Debtor: "Well, if you insist. But I'll tell you what, I will talk to my attorney directly, or if you want to, you can call him yourself."

Collector: "That's okay, Mr. Debtor. I would prefer to air our grievances through a conference call. That way we might save a lot of unnecessary calls, and perhaps we can conclude this matter in a few minutes." (Push for a conference call. If you cannot get it, then call the debtor's attorney directly.)

Collector: "Mr. Attorney, I understand that you are counsel of record representing William Pastdue. I represent _____. I can certainly appreciate that you have your client's best interests at heart. I know you do your utmost to represent him to the best of your ability." (Notice how the collector bolsters the attorney's ego and starts to condition his frame of mind.) "Mr. Attorney, a problem has arisen that requires your attention concerning . . ." (Explain the problem.) "I know that your relationship with your client is sacred, and it was my suggestion that you should be involved. I know that we can work this out amicably."

The collector then skillfully manipulates the attorney, continuing to inflate the attorney's ego by employing empathy-building statements, allowing the attorney to talk, and listening attentively. There are many variations of this technique—some soft-sell, others hard-line—but in all cases, the debtor's attorney should be viewed not as your adversary but as your liaison to a successful collection. In the end, the debtor's attorney may act as your salesperson.

Attorney-to-Attorney Respect: You are a collector, not an attorney. Many attorneys resent collectors. Some attorneys will chew you up and spit you out without a second thought. You have little chance of moving this kind of attorney off dead center. But there is an unwritten law that attorneys recognize and respect. Basically, this unwritten law mandates cooperation between attorneys even though they are on opposite sides of the fence. As a matter of good business practice, you should have at your disposal an attorney whom you can call on when the need arises. Direct communication by your attorney may be your only chance to salvage an unpaid debt. If your attorney is a proficient negotiator, understands the art of applied psychology, and does not buckle under pressure, he might be your most important link to deal with another attorney's "I know it all" attitude.

LAW LISTS FOR INFORMATION

Unbeknownst to creditors, a corresponding attorney may have had prior experience with your debtor. This information could be valuable, especially if you are dealing with hard-core types prone to litigation. Professional debtors know how to manipulate the legal system and shield themselves against judgment. In such cases, litigation would be an exercise in futility. Some debtors will pay only at the eleventh hour, when the sheriff is knocking on the door.

The attorney you choose to handle a claim is also receiving claims from other creditors and collection agencies. If your debtor is already being sued by the same attorney, the attorney will group the claims together. This will not only lower your litigation costs but may also increase your chances of success. It is always more economical and to your advantage to group claims together. What is more important, much of the preliminary work, including verification of a business entity (to avoid defects in legal pleadings) and searches for judgments and/or tax liens, would have been completed. The attorney may have commenced discovery (i.e., subpoenas, interrogatories, and depositions), which will further enhance your position. The law firm's prior experience with your debtor can be very useful to you.

LAW LISTS—COMMERCIAL AND CONSUMER COLLECTION ATTORNEYS

The General Bar, Inc.
25000 Center Ridge Road
Cleveland, OH 44145-4108
(440) 835-2000 or
(800) 533-2500
www.generalbar.com

American Law Quarterly
853 Westpoint Parkway
Suite 710
Cleveland, OH 44145
(800) 843-4000
www.alqlist.com
User: alq#1
Password: 1899

The Forwarders List of Attorneys
400 Windsor Corporate Park
50 Millstone Road
Suite 200
East Windsor, NJ 08520-1415
(800) 638-9200

Wright Holmes Inc.
1020 8th Avenue South, Suite 10
Naples, FL 34102
(800) 882-5478
www.collectioncenter.com

Campbell's List
P.O. Box 428
Maitland, FL 32751
(800) 249-6934 or (407) 644-8298
www.campbellslist.com

Note: Law list publishers provide their directories free of charge to qualified users. The code of ethics mandates that publishers provide their law lists to collection agencies and other third-party collection sources. They are reluctant to give copies of directories to creditors. Some will, although they may require you to submit a letter affirming that you do not use collection agencies. Creditors may have trouble getting law lists, but they can probably get copies through collection agencies or by creating their own in-house collection agencies (see Chapter 4). Law lists are invaluable tools that are essential when litigation becomes necessary.

Understanding the Basic Principles of Law

Civil and criminal procedures vary from state to state, but certain principles are almost universal. To be effective, a professional collector must have a working knowledge of basic legal remedies. For example, most states have laws that prohibit lawyers from using threats of criminal prosecution to resolve civil matters; however, collectors and creditors often use the implied threat of criminal sanctions to stimulate a debtor to make payment. You can convey information to a debtor and/or the debtor's attorney where you suspect the debtor of criminal improprieties, but it is imperative that you remember that you are not practicing law. The information contained in this section is not intended as a law primer, but is submitted for information purposes only to help you formulate legal strategies to maneuver debtors toward payment. It is urgently recommended that collectors become familiar with state and federal rules and regulations *before taking any action to collect debts*.

Summary (Accelerated) Judgment

The U.S. Constitution and state constitutions grant all litigants the right to a day in court; however, if either party can convince a court that there is no material issue of fact in a dispute, the courts can make a ruling without going through the complex discovery process and a protracted trial. This strategy, known as "summary" or "accelerated" judgment, is the procedural equivalent of judgment after trial. It is a harsh remedy. A motion for summary judgment will not be granted unless an overwhelming preponderance of the evidence clearly establishes that *there is no defense*. If a motion for summary judgment is granted, it will generally put an immediate and permanent end to the case. Collection matters are especially suited to summary judgment. In many jurisdictions, if a claim is based on an unconditional promise to pay money (i.e., goods sold and delivered) or other evidence of indebtedness, the creditor may serve with the summons a notice of motion for summary judgment and the supporting papers instead of a formal summons and complaint.

If your claim is based on goods sold and delivered and the amount is long past due, the burden is on you to establish a valid claim against the debtor. Once established, the burden shifts to the debtor, who must prove that a material issue of fact would preclude summary judgment. In some jurisdictions, the court will grant partial summary judgment. In that case, the court will not issue a judgment for damages, but will issue a *partial* summary judgment establishing *liability*. Thus the dispute must still proceed to trial to settle the issue of damages.

For example, assume that a debtor owes you $10,000. Payment is long past due, the receivable is amply documented, and to your knowledge there is no dispute over the indebtedness, nor has the debtor imposed any counterclaim. Under those conditions, the matter is ripe for summary judgment. If you are pursuing the debtor directly, the summary judgment technique can be used to compel the debtor to come to terms. If you are acting on behalf of a collection agency, you might refer to the corresponding counsel who would exercise this remedy. Consider the following conversation:

Debtor: "Mr. Collector, I have listened to everything you said, and if I were financially able, I would make payment. But due to circumstances beyond my control, I can't meet this obligation. There is nothing I can do . . ."

Collector: "Ms. Debtor, I understand that you are going through a tough time" (assuming the collector has verified that the debtor's grievance is real). "But perhaps you are mis-informed, believing the myth that any lawsuit commenced to collect this debt will linger in the courts. Ms. Debtor, are you aware our attorney is preparing a motion to prosecute this case via summary judgment?" (Pause.) "Are you aware also of the con-sequences should this motion be granted?" (Pause.) "Ms. Debtor, a motion for sum-mary judgment compels the court to determine whether there are any material issues of fact that require trial before a judge and/or jury. Ms. Debtor, these accelerated pro-ceedings take just a few weeks, not several years. Let me ask you, Ms. Debtor, are you going to remain idle and permit an accelerated judgment to ensue?" (Wait for answer.)

Analysis: If you do not get a favorable response, it may be that the debtor is judgment-proof or is about to become judgment-proof. If the debtor responds positively and is rep-resented by counsel, you have created a more positive climate. Continue as follows:

Collector: "Ms. Debtor, attorneys are not cheap. The extraordinary remedy of accelerated judgment requires not only preparation and service of a summons and complaint, but also a motion, supporting affidavits, and other documentation of the claim. Even if we are unsuccessful in getting the entire relief we seek, which I doubt, there is always the possibility that the court will grant partial summary judgment. That is, Ms. Debtor, the court may determine that the debt is valid, leaving only the amount of damages to be computed by a judge. Either way it will be expensive for you. It seems foolish that you would spend money on legal representation when those same funds could be used to resolve this thorny problem. Don't you agree?" (Pause.)

Many times when attorneys argue for summary judgment, the court will grant only par-tial summary judgment, thus establishing liability and leaving the extent of damages to be determined at a plenary trial or inquest. Take your debtor on a mental journey into the morass of legal expenses, confrontations, and oral hearings before the court. Point out that it is quite possible for a court to enter judgment against the debtor in a relatively short time. This will strengthen your bargaining position and create leverage for a more satisfactory resolution of the debt.

Reminder: Third parties, including attorneys, collecting *consumer* debts must not threaten action on which they are not prepared or legally permitted to follow through.

Extraordinary Remedy of Attachment

Under certain circumstances a court may order a debtor's property and/or assets to be seized and brought into the custody of the law. The courts are naturally reluctant to attach a debtor's assets *before judgment,* but where the facts indicate that a debtor might act to dispose of funds or property so as to make any judgment against the debtor worthless, the court may issue a writ of attachment against a debtor's property to gain jurisdiction over that property to ensure that it will be available for execution and sale should judgment be obtained against the debtor.

Attachments are not final judgments, but provisional remedies. When they are granted, the plaintiffs (creditors) must usually post bonds or other security worth as much as or more than the assets to be attached. Each state has its own rules and procedures for granting writs of attachment, and creditors must establish the facts in accordance with the requirements of their individual state statutes. The referenced letter with CPLR excerpt, while New York procedural law, is similar in most states.

If a debtor has hidden property, is disposing of personal assets, is about to liquidate or transfer business assets, or is engaged in other activities that would permit a court to issue a writ of attachment under state statute, attachment can be an excellent collection strategy. If you think that you will be unable to execute a judgment obtained against your debtor if the debtor is allowed to hold onto his property, present your attorney with any evidence that supports your position and suggest that your attorney apply to the court for a writ of attachment. If you have done your homework and meet the necessary criteria for an order of attachment, you might use this strategy: Communicate your intent to pursue a writ of attachment to the debtor directly or to his attorney. Consider how startled your debtor will be as you recite the provisions of the applicable statute. Of course, the threat of attachment can be implemented only through your attorney. But as a tactical approach, you can make it clear to the debtor that you intend to pursue the attachment option. Properly executed, this approach might cause the debtor to realize that the best option is to settle the debt.

Bear in mind: Creditors should not attempt to attach a debtor's property unless they are absolutely certain that they are on firm legal ground. It would be an expensive and embarrassing mistake to exercise this remedy if you do not meet the legal criteria.

One area where attachment has applicability is Long-Arm Statute jurisdiction. Sophisticated creditors have written into their sales agreements/personal guarantees ironclad legalese where if a customer defaults, and the debt is pursued in the courts, the debtor is legally bound to submit to the jurisdiction as designated. Forcing your nonpaying customers to incur the increased expense of defending a creditor-initiated lawsuit within its jurisdiction provides a powerful tactical advantage, but it does have one drawback.

Assume for argument's sake that your debtor does not defend a lawsuit filed in your state, resulting in judgment. For example, the creditor files suit in California, and the debtor, who is domiciled in Ohio, fails to answer the complaint. A default judgment is forthcoming in California. A legal victory, yes, but possibly no recovery. Although the debtor is legally obligated to submit to his creditor's jurisdiction (i.e., California), the creditor most likely has limited power over the foreign Ohio judgment debtor. The remedy might be attachment. Also, depending on the rules of each state, the creditor may exercise conventional judgment recovery procedures.

To a California attorney, in possession of a judgment, who then exercises it as an attachment in Ohio, the process is two-fold. Because a judgment is a conclusive legal decree, the Ohio court, while it possibly may not be able to execute a California judgment, instead issues a writ of attachment. Once the debtor's assets are attached in Ohio, it is very unlikely that the Ohio court will not release them or set aside the California judgment. Depending on each state's rules, foreign judgments may be executable within its jurisdiction. The process, while costly, is extremely potent. Attachments are very risky; for although they are legal remedies, they do not have the same force and effect as a judgment.

The author has had considerable recovery success representing creditors who exercised their state's Long-Arm Statutes. On the plus side, most debtors who are sued from a foreign state will either pay up or consent to default judgment in the creditor's locale. The advantage is that Long-Arm Statute jurisdiction will generally succeed in greater proportion to offset its increased costs. The disadvantage is that a creditor may have to exercise the supplemental remedy of attachment in the debtor's state and/or domesticate a foreign judgment. If the debtor does not answer a creditor's complaint filed within its jurisdiction, default judgment ensues.

Creditors should consult with an attorney to incorporate legalese within their sales contracts, sufficient to compel a potential defendant to submit its jurisdiction, including fulfillment of the minimum contact rule. Make sure your attorney has experience in this area, and take particular note to include airtight language that will withstand the acid test of judicial rule.

Drawbacks to the attachment technique: Among the disadvantages of an attachment proceeding are that the burden of proof (to show why a writ of attachment should be issued) and the bonding requirements make it a very expensive remedy. Most jurisdictions require that you post a bond or an undertaking for double the amount of the attachment. The creditor is put in a position of having to spend large sums of money in an attempt to insure the writ. Another major disadvantage is that even if a writ of attachment is obtained, it is temporary, pending a hearing that must follow within a short period to determine whether the attachment order should continue in force or be vacated. If the debtor can convince the court that you have not met the statutory criteria, the order will be vacated. In that event, you will be liable to the debtor not only for his attorney's fees, but also for any costs or damages incurred as a result of the attachment. Such damages sometimes far exceed the amount of the debt.

Most attorneys will not seek a writ of attachment—even when the criteria can be met—unless substantial sums are at stake and the attorneys consider it a legal certainty that attachments will be granted and sustained. I have known many collectors with paralegal training who are more knowledgeable about the remedy of attachment in their states than most practicing attorneys. Astute collectors will use this knowledge to bring the debtor to the bargaining table. The remedy of attachment is just one more tool that separates the average collector from the pro. Only in situations where a creditor has obtained a foreign judgment is an attachment likely to be sustained.

Involuntary Bankruptcy

Bankruptcy is a highly specialized area that certainly has its place in the debt collection process. A debtor can be put into involuntary bankruptcy under Chapter 7: liquidation or Chapter 11: reorganization. Refer to legal counsel for statutory limits.

Sometimes involuntary bankruptcy does present a viable collection opportunity. Maybe you have witnessed a debtor "melt under the gun" when a collector found the debtor's hot button. Sometimes just letting the debtor know that you are considering an involuntary petition will be enough to induce the debtor to pay, especially if the debtor fears bankruptcy or knows there are other creditors who could join in a petition to fulfill the statutory requirements. If the debtor still will not budge, you can act as the catalyst—putting together all of the legal criteria, even retaining counsel—to actually bring about an involuntary petition in bankruptcy.

One word of warning: Creditors that file involuntary petitions in bad faith (e.g., to harass or embarrass debtors or to compel them to make preferential payments to your clients) may be liable to the debtors for actual and punitive damages. Creditors that file involuntary petitions may also be liable for costs, attorney's fees, and damages if their petitions are dismissed. A collector should not arbitrarily contact creditors of the debtor about a possible involuntary petition. Rather, the collector should establish a relationship with an attorney, preferably a bankruptcy attorney. Then, assuming the client is interested in going the involuntary bankruptcy route, the collector can communicate with other creditors.

Injunctions

Injunctions are another provisional remedy under statutory law. These are court orders that forbid debtors to take certain actions. Injunctions are available in cases where a debtor threatens to destroy or remove the specific subject matter of a lawsuit, or where the debtor threatens, before the matter can be adjudicated, to commit the very act that the suit seeks to prevent. The interim relief grants the creditor a measure of security, but the remedy is drastic and will not be granted unless there is a convincing showing that the creditor is likely to prevail in court and that there is risk of "irreparable injury" to the creditor's interests if the injunction is denied. ("Irreparable injury" is an injury for which a monetary award alone is not adequate compensation.) Injunctions are not available in actions to recover only sums of money.

There are three types of injunction:

1. Temporary restraining order
2. Preliminary injunction
3. Permanent injunction

A temporary restraining order may be issued where, upon a motion for a preliminary injunction, the creditor can show substantial evidence that immediate and irreparable injury, loss, or damage will result unless the debtor is restrained from certain actions *before a hearing can be held.* A temporary restraining order, unlike a preliminary injunction, may be issued without prior notice to the debtor. When a temporary restraining order is issued, the court will set a hearing at the earliest possible time to consider a preliminary injunction. Unless the court orders otherwise, the temporary restraining order, together with supporting documents and notice of the hearing on the motion for a preliminary injunction, must be served to the debtor in the same manner as a summons (i.e., in person). Before issuing a temporary restraining order, the court may, at its discretion, require the creditor to provide a bond or other security in an amount to be fixed by the court.

A preliminary injunction is usually granted while the court considers a motion for a permanent injunction. A creditor can move for a preliminary injunction at any time from the commencement of the action until final judgment. In a motion for a preliminary injunction, the creditor must prove there is a genuine risk that the debtor will, during the lawsuit, perform some act that the creditor has gone to court to prevent, thereby rendering any final judgment sterile. Again, if a preliminary injunction is granted, the creditor will be required to post a bond or other security in an amount to be fixed by the court. If it is finally determined that the creditor was *not* entitled to an injunction, the creditor will be required to pay all damages, costs, and attorney's fees that the debtor sustained as a result of the injunction.

A permanent injunction—ordering that all (or some) elements of the preliminary injunction be sustained—is usually granted after a full trial.

It must be evident that the injunction remedy is an expensive procedure that will not be readily granted by the courts; however, if a court does grant a preliminary injunction, or even a temporary restraining order, the situation can pose monumental problems to the debtor.

Legal note: This chapter is intended merely to familiarize the collector with provisional remedies that may be available with recourse to legal proceedings. If exercised properly, they can be valuable to effectuate collections at the earliest possible time, but these provisional remedies should not be undertaken, or used to coerce debtors to make payment, without benefit of legal counsel.

The remedy of injunction is a valuable recovery tool, applicable in situations wherein a debtor is engaging in or contemplating an act detrimental to a creditor. The most common application for a debtor pursuing injunctive relief is the sale of a business or liquidation of assets. Generally, a creditor's position must be secured and the debtor about to commit an act prejudicial in order for the remedy to be applicable.

CHAPTER 10

Enforcement of Money Judgments and Investigatory Skills

A scorpion was taking in the sun along a riverbank, desirous of crossing it. About that time, a tortoise descended to the foot of the water in readiness to plunge into it. "Hey," notioned the scorpion, "can you do me a favor?" The accommodating tortoise replied: "What can I do for you?" A conversation ensued:

Scorpion: "I'd like to cross the river. Can I climb on you and hitch a ride?"

Tortoise: "Are you crazy? I'm a turtle, and you're a scorpion. How do I know that once we get out into the water you won't sting me?"

Scorpion: "My venom is lethal, but I assure you that I only want to cross the river. Why would I kill you at the expense of drowning?"

Tortoise: "OK, get on my shell and hold on. I'll get you to the other side."

All was fine until about midway across the river, when the scorpion injected the tortoise with its deadly poison. As the two began to drown, the tortoise demanded an explanation.

Tortoise: "Why did you sting me? Now we're both going to die."

Scorpion: "I couldn't help it. It's my nature!"

Our landscape is cluttered with the bodies of deadbeats, credit criminals, bad check passers, manipulators, and judgment-proof debtors. These bastions of deceit thumb their noses at adversaries and defy our legal system. For judgment creditors, these deadbeats represent a paradox of conflicting dimensions. On the one hand, they enter into credit relationships representing honorable intent. On the other hand, they make a mockery out of our judicial system. For frustrated creditors, the result is a paper victory and no money.

UNCOLLECTIBLE JUDGMENT SYNDROME

No one knows exactly how many judgments are either uncollectible or unenforceable, but conservative estimates indicate that the number averages about one in three. Imagine, almost one-third of legal decrees are never converted to money. Translated to numbers, the volume of unsatisfied legal decrees is in the billions of dollars. One source estimates that if all the uncollected judgments were converted to money, it would be enough to satisfy about 20% of our national debt.

Within this melting pot are creditors who, like you, have exhausted due process only to end up with zero money. The pain is excruciating, for you have not only written off the original indebtedness, but worse, you have expended good money after bad.

Why are so many judgments uncollectible? The problem is a combination of inferior credit management, less than quality legal representation, and the lethargy of the judicial system, coupled with hard-core debtor mentality. Add to this the countermeasures that can easily be implemented by an astute judgment debtor and the result is that *anyone* can frustrate the enforcement of a money judgment.

The following section examines the causes for noncollectibility together with quick-fix solutions:

Typical Credit Management	Astute Credit Management
Too many creditors are lenient, extending credit by the seat of their pants. Anxious to make a sale, they fail to perform an investigation into the customer's financial history. The approval process is haphazard at best. Worse, security instruments are either overlooked or structurally weak. The result is a house-of-cards transaction, subject to the vagaries of your customer. Will he pay or won't he?	Thorough credit investigation including evaluation by cross reporting National profiles Personal guarantee, assignments, waiver, or confession of judgments Electronic debit and credit card authorizations Intuition and gut feeling

Inferior Legal Representation	Quality Attorney Representation
An attorney/client comfort zone. Most lawyers are *not* skilled in judgment recovery. Securing a judgment and collecting it are two entirely separate procedures.	"Choose your love and then love your choice," is more than a metaphor. It also applies to the people we choose to represent us. All lawyers are trained to litigate your dispute to judicial finality (i.e., judgment), but few maintain the investigative resources to enforce it. Always select a lawyer who *maintains experience in collecting money judgments.*

TRAINING DAY: THINK CREATIVELY!

Imagine you are employed as Vice President of Finance for the once prestigious Ball Bearing Company, which transitioned into bankruptcy. You are over-inventoried and knee-deep in debt; liquidation is imminent. The events leading to your company's demise are anchored in a declining use of your product, ball bearings. Faced with collapse, the inevitable day of reckoning is fast approaching. Soon you will be unemployed.

Meanwhile, there are millions of dollars of unsold ball bearings in the warehouse—inventory that must be liquidated for scrap. With doomsday fast approaching, you are struck with a novel idea. Why can't you sell ball bearings for unconventional uses? Your hair-brained scheme foments, eventually crystalizing into a full-fledged marketing plan. Your list of potential ball bearing uses includes the following:

Weights	Toys
Curtains	Roller skates
Exercise equipment	Games
Underwater gear	Contests (fill a fishbowl and guess the quantity)
	Fillers
	Decorations
	Flower pots

Armed with a list of ready prospects, you cross-market your inventory while raising much-needed cash. Surprised, you eventually penetrate new markets, regain lost business, and emerge from bankruptcy to a bright future.

The above scenario is not hypothetical, but based on a real-life bankruptcy. While creditors, lawyers, and the bankruptcy court were litigating the collapse of this multimillion-dollar company, one CFO was implementing a novel game plan for survival and rebirth. A resourceful executive accomplished what the courts and the lawyers could not. The lesson learned is significant because the application of creativity coupled with bulldog determination saved the day. Applied to the recovery of money judgments, you are going to learn how to "pass go and collect $200."

The recovery of money judgments is the extreme of commercial receivable management—an inexact science for which even attorneys lack proficiency. It is an art form, a specialty requiring the practitioner to think outside the box. Although judgment recovery is far removed from your day-to-day responsibilities, it is nevertheless the final frontier. If you can collect money judgments, you can recover virtually *any* receivable!

Judgment debtors who do not voluntarily honor a court decree are consistent with attorneys who secure the writ, but fail to convert it into money. The reason? Discovery within a lawsuit is extrajudicial (i.e., the voluntary submission of information during or post litigation). Most often, judgment debtors submit "icicles in wintertime," with frustrating consequences for judgment creditors. Typically, creditors secure a paper victory (i.e., a judgment, but no money).

The following are three actual case histories, which are a radical departure from typical lawyering (i.e., conventional execution attempts of money judgments). All three initially failed. These case histories provide a synopsis of three judgment-proof debtors and a more detailed explanation of the creative penetration that resulted in their recovery.

1. *Johnson Worldwide Associates v. Taylor Rental* [NOTE: This case reflects only one Taylor Rental franchise.]—$22,697.18. Two attorneys failed to collect the money judgment. Conversely, we arranged for an embarrassing levy of commercial tents to be levied during the graduating class of a major university, augmented with a newsworthy press release. When confronted with this dilemma, the humiliated debtor not only wired the $22,697.18, but also paid an additional interest of $1,623.18, and sheriff fees of $425.00, all simultaneous to threats from the debtor's attorney that his clients "rights were violated."

2. *23rd Century v. Mullins/Rubinstein*—$40,862.00 for property damage. The attorney erred in submitting the execution to the local sheriff, relevant to the employment of one defendant. Because this defendant worked for a large corporation, its offices were out of state—and out of reach of the local sheriff. Resubmitting the judgment, it was processed via the Secretary of State, which was *within* the constable's jurisdiction. As a result, the levy was successful.

3. *Stone Mountain Enterprises v. Dorothy Hughes and Hughes Advertising*, defunct. Sixteen creditors wrote off judgments (exceeding $900,000) due to liquidation; however, we uncovered that the judgment debtor was laundering monies in collusion with a real estate development company by obtaining microfiche copies of checks cashed by a property manager who was taking kickbacks. The real estate firm voluntarily paid $60,000 of a $68,372 judgment on behalf of out-of-business Hughes Advertisement.

In all three cases, attorneys representing creditors did *not* excavate crucial evidence that would have resulted in converting these judgments into money. In the *23rd Century v. Mullins/Rubinstein* execution, the attorney submitted the execution to the local sheriff, which seemed appropriate, but the judgment debtor's corporate office was out of state, so the writ was returned unsatisfied. This is not an attorney error, but rather the lack of excavating crucial information that would have resulted in recovery.

Let's examine these three judgments, making note of the unconventional techniques that were employed to checkmate these hardened debtors, and particularly the creativity that resulted in recovery:

1. *Johnson Worldwide v. Taylor Rental.* Johnson Worldwide Associates' first attorney secured judgment by default. The second attorney petitioned the judgment debtor to post judgment examination, wherein the proprietor lied under oath (about

assets). The third attempt by the collection consultant also failed because the judgment debtor's assets were not in his name. The fourth attempt was bold and successful. Creditor Johnson Worldwide Associates did not want the commercial tents because its depreciated value was about 20% of judgment. Our strategy deviated from protocol, wherein arrangements were coordinated to levy the commercial tents smack within Taylor Rental's prime graduation rental season. The constable's levy was simultaneous with graduation ceremonies. The sheriff appeared three hours before the invited guests, while the news media were desirous of interviews. A stunned Taylor Rental threatened unfair practices and harassment, which was responded to with compelling street methodology. Checkmated, we secured payment in full via wire transfer. When appropriate, execute a Human Interest Press Release, sending copies to local media.

2. *23rd Century v. Mullins/Rubenstein.* Wage garnishments can be tricky, especially if the judgment debtor works for a corporation whose headquarters are out of state (exception, U.S. Post Office, Minneapolis). For example, assume that the judgment creditor is in Connecticut. The debtor works for a Hess Service Station in Suffolk County, New York. Hess's corporate office is in Woodbridge, New Jersey. The judgment creditor submits execution to Hess's Woodbridge office, which is *outside* the sheriff's jurisdiction; the writ is returned unsatisfied. By contrast, we served Hess Corporation's New York registered agent (i.e., the Secretary of State). Because the judgment creditor is registered to do business in New York, the sheriff has jurisdiction. This is a minor technicality, but it will make the difference between success and failure.

3. *Stone Mountain Enterprises v. Hughes Adverting.* This was an example of serendipitous enrichment. We were discharged from representation per creditors World Color Press's Vice President, whose company was owed in excess of $120,000. (The VP opted not to pursue our drastic remedy.) As we had completed an investigation per Hughes's belated public filings, including photocopying of a myriad of unsatisfied judgments, we were well-acclimated with this mastermind credit criminal. Sixteen-plus judgment creditors were attempting to recover from a defunct corporate entity, all of which wrote off their judgments as uncollectible. Conversely, the Hughes/real estate development firm relationship was very suspicious (i.e., the real estate firm refused to withhold approximately $55,000 due to Hughes, their ad agency, for vendor World Color, who printed their full-page ad in *Parade* magazine). A legitimate vendor would have voluntarily cooperated by withholding remittance for 30 days to permit an impleader complaint (and $55,000 to World Color). Conversely, this real estate firm threatened litigation, charging "harassment." World Color would not endorse our "creative penetration" (i.e., an impleader complaint), nor would it authorize investigation into the unscrupulous practices of the ad agency/client. After having expended many hours assembling documentation, and the wimpy posture of the creditor (i.e., afraid of a "harassment" lawsuit), the endeavor became a salvage

operation. The second largest creditor who maintained a $68,372 judgment was solicited, albeit with a purchase option. Once the culprits were confronted with exposing the scam, the $68,372 judgment was settled for $60,000. (World Color could have recovered their $120,000 had they not been intimidated by the bluff.)

INFORMATION SUBPOENAS: AN UNCONVENTIONAL APPROACH TO DEVELOPING INFORMATION

Our legal system provides for a cross mixture of discovery devices: notices to produce, depositions, examinations, interrogatories, and subpoenas. Its relation to potential garnishees, the recovery of money judgments presents a multiset of problems—jurisdiction.

Assume arguendo that you are a judgment creditor in Pennsylvania. Your judgment debtor is domiciled in Illinois but has attachable assets in Florida. Assume also that you secured a default judgment in Pennsylvania. Like most states, Pennsylvania maintains a Long-Arm Statute (i.e., suing from your state and reaching into a foreign jurisdiction). The mere procurement of the Pennsylvania writ is just the beginning. Enforcement is an entirely different problem.

Notwithstanding that your judgment debtor has numerous defenses (alleging improper venue), technical problems must be overcome. These include, but are not limited to, meeting the statutory requirement of "minimum contacts" (i.e., your defendant maintained "minimum contacts" with your jurisdiction and/or "continuity and regularity of contracts").

This section is not intended to dissect the vagaries of jurisdiction, but rather the creative techniques, which are often overlooked, to penetrate and recover a money judgment. In our example—a Pennsylvania plaintiff, Illinois defendant, with Florida assets—we will assume the Pennsylvania judgment is *not challenged* (in Pennsylvania). Assuming you have secured a default judgment, here is the chronology as to how you would execute it:

1. After securing a verified praecipe for judgment in Pennsylvania, next secure a *triple seal exemplified record*. The triple seal (i.e., judge's signature, prothonotary witness of judge's signature, and authenticity) is required for out-of-state domestication.

2. Record the Pennsylvania exemplified record and verified praecipe for judgment in Illinois.

3. Illinois may treat the Pennsylvania judgment as an attachment, or you may have to initiate a new civil proceeding. *Advantage:* Illinois court *does not* have jurisdiction to set aside or vacate the Pennsylvania degree. *Disadvantage:* Illinois court can temporarily restrain the execution of the Pennsylvania judgment, sufficient to allow time for your judgment debtor to prove "excusable default" or a "meritorious defense," in Pennsylvania.

Note: Assuming the Pennsylvania judgment stands and/or is uncontested, your Illinois lawyer may proceed with its execution. At this juncture, you have two options:

1. Proceed with attempting to execute the Pennsylvania judgment in Illinois (domesticated), relying on conventional protocol (i.e., post-judgment discovery).

2. Proceed with an *unconventional* game plan of uncovering attaching assets.

Let's examine option 2 in greater detail. Reading between the lines, it is a safe bet that your nonresponsive Illinois defendant has either concealed assets and/or is judgment-proof. The fact that your defendant did not impose a defense in Pennsylvania is a tell-tale sign of its uncollectability; your defendant is not worried about potential ramifications.

By contrast, if your Illinois defendant defended your Pennsylvania lawsuit, this is an indication that your adversary has assets worth protecting. Generally, default judgments are a dead giveaway that your adversary's assets are out of your reach or protected. Overall, defended lawsuits result in a higher percentage of collectability.

Information Subpoena Ruse

Information subpoenas are a judgment creditor's best discovery resource because they reveal information without your adversary's knowledge. Depending on jurisdiction, subpoenas can either be served by an attorney, or in many cases, must be approved by a judge. Either way, one stumbling block will prevent crucial information from being revealed. In our hypothetical Pennsylvania/Illinois litigation, a judicial problem arises: Subpoena enforcement is limited to Pennsylvania. Because your adversary has *no* assets in Pennsylvania, discovery is worthless. Stated another way, your Pennsylvania judgment has value only over attachable Pennsylvania assets. On the flip side, your Pennsylvania exemplified record and domestication in Illinois now gives you subpoena power in that state. Assuming your judgment debtor has assets in Illinois, you will retrieve valuable information and possibly recover.

Cost Versus Feasibility

So far you have exercised legal rights in two states (Pennsylvania and Illinois) and engaged in a double marathon, albeit the Pennsylvania judgment was obtained at negligible cost. The real expense (i.e., collecting your judgment) is going to be consumed trying to excavate information revealing attachable assets that are out of state and then levying upon them.

An Effective Discovery Device: Mail-Order Information Subpoenas

Over the years, the author has wrestled with this problem for many judgment creditors, exercising their legal rights in various jurisdictions. The system has many flaws and many obstacles. Navigating this legal matrix is an expensive and time-consuming nightmare. Because a judgment debtor's assets may not necessarily be within his forum state, coupled with garnishee information, which may be spread out over many states—and jurisdictions—the enforcement process can be daunting.

Note: Judgments obtained in federal court are not subjected to the vagaries of state courts and are multistate enforceable.

For example, assume you issue an information subpoena (from Pennsylvania or Illinois) to a potential garnishee in Florida (as per the example). In all likelihood, the Florida garnishee will respond that neither Pennsylvania nor the Illinois court maintains jurisdiction, thus rejecting your subpoena. If the Florida source maintains crucial information sufficient to levy the judgment, and will not honor it, you have hit a stone wall. This is a major problem analogous to delivering the ball to the one-yard line and not being able to score a touchdown. For the judgment creditor, this means hiring Florida counsel to further domesticate your Pennsylvania judgment, gaining jurisdiction over the judgment debtor's assets in Florida. In this scenario, the judgment creditor would sustain the costs of legal representation in three states: Pennsylvania, Illinois, and Florida. How may creditors are willing to multistate litigate?

An Ingenious Strategy: How to Obtain Information Using Mail-Order Psychology

One little-known strategy combines marketing savvy with psychology. On average it's 50% effective and intended to circumnavigate these roadblocks. Here is the chronology to develop vital information while suppressing the jurisdiction issue. First, secure a supply of information subpoenas from a legal forms retailer, the court, or on the Web. The more official looking they are, the better. Next, secure a rubber stamp with large red letters that says: Attn: Credit Department.

Equipped with these forms and stamp, you will need to acquire a credit report and national profile for your subject. (A national profile differs from a credit report because it reveals information *retroactive* 10 years as matched to your subject's Social Security number and is not reported as an inquiry.) If your subject is credit active (a good sign that increases your chances of success), you will note that the last page provides the names, addresses, and phone numbers of reporting creditors. These names and addresses combined with a national profile are your best sources for serving information subpoenas because each one has or currently maintains a financial relationship with your judgment debtor. Most maintain copies of checks, credit applications, client histories, and/or employment, every one of which can provide you with crucial information to levy your judgment.

Prepare information subpoenas for each and every source listed on both the credit report *and* national profile, each addressed to the Credit Department. *Warning:* Never address your information subpoena to a legal department. Simultaneously prepare two cardboard, Priority Mail envelopes. Affix the mailing envelope with $3.85 in commemorative stamps and labeled for return of documents. Never use a postage meter idesia. The reason will be explained later.

Note: Generally, the movant to vacate a default judgment must meet two criterion: (1) Establish a "meritorious defense" and (2) "excusable default." Assume that your adversary can prove he was in the hospital undergoing an operation at the time of service of your lawsuit; this would constitute "excusable default." Next, assume that your merchandise was not delivered timely, providing a defense (frivolous or genuine). Even if the purported delivery was untimely and your adversary could prove economic damage, the motion would be denied. Why? Consider if you sold widgets in January, the account defaulted in February, and it took you until December to sue—and this was the *first* defense representation—the motion to vacate would likely fail. Add to this the creditor's immunity from the debtor's time-dated requirements, and the burden of satisfying a "meritorious defense" is not met. A prudent court would likely uphold the default and deny a motion to vacate. Although your defendant would have met the burden of "excusable default" (i.e., convalescing in a hospital), the second criteria of a meritorious defense would not be satisfied. Both "excusable default" and a "meritorious defense" are mandatory criterion to vacate a money judgment, applicable in most jurisdictions.

Mailing Your Information Subpoenas

Attach to your information subpoena a credit report and/or national profile excerpt and highlight relevant information as reported. Enclose a cover letter. Send it via Priority Mail with a commemorative stamp affixed for $3.85. (Make sure the front of the envelope is marked Attn: Credit Dept. or Credit Manager. This is important because you intentionally want to avoid it being passed on to the legal department.) Your cover letter should contain the information shown in Exhibit 10.1.

Assume that you have subpoenaed 20 sources on the credit report and 10 excerpted from the national profile, for a total of 30. What are your chances of success? Overall, you should receive favorable responses from at least 15, or about half. The other half will reject your subpoena claiming a "jurisdiction defect." What is important is *not* the 50% rejections, but rather the 50% compliance. The one-half that comply may yield the information required to effectuate recovery of your judgment.

EXHIBIT 10.1   INFORMATION SUBPOENA LETTER: SAMPLE

To Whom It May Concern:

Enclosed are:

- Information Subpoena
- Account Information excerpted from credit report
- Civil Judgment (or domesticated exemplified transcript)
- Self-addressed return envelope

Please provide copies of remittances, credit application, and debits. If place of employment is known, please provide.

Your compliance with the enclosed subpoena within 20 days will negate legal intervention. For your convenience, a stamped, flat-rate Priority envelope with $3.85 postage is affixed (valid for up to 2 lbs.).

Your cooperation is greatly appreciated.

This procedure differs from mailing your subpoenas in a plain white envelope, affixed with a postal idesia, and addressed to the legal department. If you subscribe to protocol, it is a sure bet that more than 95% will reject your subpoena(s) as being jurisdictionally defective. Why the difference? The answer as to why this technique works has more to do with psychology and marketing strategy then legal compliance.

Compliance Factor

Why does this technique work? You have presented your subpoena to the credit department, which is removed from the lawyers; a clerical person is more likely to respond favorably than a lawyer, who will impose legal technicalities and rejection. You have also highlighted relevant reporting information excerpted from credit reports/national profile (i.e., Social Security number, account number if known, date of birth, address, and payment experience); the result is expeditious retrieval of information. As a further inducement, you have employed marketing savvy and convenience. By mailing your subpoenas Priority Mail in a colorful plastic wrapper, labeled "Attn: Credit Manager" or "Credit Dept.," you have not only circumnavigated the legal gurus, but your package also stands out among other competing mail. In all likelihood, a clerical person will process your subpoenas.

The icing on the cake is your self-addressed, stamped return Priority flat-rate mailing envelope affixed with $3.85 in postage (whatever the sender can stuff in the envelope, the post office will deliver), decorated with commemorative stamps on both the sending and return envelopes.

The commemorative stamps adds a touch of elegance to the mailing package. Important: A return postage idesia is *not* acceptable and in violation of postal regulations. Metered mail can only be sent from the originating post office.

How to Obtain a Mortgage Application

If your subject owns or has refinanced a home, the mortgage application is the ultimate tell-tale document. Mortgage applications reveal everything about your subject's finances, income, investments, real estate owned, employment, and so on. A mortgage application is a protected document requiring a subpoena signed by a judge. It is one of the most difficult documents to obtain—and one of the most valuable.

Consider that a mortgage application may also deviate from testimony provided by your judgment debtor. Because a mortgage or refinance is a significant capital obligation, the borrower will reveal everything about his finances. Often, the information contained in a mortgage application *contradicts* what your adversary reveals to you as judgment creditor.

Criminal Penalties

Mortgage applications also contain severe civil and criminal penalties for false representation; misrepresentations are punishable per Title 18, Section 1001, of the U.S. Code.

Incredibly, despite the extraordinary protection afforded a mortgage application, clerical personnel are often duped into copying these documents. Overall, the author has averaged about a 50% success rate obtaining these privileged documents—information that often showcases a judgment debtor's assets. A shrewd practitioner would be wise to utilize contradictory information contained in a mortgage application to ambush your adversary. In some instances, it can even be used for criminal prosecution (i.e., making false material statements). You too can beat the system and penetrate numerous obstacles that frustrate the recovery of money judgments. As demonstrated, virtually everything about your subject is discoverable—if you know which buttons to push.

These strategies are far removed from protocol and are very creative. The practitioner can circumnavigate a regimented system stymied with legalese and frustrated with obstacles. By implementing ingenuity seasoned with determination, you can outmaneuver the system and bypass the legal gurus, whose job it is to prevent you from passing go and collecting $200. Just as the ball bearing executive implemented a novel game plan to rejuvenate his company, so you too can succeed.

NATIONAL PROFILE (AKA INSIDER REPORTS)

The opposite of a credit report, a national profile provides expanded and valuable information—data that may reveal attachable assets. Unlike a credit report, which reveals payment history per inputting creditors, National Profiles (aka insider reports) electronically match the subject's Social Security number to most transactions (except investments and payment of taxes) retroactive 10 years. Insider reports *do not* publish an inquiry (the subject never knows information was accessed), which further embellishes their usefulness. Insider reports vary in size from a few pages to small tomes. They are sold by information providers, electronic search firms, and most detective agencies.

Depending on the databases accessed, their use as a discovery device is unparalleled. Comprehensive insider reports contain the following information:

- Subject's Social Security number matched to genre, including possible associated Social Security numbers
- Driver's licenses numbers and addresses
- Registered motor vehicles
- Real estate owned, assessed value, date of sale, and seller's name
- Deed transfer
- UCC filings and liens
- Bankruptcies and judgments
- Criminal history
- Business and corporate affiliations with officer match
- Possible relatives with Social Security numbers and telephone numbers

- Cross-numeric address search with alternate names
- Neighbors with nearby addresses and phone numbers

The last page of an insider report indicates the databases assessed.

Two recommended search firms that can provide you with this service are the following:

The Finders
P.O. Box 261
Croton Falls, NY 10519
Tel: (800) 834-2141 or (845) 278-4206
Fax: (845) 278-4206

North American Information
2401 E. 32nd Street, #10-233
Joplin, MO 64804
Tel: (888) 296-2292 or (417) 626-2292
Fax: (417) 626-8228

The utilization of a national report is not limited to the recovery of money judgments. They are marvelous research tools. As a resource for information subpoenas, they provide judgment creditors with a smorgasbord of potential information.

INFORMATION SUBPOENA PACKAGE

The following are the components of an information subpoena package. (Sources are derived from credit report and national profile.)

- Cover letter
- *Subpoena duces tecum* or information subpoena (refer to Chapter 9)
- Statement or transcript of judgment
- Credit report revealing Social Security number, date of birth, with excerpted creditor account number and payment history (refer to judgment debtor's credit report for sources of information)
- Priority Mail envelope addressed to Credit Manager or credit department. (Never address your subpoena to the legal department.)
- Self-addressed, stamped return flat-rate Priority Mail envelope
- Both mailing envelopes affixed with commemorative stamps

Credit reports and national profiles are necessary research tools because they reveal a financial picture of your adversary, together with account numbers and addresses.

Despite a persuasive subpoena package, you will elicit a percentage of "drop dead" non-compliance letters; however, despite the rejections, about 50% will comply, photocopying documents that may be useful to a judgment creditor.

CHAPTER 11

Case Studies

This chapter will introduce you to the dark side of the collection industry, where unscrupulous debt collectors resort to unethical and illegal conduct to trick or scare debtors into paying. Of course, the games these collectors play to recover receivables are in blatant violation of numerous federal and state statutes. Many creditors turn over their uncollected receivables to collection agencies without inquiring about the collectors' backgrounds or their modus operandi. You may feel that how your collection agency goes about its business is no concern of yours. But, in fact, collectors who overstep legal boundaries expose the companies that hired them to liability for damages. The information presented here will make you aware of the criminal element in the collection industry. You will learn what to watch out for to avoid legal consequences.

Some collectors are master impersonators. You will learn how some experienced collectors impersonate sheriffs and attorneys. They may "double-team" debtors to get them to meet their obligations out of fear of the legal consequences should they refuse to pay. This is a game of Russian roulette, however, because debtors under such circumstances have every right to turn around and sue the collectors and their creditors. Thus this approach can destroy collection potential and subject collector and creditor to liability.

You will learn the difference between the legal use of aliases by collection personnel and illegal impersonation. In one outrageous example, a collector actually represented himself as a state supreme court justice. The debtor bought the hoax and ended up paying the debt plus interest.

Most cases of outrageous conduct on the part of debt collectors involve large receivables, simply because it would not be worth the trouble or the risk to break the law in pursuit of small accounts, but there are exceptions. Find out how one woman collecting small-balance accounts collected more than 80% of the outstanding accounts by making one phone call to past-due debtors.

What would you do to collect from a foreign buyer who refused to pay? You would be ill-advised to go to the lengths of one veteran collector who broke every rule in the book by impersonating an agent of the U.S. Customs Service.

In short, there are collectors who will stop at nothing to collect their accounts. Any creditor who hires such people is wielding a dual-edged sword. Some would not be averse to ripping off their clients, other collection agencies, or even law firms. In many cases the nefarious practices of irresponsible collectors succeed where the legal system would have failed. But at what cost, and at what risk? These unethical collectors are generally unconcerned about the consequences of their illegal acts. They know the chances are slim that they will ever be prosecuted. If things get too hot, they can simply pack up their bags and move on. They could not care less that their clients are left holding the bag.

CONFESSIONS OF BILL COLLECTORS

Debt collection is a regulated industry, and no book on collecting accounts receivable would be complete without a few war stories. The Fair Debt Collection Practices Act strictly regulates third-party collection of *consumer* debts. Other legislation, including the Fair Credit Reporting Act, the Fair Credit Billing Act, the Federal Trade Commission Act, and numerous state statutes also regulate consumer collectors and, in some cases, commercial collectors and creditors. But despite these laws and regulations, some collectors still resort to unethical and illegal conduct. The purpose of this chapter is not to teach these illegal tactics. Rather, this chapter is included:

- To help creditors better understand the games collection agencies play to recover their receivables, so you will know what to watch out for to avoid possible legal consequences
- As a source of information

Fortunately, most collectors do adhere to state and federal laws, but there is a small minority who step out of line, thumbing their noses at the law and making their own rules. Of course, every industry has its criminal elements. In medicine they are known as quacks. Attorneys who bend the law are shysters. Salespeople who knowingly sell unsuspecting customers a pig in a poke are known as pitch men. Alas, there is also a criminal element in the collection industry.

Names have been changed to protect the guilty. Collectors who engage in criminal activities are calculating and cunning. Master impersonators, they are very creative in their collection calls. The following experiences, derived from interviews with many veteran collectors, might best be termed "war stories." Names and details have been changed to protect the privacy of those involved.

DEPUTY LANO

One of the more interesting characters in our industry is Hernandez Salvatore—better known among his peers as "Deputy Lano." Hernandez, a veteran of 30-plus years' collection experience, got his start in the finance industry. He is probably one of the best impersonators in the business. Hernandez, together with his partner in crime, uses a very simple yet effective ploy to motivate debtors. Hernandez, impersonating a sheriff (or marshall, constable, etc.), prompts the debtor to call another collector who is posing as an attorney.

Through this double-team strategy, Hernandez and his cohort instill in the debtor's mind a fear of devastating legal consequences. Here is how the collectors implement their technique:

> *Hernandez:* "Mr. Pastdue? Mr. William Pastdue? This is Deputy Lano of the New York Sheriff's Department. We received papers for the execution of a writ of attachment that was filed by attorneys Rubinstein & Rubinstein against you in the amount of $5,287.36, plus court costs and disbursements representing $387.42, for a total of $5,674.78. Mr. Pastdue, the New York Sheriff's Department does not have jurisdiction in New Jersey, and I must send these papers to the sheriff in Essex County to be served against you. Is there a problem, Mr. Pastdue, that the matter has gotten to this point?"

Analysis: If the debtor really believes that the sheriff is about to knock on the door, he might be inclined to pay. If that is the case, the con proceeds as follows:

> *Hernandez:* "Well, Mr. Pastdue, I recommend that you contact the attorney representing the creditor in this matter immediately. His name is Mr. William Rubinstein, and his telephone number is (212) 555-1680. Either get this matter resolved or retain counsel, Mr. Pastdue, as it will take less than 72 hours to execute the writ against you."

If all goes according to plan, the debtor will then call the "attorney," in which case the other collector, Hernandez's partner, will impersonate an attorney and structure the call to move the debtor to meet his obligation.

Of course, not all debtors fall for this con. Some are familiar with legal processes and know how difficult it is to secure a writ of attachment. All too often, a debtor, acting out of fear or recognizing the con, will call his own attorney. Hernandez then tries to manipulate the debtor's attorney into believing the legal machinery has gone forward "ex parte" (without notice to the debtor). Hernandez might then cite the appropriate statutes, perhaps telling the attorney that a bond has been posted and that the creditor will be moving for a writ of attachment; however, if the debtor's attorney is astute and knows appropriate procedural law, he will ascertain that there is in fact no "attachment" and that no "legal papers" have been processed.

Depending on the debtor's situation, vulnerability to judgments, and other factors, the technique is effective perhaps 20% to 40% of the time, according to Hernandez. The problem with this technique, he warns, is not how to implement it, but rather how to get out of it. If the debtor's attorney persists in an investigation and finds out that the collectors' statements are false and that they are not who they say they are, the debtor is in excellent position to turn the tables and bring charges against the collectors, with every likelihood of success.

TRIAL OF HERMAN DEADBEAT: OVER THE PHONE

The practice of using aliases among individual debt collectors is prevalent in the collection agency industry, although some creditors also have employees use aliases when they collect accounts. This practice, permissible in most instances under federal law, should not be confused with illegal impersonation. Some unscrupulous collectors are notorious for representing themselves as sheriffs, marshalls, constables, attorneys, IRS agents, and even judges. In one humorous, if not bizarre, case, a debt collector actually convinced the debtor that a "trial" was going to take place over the telephone. The collector, holding himself out as an attorney, advised the debtor that "service of process" had been accomplished via "publication" (i.e., a legal notice in a newspaper), that he, the attorney, was actually in the courtroom, and that a trial to settle the debt was about to commence. Incredibly, the debtor believed this outrageous lie and prepared to defend himself over the telephone. The collector enlisted an accomplice to play the role of the judge, and a three-way conversation ensued. The collector playing the attorney cross-examined the debtor with respect to the indebtedness. After about 10 minutes, the judge (the other collector) told the debtor that he would "retire to his chambers" to review the evidence and render a verdict. While this was going on, the attorney (the first collector) kept the debtor on the phone. Within a few minutes, the "judge" returned with a verdict, telling the debtor something to this effect:

"After reviewing all of the evidence, we conclude that the plaintiff has presented sufficient proof, including documentation, to substantiate the claim that it sold and delivered goods to the defendant, and that defendant did not pay for those goods. Since the defendant has presented no valid defense to this claim, it is the order of this court that the defendant shall pay to the plaintiff $3,127.16, together with interest representing 6½% per annum, calculated from the 2nd day of June, 20____, to October 25, 20____, reasonable attorney's expenses of $300, and all costs of this action. The defendant is hereby notified that he may appeal this decision, provided a notice of appeal is filed with the appellate court within 30 days. So ordered, the Honorable Justice William O'Casey, Superior Court Judge, Marian County Courthouse, Marian County, South Carolina."

The debtor, who actually believed that he had been tried over the telephone, was devastated. He not only bought the hoax but actually paid the debt—and the interest as well.

FLYING WITH THE FEDS

Bill Stokes, a veteran collection specialist of 20 years' experience, was collecting a debt from a small regional airline that owed an oil company approximately $8,000 for fuel. The airline, which was experiencing severe financial difficulties, had already been named in several lawsuits. All conventional collection techniques had failed, and it appeared that attorney intervention would only result in an uncollectible judgment. Stokes, a virtuoso intimidator, set the stage for his collection strategy by telling the president of the troubled airline that he was aware that the airline operated a charter service and that he would be filing a complaint with the Civil Aeronautics Board and the Federal Aviation Administration, along with an application for an order to show cause why the airline's charter privileges should not be revoked.

The airline president burst into a rage. Charging harassment, he threatened to take the collector and the creditor to court. Stokes, standing his ground, advised the airline president that the creditor had retained counsel to conduct an investigation. He advised the president that the attorney's findings would make it impossible for the airline to stay in business and that the attorney would file a complaint with the regulatory authorities. "If you want to jeopardize an entire airline for an $8,000 fuel bill, fine. Let the chips fall where they may," the collector threatened.

Stokes let some time lapse to boost his credibility and then had another collector in his office call the airline president. The conversation went something like this:

Collector (impersonating a federal officer): "Mr. Jack Smith, president of Suburban Airlines? This is the Federal Aviation Administration. We have a verified complaint concerning the airline's indebtedness along with a complaint from employees charging that routine maintenance has been neglected and that your company's aircraft are unsafe. The complaint further challenges your right to hold a charter license under federal law. Are you represented by counsel, Mr. Smith?"

Smith: "Yes."

Collector: "A hearing has been scheduled for June 11, at which time you will have an opportunity to defend against these charges. The primary complainant is XYZ Oil Company, which has submitted certain findings with its complaint . . ."

This impersonation was so well performed by Stokes's accomplice that the president of the company immediately called his attorney, who in turn contacted the oil company. A heated debate followed. The creditor refused to communicate with the airline attorney, forcing the attorney to call the collector, Stokes. According to Stokes, the conversation went something like this:

Stokes: "Counselor, certainly you have a right to exercise your legal rights. That is why we have courts. However, I have carefully reviewed this matter. I have communicated with employees of the airline and have sought the advice of a competent aviation attorney. I was advised that we have a right to file a complaint even though it has nothing to do with the airline's debt. We're taking this action, counselor, because a search of the public records has revealed other litigation pending against your client. A lawsuit would probably result in an uncollectible judgment. Probably your client will go out of business. We would not have taken this harsh action, if not for the belligerent, hostile attitude of your client. The president of the airline will not admit that the company is faltering. He has made numerous promises, all of which have been broken. He has lied to us and is obviously doing everything in his power to evade his creditors. If we are playing hardball, counselor, it's only because your client has used false and misleading statements to try and put one over on us. We are simply fighting fire with fire. Now, if your client wishes to jeopardize valuable licensing privileges for $8,000, so be it. We have nothing further to discuss. You do what you have to do, and we will do what we have to do. Even if we don't recover a dime, there will certainly be ramifications at the regulatory level. Now you can either be a hero and put this matter to rest, or you can accelerate the airline's demise."

The airline paid for the fuel. Shortly thereafter, it filed for bankruptcy and ultimately went out of business.

SAY IT WITH FLOWERS

Pamela White got her start in the agency business working with a national collection agency as a small-balance collector. White got the accounts nobody else wanted, mostly small balances less than $100. One of the agency's accounts was a major distributor of floral arrangements, which were sold on credit at the retail level. The average receivable was about $60. From an economic standpoint, the agency could not spend much time on these receivables. The routine was simply to bombard the debtors with letters. When White took over these accounts, she started calling the debtors, but she soon discovered that the economics did not justify the means. It just was not worth several phone calls to collect $60 from a man who sent flowers to his girlfriend. There had to be a better way.

White revised her collection approach, implementing a very potent tactic against these debtors. Here's how Pamela conducted her collection calls:

> *White:* "Mr. Pastdue, this is Pamela White. I am calling in regard to a floral arrangement that you had us send to Miss Sandra Linn. These flowers have not yet been paid for." (Usually, at this point, the debtor is quick to offer excuses or make promises that in all probability will never be kept.) "Mr. Pastdue, I will not call you again, for if I do not receive a check in my office within 24 hours, I am going to call your girlfriend (or whomever the debtor sent the flowers to) and tell her the flowers have not been paid for. Quite frankly, I am going to press for payment from the recipient of the flowers!"

White used this illegal tactic quite effectively. She recovered more than 80% of these obligations on the first phone call. White never carried out her threats if the debtor failed to pay. (From a legal standpoint, this does not matter. The mere threat that she would communicate the indebtedness to the recipient was a violation of the Fair Debt Collection Practices Act.) But the debtor believed that White would call the recipient, and that is what was important from a collections standpoint.

If a debtor had sent flowers to his mother in the hospital, White might soften her approach, saying something to this effect:

> *White:* "Mr. Pastdue, I know you sent these flowers to your mother in the hospital. I certainly will not call her until she returns home and has recuperated. However, I do not intend to keep calling you. I am going to check with the hospital and find out when your mother will be released. Upon her return home, I fully intend to contact her, tell her that these flowers were not paid for, and invoice her for your debt!"

Obviously, when debtors thought that the collector would embarrass them by contacting the recipients of the floral arrangements, they were motivated to pay. Needless to say, there were complaints. But most of these never amounted to anything, because White never did in fact contact any of the recipients. But, again, it was a violation of federal law, and in all probability state law, for her to even suggest that she was going to contact the recipients.

EXTRADITION TO THE UNITED STATES: THE STING

One of the most entertaining stories comes from Roger Steinfeld, a top-notch commercial collector with 22 years of experience. These events happened several years ago, but the tale of Rodriguez Pasquale is still being told today. Pasquale, the owner of an import/export firm, routinely purchased hundreds of thousands of dollars' worth of foreign merchandise and shipped it to the United States. Pasquale was an unethical businessperson who had taken many credit grantors to the cleaners. Nonetheless, his credit report showed a good payment record because he did pay those vendors that had saleable products Pasquale needed. But if a product he purchased did not sell, or if he thought he could get away with it, Pasquale simply did not pay his bills. He routinely changed his corporate entity to make himself judgment-proof.

In one case, Pasquale successfully bilked a vendor out of more than $60,000. When the account was about a year past due, it was placed with Steinfeld's collection agency, but all conventional collection efforts failed. Even when Steinfeld was successful in getting Pasquale on the phone, the debtor would not budge. A lawsuit would not have been in the creditor's best interest, and service of process would have been virtually impossible because Pasquale traveled extensively and was usually in foreign countries at least six months of the year.

Steinfeld decided to turn a disadvantage into an advantage and have a little fun with Pasquale. Steinfeld learned that Pasquale was participating in an international buyers' convention in Mexico City. He found out that Pasquale intended to transact a significant volume of business and that he would be making a presentation at a specific time. That was all Steinfeld needed to know. Steinfeld did a little homework and learned that when Pasquale shipped goods into the United States, through scheming and corporate manipulation he routinely managed to evade duty taxes, which had been advanced by the freight forwarders. When shipments arrived in the United States, Pasquale would quickly liquidate the goods for cash. He never paid the freight forwarders, thus beating them out of shipping charges and duty taxes.

The Sting: Remember the movie *The Sting,* with Robert Redford? With as much attention to detail, careful planning, and the judicious use of pertinent information, Steinfeld wove a devastating con that—if successful—would scare the pants off Pasquale and prompt him to pay. On the day of the big international buyers' convention, Steinfeld had his secretary impersonate an international operator handling a call that was placed to the convention center in Mexico City. This was done precisely when Pasquale was making his presentation. Naturally, Pasquale was not to be interrupted. But the secretary, claiming that the situation was a dire emergency, left a message that the U.S. Customs Service had filed extradition papers against Pasquale and was looking for him in Mexico City to take him back to the United States to stand trial for nonpayment of duty taxes and illegal possession of merchandise. Steinfeld immediately followed this call with one of his own, in which he presented himself as a U.S. customs official. His call was quickly forwarded to the conference room, where Pasquale was making his presentation. Initially, the call was answered by a prospective buyer. Steinfeld, impersonating a federal officer, said something along these lines:

"My name is William Henley. I'm with the U.S. Customs Department. We have an international warrant for the arrest of Rodriguez Pasquale. He allegedly has received hundreds of thousands of dollars in merchandise on which he failed to pay duty taxes. We understand he is in the hotel. We have a warrant to extradite him to the United States to stand trial."

You can imagine the devastation this caused when the buyer handed the phone to Pasquale. Not only was his entire business trip ruined, but his credibility was severely damaged. When Pasquale found out that the "warrant" had been issued as a result of Steinfeld's investigation, he called Steinfeld at his office. Steinfeld then hit Pasquale right between the eyes with the "sting." Pasquale begged Steinfeld for "permission" to come back into the United States. He offered to pay half the $62,000 via a money transfer and the balance a short time later. Steinfeld, however, knowing that he had Pasquale scared, did not budge. He insisted upon payment in full before he would sign an "affidavit of satisfaction" with the customs service. Steinfeld had Pasquale exactly where he wanted him. Devastated, Pasquale arranged for a money transfer from his bank in London to pay the entire $62,000. It took several hours to complete the transaction, and during this time, Pasquale kept calling Steinfeld to verify that the payment was in progress, fearing that he would be "extradited" if he tried to board a plane in Mexico.

The collection fraternity still talks about Pasquale's numerous phone calls trying to ascertain when it would be safe for him to return to the United States. Steinfeld broke every law in the book, but he did succeed where the legal system would have failed. Interestingly, the credit grantor was aware of the sting and even helped Steinfeld carry it out.

CASE OF PAROLE

In a fairly routine collection procedure, Dennis Cummings, a collector on the West Coast, was pursuing a deadbeat who owed approximately $7,000. In the course of routine inquiries, Cummings discovered that the debtor had been convicted of a series of white-collar crimes and was out on parole for good behavior after serving four years of a seven-year sentence. The debtor had a long track record of passing bad checks, corporate manipulations, schemes, pyramids, and other white-collar crimes. Cummings also learned that the debtor was still reporting to a probation officer at regular intervals.

Cummings simply confronted the debtor with this knowledge. But Cummings twisted the facts to make it sound as if the debtor had acted illegally when he incurred the debt that Cummings was trying to collect.

"Mr. Pastdue, obviously you have much to lose. In my investigation, I have found out from my informants that you are currently on parole and under the supervision of the court. Your past track record of convictions is enough grounds for us to report this fraudulent transaction to your parole officer and file formal charges. You are in violation of your parole. You could be required to serve the remaining years of your sentence."

Obviously, the debtor was angry, feeling that his back was against the wall. Cummings used the implied threat of a complaint from a legitimate creditor to instill in the debtor a fear that he could be sent back to prison. *This was blatantly illegal.* Certainly Cummings had no right to use the implied threat of criminal proceedings to resolve a civil matter. Nonetheless, the strategy worked, and the account was paid in full.

SAILING ANYONE?

By now, you should be getting a bad taste in your mouth from some of these underhanded tactics. Here is yet another nominee for the collectors' "hall of shame." Willie Smith came into the collection business with a strong background as a repossession agent. One of his clients, a marine facility that did repairs on yachts, turned over to Willie a number of uncollectible claims, mostly from transient boat owners. These people sailed to the coast of Florida, had repair work done, and then sailed off, ignoring the bills.

These debtors, once the time and materials had been invested in their extravagant yachts, assumed that there was little the creditor could do to collect. Compounding the problem was the fact that most of the debtors were wealthy individuals or corporate executives who traveled extensively and were difficult to pin down. Smith was not about to subscribe to conventional collection methodology. A proficient skip tracer, Smith always found his target and established communication with the debtor. Instead of attempting to collect the debt, Smith would impress upon the debtors that there were mechanic's liens on the boats, that legal papers had been filed with the Coast Guard, and that the debtor's boats would be seized.

If a debtor still would not bite, Smith said that it would do no good to move the boat or conceal its whereabouts because a "multistate mechanic's lien" had been filed in a 13-state region. Smith impressed upon the debtor that whenever or wherever he came in for service, the boat would be seized. This usually did the trick. In fact, Smith was so successful with this technique that payment was often delivered in person in cash, or expedited by overnight courier.

CONTAMINATION AND THE FDA

Mike Davis worked for a small collection agency in a big city. Now, collecting money in a big city is very different from collecting in rural areas. City debtors tend to be streetwise and not susceptible to normal collector cons.

A creditor approached Davis with a serious problem. It had extended $35,000 worth of credit to a syrup manufacturer more than a year ago and had not been paid a nickel. Davis tried every trick in the book, but he could not budge the debtor. The debtor was not only evasive, but it also regularly changed its corporate structure. The manufacturer had been sued many times but had always managed to avoid the local sheriff. Undaunted, Davis secured a list of the syrup company's primary customers, most of which were sweet shops, cafeterias, hospitals, and restaurants.

Threat of recall: Davis had already tried the implied threat of litigation. As a matter of fact, the creditor's attorney had worded a strong letter outlining potential legal ramifications. Still, there was no response from the debtor. As a last resort, Davis proceeded to call every customer of the syrup company, posing as an investigator from the Federal Drug Administration (FDA). Davis's script:

Davis: "Is this Reed's Ice Cream Parlor?"

Customer: "Yes."

Davis: "This is Robert Meyer of the Federal Drug Administration. We've been conducting an investigation of the XYZ Syrup Manufacturing Company, and we understand that you carry that company's product. Is that correct?"

Customer: "Yes."

Davis: "We have evaluated the product and determined that it is contaminated. The FDA is recalling all syrups manufactured by XYZ. I need to know what labels you have on your shelves."

Customer: "You mean the product is contaminated?"

Davis: "I'm afraid you've got a serious problem. You may expose yourself to possible liability should you continue to sell the contaminated product."

This approach was devastating. Davis called no fewer than 20 of the manufacturer's best customers, all of whom ceased doing business with the syrup company. The debtor assumed that this was the work of a vindictive creditor, but it did not know which one. When Davis finally did confront the debtor in a subsequent call, he first advised the creditor that an investigation was under way and that his collection agency was cooperating with the authorities.

Davis ultimately collected the whole debt, but what a tremendous risk he took! "Two wrongs do not make a right," and the potential exposure was not worth the gamble. This debtor could have closed down Davis's agency and subjected him to criminal prosecution. The creditor that hired him could also be liable for damages. Imagine what it would have had to pay if a court found that Davis's slanderous statements forced the debtor out of business.

ONE WHO PRACTICES TO DECEIVE

The noted comedian Rich Little gets some stiff competition from collector Bill Greene, a virtuoso impersonator and master of the art of disguise. The scope of Bill Greene's talents are virtually limitless, for he has an uncanny ability to duplicate another person's voice almost perfectly after listening to that person for just a few minutes. On the phone, Bill Greene is a conjurer who delivers remarkable performances. For example, when debtors voice complaints that require third-party verification, most collectors would tell the debtors that they will call them back after verifying the dispute. Not Bill Greene! He advises complainants that he is "arranging conference calls" with the third parties. He puts the debtors on hold and then, a couple of minutes later, acts out two personalities with two entirely different voices. The debtors believe they are engaged in three-way conversations.

Greene often commits multiple felonies to collect a debt. He has even been known to structure collection calls by recording the voice of a debtor's attorney, waiting for that attorney to be out of the office, and then proceeding to contact the debtor using the attorney's voice. The debtor believes he is talking to his attorney! Greene advises the debtor that he, the attorney, has been served via "remedial process" and recommends immediate money transfer or overnight transmittal of money to the collector. Obviously, this is blatantly illegal, and complaints have been filed. But, of course, Greene denies the debtors' allegations.

Bill Greene not only resorts to subterfuge and deception, but he is also a master forger, embezzler, and con artist. Allegedly, Greene researches civil court matters and the disposition of uncollectible judgments. He then traces the debtors, implements some kind of con—usually impersonating a sheriff or a marshall—collects the funds, and keeps the money. He has stolen money from at least two collection agencies and one law firm, not to mention the many innocent debtors who have been bilked out of their money, including creditors who did not get a dime.

Unfortunately, there are other unethical, criminally minded collectors like Bill Greene. They make up only a small minority, but they give the entire collection industry a bad name. Usually, they are not prosecuted for their heinous crimes of embezzlement, fraud, impersonation, and forgery. Even when their crimes are discovered, collection agencies are not likely to press charges for fear that any adverse publicity might affect their own good reputations.

A MASTER CREDIT CRIMINAL

"Bustouts" are a common problem nationwide. These scam operators falsify business records and tax ID numbers; some even incorporate under a name similar to that of a reputable firm with the sole intent of wangling merchandise on credit, with no intent to satisfy the obligations. Bustouts range from small-time scams to multimillion-dollar operations. They bilk legitimate companies for billions of dollars each year. A certain collection consultant tracked down and confronted a professional credit criminal who had ripped off almost $500,000. The victim of that particular bustout had secured a money judgment, which had to that point been uncollectible. But after a Herculean effort, consuming more than two years of blood, sweat, and tears, the debtor was brought to the table to meet his obligation.

The creditor was a large insulation company. The debtor, Mr. Snake, had already ripped off other creditors to the tune of some $3 million. The debtor belonged to a prestigious athletic club, maintained residences in three states, drove a Rolls Royce, and always managed to stay one step ahead of the sheriff. Protected by his family, Mr. Snake was for all intents and purposes out of reach. He even managed to outmaneuver the government—

the IRS maintained a $75,000 unsatisfied lien against him. His family, proprietors of an insulation business, went to great lengths to conceal his whereabouts. After tracking down hundreds of leads, representing thousands of phone calls and numerous field contacts, the consultant finally uncovered Mr. Snake.

Once it was learned that Mr. Snake was a member of a distinguished athletic club, the collection consultant subpoenaed the membership records of the club and submitted this information to the IRS along with a Form 211 (Application for Reward for Original Information). The IRS sent agents to the club and ultimately recovered the $75,000 tax lien with penalties.

As for the $500,000 indebtedness, this was negotiated and settled for $200,000. Unfortunately, Mr. Snake, who allegedly had ties to organized crime, subsequently threatened a high-ranking corporate officer with harassing litigation and demanded that the creditor sign a release letting Mr. Snake off the hook for a measly $10,000. At the time, this major corporation, which had been hit with many lawsuits, had filed for bankruptcy, so Mr. Snake would not have been successful with any harassment litigation. But the corporate officer buckled under pressure, and this major Fortune 500 company wrote off the $500,000. Creditors sometimes do more damage to the recovery effort than the debtors themselves.

ALIAS AND FAIR DEBT COLLECTION

The Fair Debt Collection Practices Act recognizes that collectors need to use aliases in the fulfillment of their duties, and the use of a fictitious name in itself would probably not have any legal consequences; however, false statements by a third-party collector about his employer, profession, or job title are *expressly prohibited* under federal statute. State statutes may extend those prohibitions to cover creditors as well. Note that commercial creditors and debt collectors are not off the hook either. The Federal Trade Commission Act prohibits unfair methods of competition and unfair or deceptive acts or practices in or affecting commerce.

HOW DO YOU FIND THE BEST COLLECTION AGENCY?

You are responsible for your collection agency's acts. Make sure the collection agency you choose will not expose your company to possible legal action or skip off with your retrieved funds. Here are some useful tips to consider:

- *Check on how long the company has been collecting overdue accounts.* This does not mean that new agencies are not good, but if an agency has been in business for 5, 10, or 15 years, it must be doing something right.

- *Get recommendations from people who have used the agency.* Do not give an unknown agency a try just because someone called you on the phone. Get references. You want to know what kind of experience other creditors have had.

- *Meet the principals.* Deal with people you are comfortable with and you feel you can trust.

- *Do not think you are locked into the local area.* The important thing is how an agency performs, not where it is located.

- *Insist on being kept up-to-date.* Find out what kind of reports you can expect. Agencies should remit every 30 days.

- *Make sure the agency is bonded.* Bonds are intended to protect customers from the widespread default that was common in the collection industry. Also find out if the agency maintains a separate trust (escrow) account for each customer.

- *Find out whether the agency is a member of a reputable association.* For example, agencies that belong to the International Association of Commercial Collectors, Inc. (4040 West 70th Street, Minneapolis, MN 55435) adhere to a rigid code of ethics, are bonded, and have been in business for at least a year. In retail collections, membership in ACA International-the Association of Credit and Collection Professionals, formerly the American Collectors Association, (P. O. Box 390106, 4040 West 70th Street, Minneapolis, MN 55439) similarly ensures that an agency has met certain basic requirements.

CHAPTER 12

Conclusion

Throughout this book you have learned many cash-producing techniques. To recap, we present several invigorating strategies together with an accounts receivable exam. The latter will accelerate your learning process to the highest plateau of accounts receivable success. Let's begin with a common problem: Your debtor is cash starved. It is human nature for a slow-paying customer to make their financial problems yours—a happenstance that is not only frustrating, but also detrimental to the wallet. Although most debtors lack the capability to borrow money, a respectable percentage do. Debtors are not inclined to borrow money to pay their debts, preferring instead to capitalize on their creditors to finance them. In effect, a customer who pays a negligible sum over long periods is deriving the use of his creditor's money. A shrewd creditor would be wise to determine a customer's borrowing capability; the more creditors know about their customer's finances, the better.

Case in point: Outback Archery was indebted to North American Archery Group for $6,465.26. The obligator was employed as a janitor (who maintained an after-hours sporting goods business), who over a long period whittled down the debt by $820.00 to $5,645.26. The creditor's telephone log amply documented the creditor's ongoing frustration for accelerating payment. The debtor was a creditworthy individual who at the consumer level maintained an exemplary payment history. Although this creditor could have elected to reduce the debt to judgment, a far more productive course of action was undertaken. Because the debtor was a sole proprietorship (i.e., individual liability), a consumer credit report was obtained. The report revealed that the debtor was honorable in meeting his primary obligations. It also showcased several transactions with a local bank—First Bank and Trust. Armed with this valuable information, aggressive collection activity ceased and creative resolution began. In view of the customer's proven track record, it was suggested that his bank would in all probability extend a loan equal to the creditor's claim—$5,645.26. Initially, the debtor resisted, claiming he did not want to damage his relationship with his local bank; however, when the slow-paying customer was reminded of the following dire consequences, his attitude changed from resistance to cooperation:

1. Our client was committed to sue.

2. Detrimental data would be interfaced on his credit report, which would adversely affect his credit reputation for seven years. Productive negotiations ensued. A conference call was arranged between the collector, creditor, and the bank (with the debtor's permission). Because the debtor's bank had experience with its customer, it was receptive to granting a loan. *Warning:* This technique is applicable to commercial debts only. In a consumer situation, the creditor should obtain written permission from the debtor before contacting a third-party lender.

The conference call took about 10 minutes for both the collector and the slow-paying customer to convince the banker to approve a loan equal to the debt. As an inducement, in exchange for the bank processing the loan within one week, North American agreed to forfeit the debtor's contract liability collection fees that were equal to 25% of the principal sum of the debt, or about $1,411. Therein, the banker conducted its own credit investigation and was satisfied with its customer's ability to fulfill the terms of the loan. In just a few days, the loan closed and the banker issued its check directly to the collector, which satisfied Outback Archery's debt.

How productive is this technique? Virtually any customer that maintains good credit is a candidate. The key ingredient is that the collector take the initiative. Convince the debtor of dire consequences in greater proportion than the debt owed, make concessions (i.e., warding off a lawsuit and/or agreeing not to interface derogatory data), and the end result is a win/win environment.

COMMUNICATE WITH DEBTORS WHO ARE AVOIDING YOU

How many times have you attempted to communicate with a debtor only to be confronted with a gatekeeper or voice mail? No doubt you have been stopped dead in your tracks by an evasive debtor who intentionally avoids communication. Until the late 1990s this was a major problem, but today modern technology provides an answer. The cell phone revolution has created unlimited opportunities—the wherewithal to communicate with virtually any debtor. Cell phone numbers, unlike landlines, are not directory listed. As a result, subscribers discriminate as to whom they provide their confidential numbers. Generally, subscribers maintain control of who will have possession of their unlisted number; however, the three major credit reporting agencies—TransUnion, Equifax, and Experian—have all accessed this vital information and sell it for minimal cost.

The TransUnion Phone Append solution is a boon to creditors. Applicable to *consumer debts,* as an add-on to a credit report, a creditor can secure a header, the *nonfinancial* top portion of a credit report, which reveals the following data:

- Debtor's home and/or private phone number indicator (60% success rate)
- Up to two previous addresses (valuable as a location and/or service of process resource)

- Social Security number, which is mandatory to electronically access a multitude of public and/or confidential records
- Date of birth
- Spouse's name (Good guy/bad guy routine and/or influential source)
- Possible place of employment—additional contact/garnishment of wages

Imagine the euphoria when a debtor, who intentionally avoids his creditor(s), is unexpectedly confronted by an astute creditor who secured and communicated with the evasive debtor. Their response? "How did you get my number?"

The cell phone revolution has equipped the populace with a remarkable resource. Virtually everyone uses cell phones (contrary to common perception, it is legal to communicate with a corporate debtor at other than a place of business). Today creditors have the wherewithal to communicate with evasive customers anywhere, anytime. Communication is instrumental to debt recovery.

For creditors, this is a valuable resource. For evasive nonpaying customers, it forever removes their veil of security (e.g., voice mail, gatekeeper, and so on). The TransUnion Phone Append database is one of several that virtually guarantees an alternate phone number contact—all for a small cost over and above the negotiable cost of a credit report. Exhibit 12.1 explains the TransUnion Phone Append in greater detail. Equifax and Experian offer a similar service.

THE INSTANT GRATIFICATION SYNDROME

Debt collection is viewed as serious business (i.e., the extraction of money relevant to a service performed or merchandise delivered). There are many reasons why customers default, one of which has to do with the instant gratification syndrome. How does instant gratification impact you, the creditor? Consider your own spending habits. Assume that you and your spouse decide to redecorate your home, opting to replace both your living and dining room with new furniture. You have canvassed the marketplace considering a huge selection offered by local merchants.

Eventually, you are enticed by a TV commercial that offers no interest financing for one year—you are hooked. Visiting the showroom, you purchase a gorgeous sofa, love seat, coffee and end tables, complemented with decorator lamps. For your dining room ensemble, you commit to an expensive mahogany table and chairs, with matching china closet. The bill totals $8,396—a sum about double your original budget; however, you justify the purchase because of the 0% introductory rate and no payments for 12 months (which increases to 18% after one year.) Two years later, your original $8,396 obligation has ballooned to $9,850, or $1,454 above your original purchase. Worse, your once-gorgeous sofa and love seat are marred with stains and cigarette burns, while your beautiful dining room table and chairs have scratches. The instant gratification for decorating your living and dining room has evaporated, and now you are burdened with almost $10,000 in debt. Even more detrimental, the 18% interest rate, like credit cards, virtually

EXHIBIT 12.1   TRANSUNION PHONE APPEND

TransUnion Phone Append

Fast access to the most reliable numbers available

TransUnion Phone Append gives you phone numbers at the same time you verify address information. Whether you're trying to locate individuals or confirm application information, Phone Append is the fastest way to access one of the most accurate phone number sources available. Used in conjunction with other TransUnion services, this add-on returns a phone number when consumer information is pulled. You'll no longer have to waste time performing additional searches to get the numbers you need.

Simplify your collections process
When added to a TransUnion report, Phone Append automatically returns a ten-digit phone number or private number indicator. The information that used to take hours of digging through multiple databases to find is now available in seconds. This single search gives you everything

you need to proceed with your collections efforts.

Streamline application processing
Verifying application data is even easier when you use Phone Append. When a consumer applies for credit or service, you need to verify their information as quickly as you can. Phone Append lets you confirm the phone number at the same time you verify the other application information. Youèll be able to minimize your risk while making the process more convenient for you and your customers.

Thorough, reliable numbers
Phone Append provides some of the most reliable numbers in the industry. Most vendors use scanned White-page information—our database is continually refreshed from multiple databases throughout the country. Phone Append also has the ability to flag private, unlisted phone numbers. While private numbers are not returned, a private-number indicator will alert you that the phone number is not available—stopping your search before you invest too much time.

For access to one of the most accurate and complete sources of phone information, Phone Append is the easy-to-use solution. For more information on Phone Append, contact your local TransUnion representative, or visit www.transunion.com.

Discover the Value of TransUnion
At TransUnion, we help our business partners reduce risk, streamline processes, cut costs and increase profits. For more than 30 years, TransUnion has been a leading provider of essential business intelligence services, including consumer data, targeted marketing, analytical models and decisioning tools. We maintain one of the world's largest databases of consumer credit information, providing value-added intelligence solutions to leading businesses around the globe.

PRODUCT SNAPSHOT
- Get phone numbers at the same time you pull other reports
- Simplifies collections and identity verification processing
- One of the most accurate sources of phone numbers available
- Returns private-number indicators

Trans**Union** ℠

© 2002 TransUnion LLC. All Rights Reserved.

555 West Adams
Chicago, Illinois 60661
www.transunion.com

A member of The Marmon Group of companies

PA001 07/02

guarantees you will be cast in debt for years to come, while the value of your original purchase has depreciated.

DEBTOR MENTALITIES

What does this have to do with debt recovery? Everything! This hypothetical example is typical of many psychological obstacles a creditor must overcome. From the debtors' perspective, they are being asked to pay for broken-down furniture at exorbitant interest rates. In the customers' minds it does not matter that they are contractually obligated, nor that they have utilized the furniture for several years—nor do customers see that they ruined their new furniture. The fact is that many debtors consider their creditors as greedy, insensitive merchants who extort monies with exorbitant interest rates. It is not fair, but this perception is one major reason why creditors elicit resistance. The next time you attempt recovery of a debt, particularly an aged one, where your customers no longer have a need for the product or service, consider the customers' frame of mind. It is not enough to think of your role as a collector, but rather you must think like a psychologist. From a recovery standpoint, the collector must zero in on the defaulting customers' phobias, taking them back to the time when they initiated the purchase, while maneuvering them into a frame of mind when the transaction was consummated. Through step-by-step psychological persuasion, the creditor must gradually change the base of the debtors' thinking sufficient to elicit confirmation of the debt.

A FINAL NOTE

Throughout this book I have revealed almost three decades of hands-on debt-recovery experience, most of it acquired from the university of hard knocks. This volume is the culmination of many failures, disappointments, and experiments—all honed to perfection. Not a single publication on debt collection showcases so many novel strategies for getting paid.

You now possess within your arsenal a comprehensive blueprint governing virtually every facet of accounts receivable management. As an encore, in the Appendix, I have included a 50-question accounts receivable exam encompassing the most intricate aspects of debt recovery. Do not be discouraged if you do not score a perfect 100, nor should you expect phenomenal results overnight. Instead, concentrate on perfecting each technique until it becomes habit. Stated another way, you could read this volume over a weekend but still fail to reap the harvest of these techniques. It will take time to develop these skills. How long? This depends on you and your commitment. Although this volume focuses on debt recovery, investigations, and legal strategy, it is by no means all-inclusive. There is no finality, for the process is lifelong. Even though your author is a street-smart veteran, I still learn new tricks. School is never out for a pro.

As you embark on the road of debt recovery, remember that every time you score a victory, your success is much more than money in the bank, for you are also contributing to our economic climate. There is also the personal gratification for obtaining restitution when some credit criminal who attempted to con you out of your hard-earned money pays you.

If you have profited from this learning experience, please drop me a line at: A. Michael Coleman, P.O. Box 6512, Harrisburg, PA 17112. Your comments and suggestions are most welcome. My very best wishes for your continued accounts receivable success and the best that life has to offer.

Fraternally,

A. Michael Coleman

Accounts Receivable Proficiency Exam

For Credit Professionals, Collection Agencies, and Personnel Charged with the Recovery of Bad Debts

INTRODUCTION

Credit management is a multifaceted responsibility. Most are proficient in the art of evaluation and extension but weak in maximizing receivable recovery. Credit professionals routinely interface with the legal profession, often unaware of the multitude of remedies at their disposal. The more adept you are at charting a strategic course of action, the greater your success.

The following 50 multiple-choice questions will gauge your proficiency at converting your receivables into cash, together with helping you become a better collector.

YOUR SCORE

There are 50 multiple-choice questions. Achieving a score of 75 is passing. Some questions have one or more answers. Gauge your results on the following scale:

Test Questions Answered Correctly	Score	Level of Proficiency
50	100	Superachiever
45–49	95	Semi-superachiever Status
40–44	90	Street-smart
34–39	85	Professional
30–33	80	Qualified
25–29	75	Indoctrinated
20–24	60	Amateur
15–19	55	Apprentice/Trainee
Under 15	50	Entry-level newcomer

Q AND A

Instructions: Circle the correct answer from multiple choices.

Credit Management, Fair Debt Practices Act:

1. **The Federal Fair Debt Practices Act is applicable to:**
   a. Consumers.
   b. Consumers and principals of corporations.
   c. Sole proprietorships.
   d. Officers of corporations who sign personal guarantees.
   e. Consumers and limited exposure to proprietors and officers who sign personal guarantees.

2. **If a debtor notifies a creditor via certified mail to "cease and desist" from collection activities, the creditor must:**
   a. Terminate pursuit.
   b. Ignore the demand and continue pursuit.
   c. Provide documentation in support of the debt.
   d. Officers or corporations who sign personal guarantees are not bound to the FCRA.

3. **The Error Resolution Process of the Truth in Lending Law provides a remedial process to resolve credit card disputes. The statutory time frames to invoke remedies are:**
   a. 30 days' written notice to card issuer, followed by 60 days to investigate dispute, during which time a temporary credit is issued.
   b. Written notice within 60 days to card issuer, followed by 30 days to investigate dispute, during which time a temporary credit is issued.
   c. Written notice to card issuer, then two billing cycles to investigate dispute.
   d. Written notice within 60 days to card issuer, then issuer has 30 days to acknowledge; statutory time expires after three billing cycles.

Small Claims Forums:

4. **Which lobbying group advocates legislation increasing small claims jurisdictional amounts (favorable to creditors for economic and expeditious resolution of debts)?**
   a. American Society for the Advancement of Judicial Reform
   b. Americans for Legal Reform
   c. National Small Claims Consortium
   d. National Association for Small Claims Reform

5. **Which state maintains the highest jurisdictional amount?**
   a. California
   b. Tennessee
   c. Pennsylvania
   d. Louisiana

6. **Creditors can circumnavigate judicial limitations and minimize legal fees, while casting debtors in a vexing legal predicament by:**
   a. Initiating two or more civil complaints proportionate to Small Claims Court jurisdiction.
   b. Waiving the amount owed and suing for the jurisdictional amount (i.e., receivable is $5,300, limit is $5,000, then $300 is waived).
   c. Splitting creditor's claim into two separate civil suits in relation to different invoices.
   d. Petitioning the court for summary judgment.

7. **Select the category that accurately depicts small claims jurisdictional limits.**
   a. CA, $5,000; NJ, $7,500; PA, $8,000; NY, $2,500.
   b. IL, $4,000; FL, $6,000; MI, $5,000; CT, $3,000.
   c. MI, $5,000; KS, $3,500; WA, $2,500; GA, $4,000.
   d. MA, $5,000; RI, $3,500; TX, $8,000; WA, $6,000.

8. **A retaliatory maneuver to cause your debtor expense and aggravation once a small claims action is filed is to:**
   a. Initiate the action pro se and retain an attorney on the eve of trial.
   b. Amend your civil complaint once it is served.
   c. Fax or e-mail a request for adjournment the day prior to trial date, but mail request to your adversary the same day. (Your adversary will make an unnecessary trip to the courthouse.)
   d. a, b, and c combined initiated over time to burden your debtor with additional expense/inconvenience.
   e. None of the above.

Litigation Strategy:

9. **Choosing the correct forum can make the difference between success and failure. Where appropriate, commencing your action in federal court will work to your advantage. What criteria must be met to commence an action in federal court?**
   a. Receivable must be over $75,000 excluding interest, together with diversity.
   b. Receivable must be over $50,000 exclusive of interest and attorneys' fees.
   c. Receivable must be subject to federal subject matter jurisdiction.
   d. Creditor has no resource in federal court unless subject matter is conducive to copyright, maritime, or labor law.

10. **Federal courts are advantageous to creditors because:**
    a. A case management plan is established.
    b. Federal courts will not tolerate frivolous litigation.
    c. Debtors are more likely to be intimidated by federal judges.
    d. Legitimate receivables are viewed more favorably by federal courts.

Long-Arm Statute Litigation:

11. **Suing your debtor from your jurisdiction is advantageous because:**
    a. Your nonpaying customer will have to retain an attorney in your state.
    b. Your debtor's legal representation costs are increased.
    c. Creditors ambush debtors.
    d. Creditors reposition the playing field on their turf.

12. **Suing via the Long-Arm Statute, litigants must meet the following legal criteria:**
    a. "Minimum contacts" with the forum state
    b. Legal agreement to venue
    c. Statutory judicial authority
    d. Continuity and regularity of contracts
    e. a, b, and c

13. **The success rate for suing a debtor in your state via the Long-Arm Statute is:**
    a. 90%.
    b. 75%.
    c. 50%.
    d. 65%.

14. **Once judgment is obtained in the creditor's state against a debtor in another state, a supplemental procedure must be performed. The legal process is:**
    a. Docketing.
    b. Execution.
    c. Transcript.
    d. Domestication.

15. **Contrary to common belief, a consumer credit report is a multifaceted investigative tool. Its most valuable resources are:**
    a. Revelation of debtor's Social Security number.
    b. Resident addresses retroactive to seven years.
    c. Payment history.
    d. The names, addresses, and account numbers of creditors for the purpose of issuing an information subpoena.
    e. All of the above.

16. **Although it is illegal to secure a consumer credit report relevant to a corporate debt, a little-known device exists wherein the top portion (the nonfinancial payment history), revealing Social Security number, date of birth, home address, spouse, and often alternate place of employment, is available. This device is known as:**
    a. Profile report.
    b. Header report.
    c. Sum and substance report.
    d. Social Security report.

17. **The cell phone revolution has resulted in service providers selling their applicants' telephone numbers—most unlisted! Incredibly, for a negligible fee, over 160 million records are electronically searched in a matter of seconds. Provided as an add-on to a consumer credit report, or trace plus, the cost is:**
    a. Under $.50.
    b. Under $1.00.
    c. $2.00.
    d. $10.00.

18. **Once a creditor secures an unlisted cell number, communication with an evasive debtor (who hides behind voice mail and/or a gatekeeper) is not only assured, but is also very intimidating (the debtor is startled when your unsuspected call is received), prompting curiosity: "How did you get my unlisted number?" Is it legal to call a corporate debtor on his nonpublished cell or home number?**
    a. Yes, but with prior written notice.
    b. Yes, but if the debtor advises you not to call again, you must discontinue further communication via the nonpublished number(s).
    c. No.
    d. Federal law permits the marketing of unlisted cell and unlisted *home* numbers. A creditor has a legal right to maintain communications to nonpublished numbers.

19. **The procurement of unlisted cell and home telephone numbers is powerful ammunition to creditors because:**
    a. It establishes communication with otherwise noncommunicable debtors.
    b. It suggests that if the creditor has secured confidential information, he probably has more data.
    c. It intimidates your nonpaying customers.
    d. All of the above.

20. **During or post litigation, why is the discovery process analogous to selling icicles in the wintertime?**
    a. The system is "extrajudicial."
    b. Courts are lenient.

   c. Sanctions are rarely imposed against litigants who fail to divulge incriminating evidence.

   d. All of the above.

21. **An ingenious and inexpensive device to circumnavigate discovery is via the information subpoena. An intuitive litigant can secure valuable information by:**

   a. Inundating your adversary with combined discovery demands.

   b. Examination via deposition.

   c. Hiring a private investigator, then subpoenaing known sources and creditors whose names, addresses, and account numbers are revealed.

   d. Issuing an official-looking information subpoena to known sources, including creditors whose names, addresses, and account numbers appear on a credit report.

22. **Experience proves that a litigant should *not* address an information subpoena to the legal department, but rather to the credit department because:**

   a. An attorney is likely to dismiss it as frivolous.

   b. Credit departments, unlike attorneys or legal departments, are more likely to respond favorably.

   c. A subpoena must be issued by a court of appropriate jurisdiction.

   d. The subpoena will be quashed.

23. **Mail-order and marketing strategy should be incorporated into an information subpoena to achieve greater results by:**

   a. Affixing in large red letters "Immediate Response Requested" on the subpoena.

   b. Enclosing a return envelope.

   c. Employing both a cardboard Priority Mail envelope addressed to Credit dept. with postage ($3.85), together with highlighted information on the subject's credit report.

   d. Writing a threatening letter demanding compliance by your attorney.

   e. a, b, and c.

24. **Credit professionals routinely interface with lawyers. The following is a list of 12 common legal terms, most of which are used in judicial proceedings. Match each word/phrase to its corresponding meaning/answer:**

Word/Phrase	Meaning/Answer
a. Writ	_____ Formal allegation that facts are as stated.
b. Voir dire	_____ As much as deserved. Usually referred to for goods or services provided and not paid for.
c. Additur	_____ Permanent home and principal establishment.
d. Demurrer	_____ Mandatory precept directing the sheriff to execute a court order.
e. Quantum meruit	_____ Claim litigated by co-defendants or co-plaintiffs.

f. Collateral estoppel	_____ The manner of operation.
g. Replevin	_____ To speak the truth. Used to screen prospective jurors.
h. Assignment	_____ Civil action for recovery of chattel.
i. Domicile	_____ Transfer of interest with full legal rights.
j. Counterclaim	_____ A counterdemand by defendant in response to plaintiff's complaint.
k. Cross claim	_____ An increase in the amount of damages.
l. Modus operandi	_____ Doctrine recognizing determination of facts litigated.

25. **The following is a list of 12 questions, which are also typical in legal proceedings. Match each word/phrase to its corresponding meaning/answer:**

Word/Phrase	Meaning/Answer
a. Venue	_____ A guilty mind.
b. Unjust enrichment	_____ What for what; something for something.
c. Addamnum	_____ Entry of judgment upon a written admission without legal formality.
d. Mens rea	Written acknowledgment of debt.
e. Declaratory judgment	_____ Forum or jurisdiction where suit can be established.
f. Quid pro quo	_____ Amount of damages or claim for damages.
g. Arguendo	_____ Claim against original obligor **and** alleged liability to third party.
h. Confession of judgment	_____ Order used to correct the record.
i. Impleader	_____ A thing decided; a matter adjudged.
j. Nunc pro tunc	_____ To put in clear light for the sake of argument.
k. Debenture	_____ Judgment to express rights of movement. Nonmonetary decree.
l. Res judicata	_____ Enriched at the expense of another.

26. **A mortgage application is one of the most revealing documents because it depicts valuable information, but it is undiscoverable unless court ordered. However, a resourceful litigant can obtain it via creative penetration. Which technique has the best chance of obtaining your adversary's application for a mortgage?**
    a. Proposed order with supporting affidavit to court of appropriate jurisdiction
    b. Threatening letter to mortgage holder
    c. Information subpoena to title company
    d. Information subpoena to mortgage holder derived from credit report and/or national profile, but submitted to mortgage servicing

27. **Mortgage applications are valuable not only because they reveal financial information, but also because adversaries tend to elaborate on their financial resources. Mortgage applications contain a criminal prosecution warning (Title 11, U.S. Code) for false statements. A shrewd creditor in possession of incriminating evidence wherein a debtor who made a false statement can:**
   a. Use contradictory evidence to one's advantage.
   b. File a complaint with regulatory authorities.
   c. Ambush your adversary with its revelation.
   d. All of the above.

28. **Contrary to common belief, personal liability can be established in corporate debts without expensive legal maneuvering and protracted discovery by:**
   a. Revelation via credit reports and national profiles.
   b. Electronic matching of Social Security numbers and/or employer identification numbers.
   c. a and b augmented with persuasive undercover communications.
   d. Discovery within the framework of a lawsuit.

29. **The legal criteria to penetrate the protection of a corporation and extend liability to individual officers are:**
   a. A subchapter "S" corporation.
   b. A registered corporation with a fictitious name.
   c. Improper commingling of corporate assets for the personal use of its officers.
   d. A decision of the court post discovery, and coherent with a judicial order.

30. **Your customer hasn't paid you because he hasn't been paid—a common occurrence. What remedy permits creditors to intercept your customer's customer's receivable, prompting remittance direct to you?**
   a. A lawsuit for quantum meruit
   b. An interpleader action
   c. An impleader action
   d. Confronting your customer's customer and demanding payment be made to you.

31. **The preparation and showcasing of the correct legal procedure to intercept your customer's customer's payment is lethal. In all likelihood, your customer will "beg, borrow, and steal" to pay you because:**
   a. You have cast your nonpaying customer in an embarrassing and expensive predicament.
   b. Possible loss of your customer's customer will ensue.
   c. You have legally damaged the customer's reputation and credibility.
   d. All of the above.

32. In addition to the potent remedies referenced in questions 30 and 31, another legal maneuver is available to creditors whose products and/or services benefit a third party (who has no direct contract with creditors), but nevertheless may subject them to liability. Under what legal basis may suit be brought under these circumstances?
    a. Tortuous interference of contract
    b. Privity of contract
    c. Unjust enrichment
    d. Breach of bilateral contract

33. Extension of credit and receivable management is conducive to contract law. Choose the correct elements that constitute a legal contract:
    a. A "meeting of the minds" and default
    b. 1. Seller has capability to deliver merchandise/render service.
       2. Buyer has capability and resources to fulfill obligation.
       3. A "meeting of the minds"
       4. Consideration
       5. Breach of contract
       6. Provable damages
    c. 1. Seller delivers merchandise/performs service.
       2. Buyer defaults.
       3. Provable damages
    d. The credit application and invoice govern contract law

34. Many unsuspecting creditors believe they have a valid contract relevant to an invoice. One element of contract law provides an escape wherein debtors can be legally exonerated from a debt. Which tactic can a shrewd nonpaying customer employ to circumnavigate your invoice?
    a. Shoddy workmanship and/or inferior service
    b. Buyer does not maintain the legal wherewithal to fulfill the contract.
    c. Filing a counterclaim
    d. Provable legal criteria to fulfill the obligation and/or coercion
    e. Fraud pleaded with particularity
    f. b, d, and/or e

35. A common term referred to in debt litigation referencing monetary damages is:
    a. Treble damages.
    b. Pecuniary damages.
    c. Punitive damages.
    d. Compensatory damages.

36. Unlike statute of limitations, which establishes a specific time frame to commence an action, a legal defense exists wherein lethargic creditors

who delay filing their claims may be confronted with the following defense:

a. Laches
b. Inchoate dower
c. Hereditary succession
d. Habeas corpus

37. **A legal shortcut for a creditor to procure judgment—without trial—is known as summary judgment, aka accelerated judgment. This device short-circuits litigation and achieves instant justice. The legal criteria for a creditor to succeed is:**

a. Telephone log proving debtor's representations to pay.
b. Credit application with provisional remedies.
c. No triable issue of material fact.
d. a, b, and c, assuming creditor has debt well-documented.

38. **During their training, lawyers are taught a confrontational attitude known as:**

a. Threaten a frivolous counterclaim.
b. Adversarial twist of the mind.
c. Make noise like a lawyer.
d. b and c.

39. **It is important for creditors to practice psychology when dealing with their adversary's attorneys because:**

a. Your debtor's lawyer is focused on his client's best interests.
b. Your debtor's attorney can be an influential source if the creditor can successfully paint a visual roadmap of legal consequences.
c. Debtors' attorneys are virtuosos at intimidation.
d. All of the above.

40. **"Customer," "client," "debtor," and "defendant" are all common names used to refer to a person or entity of a debt depending on the stage of the collection process. Once your customer defaults on a debt, under law, a legal term is applicable. Choose the term:**

a. Loco parentis
b. Damnum absque injuria
c. Tort-feasor
d. Juris secundum

41. **Limited partnerships are the wave of the future—and detrimental to creditors because liability is substantially diluted. The most common pitfalls are creditors who foolishly extend credit to the general partner, particularly where the limited partners assume the bulk of liability. The most**

sophisticated partnerships divide liability. Choose the ownership ratios most common in this growing trend:

a. Limited Partner 50%
   General Partner 50%
b. Limited Partner 99%
   General Partner 1%
c. Limited Partner 90%
   General Partner 10%
d. Limited Partner 65%
   General Partner 35%

42. **An unsuspecting creditor who extends credit to the general partner is likely to write off the receivable because of diluted liability. When considering partnerships, limited partnerships should be scrutinized with finite detail and jurisdictional problems because:**

a. Limited partners are likely to be spread out over different states.
b. Limited partnerships, like certificates of corporations, are a matter of public record.
c. Some limited partnerships are organized as trusts, rendering revelation/ownership percentage impossible to detect.
d. a and c.

43. **Limited partnerships that are transferred "offshore" are made up of trusts and are impossible to unravel, effectively rending them judgment proof. Assuming a foreign limited partnership owes you $1 million (most creditors would have been duped into extending credit to the general partner, believing it's a domestic entity), the maximum U.S. liability would be (the creditor would consume years of expensive multijurisdiction litigation):**

a. $500,000 or 50%
b. $10,000 or 1%
c. $350,000 or 35%
d. $20,000 or 2%

44. **The opposite of a consumer credit report, a national profile (aka insider report) is a valuable resource for creditors because it reveals a multitude of data on your subject, including property ownership, assessed value, closing date, corporate affiliations, licensing, judgments, residences, relatives, auto ownership, registration numbers, and even numeric addresses with phone numbers! National profiles/insider reports are retroactive for:**

a. 3 years.
b. 7 years.
c. 10 years.
d. 11 years.

45. **National profiles (aka insider reports), unlike credit reports, are not reported as an inquiry because:**
   a. The report does not illustrate payment history, nor is it used for credit scoring, and is not applicable to FCRA.
   b. They are used exclusively by detective agencies and law encodement.
   c. Multiple databases are electronically searched relevant to the subject's Social Security numbers.
   d. a and c.

46. **National profiles (aka insider reports) typically match information relevant to your subject's Social Security number derived from up to 56 databases. The report is extremely valuable to creditors to:**
   a. Develop a profile on the subject.
   b. Determine collectibility of receivable and/or judgment, minimize discovery, together with a resource for information.
   c. Gauge creditworthiness.
   d. a and b.

47. **A leviathan corporation owes you money but is intentionally not paying you. Your requests for payment are ignored. Before placing the account with a collection agency or attorney, a strategy to determine collectibility is:**
   a. Communicate with the CEO.
   b. Ascertain the names, addresses, faxes, and e-mails of CFO, purchasing agent, accounts payable, and every other person directly or indirectly related to the debt, then flood its hierarchy with a conciliatory request for remittance.
   c. Intensify communications with a responsible person.
   d. b combined with telephone appeals.

48. **The best way to avoid a write-off is not to create one. Shrewd credit grantors implement an ingenious strategy wherein customers execute an electronic debit provision authorizing transfer of funds consistent with payment terms. The process is known as a reverse electronic debit. Once implemented, the transfer of monies is performed by:**
   a. Your customer's bank.
   b. Your bank.
   c. A service bureau, which advances its money, while simultaneously debiting your customer's account.
   d. Your bank in cooperation with debtor's bank.

49. **A safeguard to ensure transfer of funds from your customer's to your account is language in the credit application and/or guarantee that the creditor may debit any account (even if the designated account is closed), relevant to bonafide invoices via other accounts. Thus, if the nonpaying customer closes the account, the creditor still has inexpensive recourse via:**

a. Threatening a lawsuit.

b. Renegotiating credit/payment terms.

c. Utilizing search firms to electronically match Social Security and/or EINs to locate and debit ancillary account.

d. Proceeding with conventional collection procedures.

50. **While authorized reverse electronic debit substantially reduces write-offs and/or lethargy, creditors must convince new customers of its benefits and ensure accuracy. As a cushion to assure customers of nonabuse, creditors often incorporate escape clauses (invoice due net 30, 15-day grace period before debit, etc.). A typical electronic debit would activate after written notice and/or a grace period. Experience proves one of the following clauses will maximize results. Choose the one proven to be the most effective:**

a. 15 days' written notice of creditor's intent to electronically debit.

b. 10 days past due date with one-half of debt debited, balance negotiated.

c. 15 days past due with entire amount debited, without notice.

d. Variations of a, b, and c, depending on circumstances.

ANSWERS TO ACCOUNTS RECEIVABLE PROFICIENCY EXAM

1. e. The Federal Fair Debt Collection Practices act is *entirely applicable to consumer* debts. If an officer of a corporation executes a personal guarantee, under the Act the debt is still considered a corporate obligation.

2. a, b, and c are the correct answers depending on whether the debt is commercial or consumer oriented. In both consumer and commercial debt, the collector *must* provide documentation relevant to the debt. If directed by a consumer debtor to cease and desist, a collector must terminate pursuit. If either a commercial or consumer debtor instructs the collector to direct *all* communications, written or oral, to an attorney, the collector must comply.

3. d

4. b

5. California $5,000, Pennsylvania $8,000, Tennessee $15,000, and Louisiana up to $20,000. The correct answer is b and d, depending on county. *Note:* California is considered "small claims," Pennsylvania, District Justice, Tennessee, General Session, and Louisiana varies up to $20,000 depending on parish.

6. Both b and c are correct depending on timing of invoices relevant to different small claims actions.

7. a is most applicable.

8. d. In many jurisdictions, a corporation may represent itself pro se (i.e., without a lawyer) but only in small claims. Thus, a creditor can file the action and delay retaining an attorney until the eve of trial. A vindictive creditor/plaintiff can secure an adjournment compelling the defendant to make an unnecessary trip to the courthouse.

9. a and b. Federal courts can only be utilized if applicable subject matter jurisdiction or if diversity of citizenship exists (i.e., plaintiff(s) and defendant(s) *must* be citizens of different states and the controversy must exceed $75,000 exclusive of interest and disbursements). In contrast, jurisdiction is also applicable if the action arose under Federal subject matter jurisdiction (i.e., Maritime Labor Law, etc.)

10. a and b, combined.

11. a and b, combined.

12. e or a, b and c

13. d

14. d. A foreign judgment *must* be domesticated. It is subject to execution only if the recipient state gives it "full faith and credit."

15. e. Contrary to common belief, a consumer credit report has multifaceted benefits. In addition to a, b, c, and d, it can also be utilized as a resource for information subpoenas.

16. b. A header report reveals *only* the subject's *identifiers* (i.e., Social Security number, date of birth, address, previous address, including possible landline phone or cell

number). Sometimes place of employment is listed. Since a header report *does not* disclose the consumer's payment history or inquiries, it is universally obtainable and *does not* require the consumer's consent. Header reports are also useful for commercial debts, including service of process, establishing communication, and so on.

17. a. TransUnion, Equifax, and Experian sell this information to its subscribers for under $.50.
18. d
19. d
20. d
21. d
22. b
23. e
24. a. Writ: mandatory precept directing the sheriff to execute a court order
    b. Voir dire: to speak the truth
    c. Additur: an increase in the amount of damages
    d. Demurrer: allegation that facts as stated—even if admitted—are not sufficient to sustain a cause of action
    e. Quantum meruit: Latin for goods sold or services provided and not paid for
    f. Collateral estoppel: doctrine recognizing determination of facts litigated
    g. Replevin: civil action for recovery of chattel
    h. Assignment: transfer of interest with full legal rights
    i. Domicile: permanent home and principal establishment
    j. Counterclaim: a counterdemand in response to plaintiff's complaint
    k. Cross claim: claim litigated by co-defendants or co-plaintiffs
    l. Modus operandi: the manner or order of operation
25. a. Venue: forum or jurisdiction where suit can be established
    b. Unjust enrichment: enriched at the expense of others
    c. Addamnum: amount of damages or claim for damages
    d. Mens rea: A guilty mind
    e. Declaratory judgment: judgment to express rights of litigant. Nonmonetary decree.
    f. Quid pro quo: what for what; something for something
    g. Arguendo: to put in clear light for the sake of argument
    h. Confession of judgment: entry of judgment upon written admission without legal formality
    i. Impleader: claim against original obligor and alleged liability to third party
    j. Nunc pro tunc: order used to correct the record
    k. Debenture: written acknowledgment of a debt
    l. Res judicata: a thing decided; a matter adjudged
26. d
27. d
28. c

29. c
30. c
31. d
32. c
33. b
34. f
35. b and d
36. a
37. d
38. b
39. d
40. c
41. b
42. d
43. b
44. c
45. d
46. d
47. d
48. c
49. c
50. d

Index